NEWSPRINT LITERATURE AND LOCAL LITERARY CREATIVITY IN WEST AFRICA, 1900s–1960s

AFRICAN ARTICULATIONS

ISSN 2054-5673

SERIES EDITORS
Stephanie Newell & Ranka Primorac

EDITORIAL ADVISORY BOARD
Akin Adesokan (Indiana University)
Jane Bryce (University of the West Indies)
James Ferguson (Stanford University)
Simon Gikandi (Princeton University)
Stefan Helgesson (Stockholm University)
Isabel Hofmeyr (University of the Witwatersrand)
Madhu Krishnan (University of Bristol)
Lydie Moudileno (University of Southern California)
Grace A. Musila (University of the Witwatersrand)
Caroline Rooney (University of Kent)
Meg Samuelson (University of Adelaide)
Jennifer Wenzel (Columbia University)

The series is open to submissions from the disciplines related to literature, cultural history, cultural studies, music and the arts.

African Articulations showcases cutting-edge research into Africa's cultural texts and practices, broadly understood to include written and oral literatures, visual arts, music, and public discourse and media of all kinds. Building on the idea of 'articulation' as a series of cultural connections, as a clearly voiced argument and as a dynamic social encounter, the series features monographs that open up innovative perspectives on the richness of African locations and networks. Refusing to concentrate solely on the internationally visible above the supposedly ephemeral local cultural spaces and networks, African Articulations provides indispensable resources for students and teachers of contemporary culture.

Please contact the series editors with an outline, or download the proposal form www.jamescurrey.com. Only send a full manuscript if requested to do so.

Stephanie Newell, Professor of English, Yale University stephanie.newell@yale.edu
Ranka Primorac, Associate Professor in English, University of Southampton r.primorac@soton.ac.uk

Previously published volumes are listed at the back of this book

NEWSPRINT LITERATURE AND LOCAL LITERARY CREATIVITY IN WEST AFRICA, 1900s–1960s

Stephanie Newell

JAMES CURREY

James Currey
is an imprint of
Boydell & Brewer Ltd
PO Box 9, Woodbridge
Suffolk IP12 3DF (GB)
www.jamescurrey.com
and of
Boydell & Brewer Inc.
668 Mt Hope Avenue
Rochester, NY 14620–2731 (US)
www.boydellandbrewer.com

Our Authorised Representative for product safety in the EU is
Easy Access System Europe - Mustamäe tee 50, 10621 Tallinn, Estonia,
gpsr.requests@easproject.com

© Stephanie Newell 2023
First published in hardback 2023
Paperback edition 2025

All rights reserved. No part of this book may be reproduced in any form, or by electronic or mechanical means, including information storage and retrieval systems, without permission in writing from the publishers, except by a reviewer who may quote brief passages in a review

The right of Stephanie Newell to be identified as
the author of this work has been asserted in accordance with
sections 77 and 78 of the Copyright, Designs and Patents Act 1988

ISBN 978-1-84701-382-8 hardback
ISBN 978-1-84701-383-5 paperback

A CIP catalogue record for this book is available on request from the British Library

The publisher has no responsibility for the continued existence or accuracy of URLs for external or third-party internet websites referred to in this book, and does not guarantee that any content on such websites is, or will remain, accurate or appropriate

For Akachi Adimora-Ezeigbo

Contents

	List of Illustrations	viii
	List of Abbreviations	xi
	Note on Spelling	xii
	Acknowledgements	xiii
	Introduction	1
1	Anglo-Scribes and Anglo-Literates in West African Newspaper History	13
2	The Time of Letters: Epistolarity and Nigerian Newsprint Cultures	31
3	'Shameless Thefts' vs Local Literatures: Dusé Mohamed Ali's *Comet*	43
4	Onitsha Pamphlets: Youth Literature for the Modern World	65
5	The Work of Repetition in Nigerian Epistolary Pamphlets	85
6	English Romantic Discourse: Women vs Men	109
7	Female Critical Communities in Nigerian Pamphlet Literature: 'Beware of Women'	127
8	Writing Time: African Cold War Aesthetics and Nigerian Political Dramas of the 1960s	143
9	Romances from the Nigerian Civil War: Veronica's End	163
	Conclusion: Local Aesthetics	175
	Bibliography	187
	Index	207

Illustrations

3.1 Photograph of the manager and staff at I. W. Oshilaja's Ife-Olu Printing Works, Lagos, where the *Comet* was produced (*Comet* Christmas Number 1933, 54) — 59

3.2 The composing room at I. W. Oshilaja's Printing Works (*Comet* Christmas Number 1933, 39) — 59

4.1 Cover of first edition of Ogali A. Ogali's (1956) bestselling pamphlet, *Veronica My Daughter* (Enugu: Zik Enterprises) — 66

4.2 Cover of Nathan O. Njoku's (n.dat.) *How to Read and Write Correct English, Better Compositions, Sentences, Proverbs, Office Routine, How to Pass Examinations and General Knowledge (For Schools and Colleges)* (Onitsha: Njoku and Sons Bookshop) — 70

4.3 Cover of J. Kenddys Onwudiegwu's (1965) *English: The Language of the Modern World. How to Write Good Letters, Better Compositions, Agreements, Good Business Letters, Applications and Teach Your Self How to Speak and Write Good English* (Onitsha: Gebo Brothers Bookshop) — 71

4.4 Back cover of Nathan O. Njoku's (1963) *The Complete Letter Writing Made Easy for Ladies and Gentlemen* (Onitsha: Njoku and Sons) — 75

4.5 A. Onwudiwe, Managing Director of Onwudiwe and Sons, flyleaf of *The Bitterness of Politics and Awolowo's Last Appeal* (1964) by Mazi Raphael D. A. Nwankwo (Onitsha: A. Onwudiwe and Sons) — 76

4.6 The author Raph Oguanobi, flyleaf of *Two Friends in the Romance of Runaway Lover* (c.1960) (Onitsha: Obi Brothers Bookshop) — 77

4.7 S. Aw. Emedolu, Manager of Treasure Press, Aba, pictured on the final page of H. O. Ogu's *Rose Only Loved my Money* (1950), with the caption, 'Hints: African authors are cordially invited to send in Manuscripts to us. We allow negotiation' — 78

4.8	Portrait of F. B. Joe, front cover of *The General Guide in English: Complete Compositions, Business Letters and 95 Modern Questions and Answers Made Easy for Elem. Schools and Colleges* (c.1965) (Onitsha-Fegge: United Brothers Bookshop)	79
4.9	C. N. O. Moneyhard in cowboy's dress on final page of *Why Harlots Hate Married Men and Love Bachelors* (c.1955) (Port Harcourt: C. N. O. Moneyhard)	80
5.1	Photograph of 'Ralph O. Ability' (probably the publisher, R. O. Egbusunwa) as a smartly dressed 'man of letters' from the pamphlet, *A New Guide to Good English and Correct Letter Writing* (1964: 29) (Onitsha: R. Egbusumh and Bros)	86
5.2	Cover of Okenwa Olisah's (1962) *How to Write Good Letters and Applications* (Onitsha: Highbred Maxwell, Students Own Bookshop)	92
5.3	Cover of N. O. Njoku's (1962b) *How to Write Better Business Letters, Good English, Applications, Telegrams and Important Invitations* (Onitsha: Njoku and Sons)	93
5.4	Cover of J. C. Abiakam's (c.1972) *How to Write Important Letters, Applications, Agreements and Love Letters* (Onitsha: J. C. Brothers Bookshop)	94
5.5	Cover of Chidi M. Ohaejesi's (n.dat.) *Quotations for all Occasions: Wise Sayings, Idioms, Proverbs, Good English and Compositions* (Onitsha: Minaco Bookshops)	98
5.6	Back cover of Benjamin O. Chiazor's (n.dat.) *Back to Happiness* (Onitsha: Highbred Maxwell)	101
5.7	Front cover of Speedy Eric's (1964) *How to Write Successful Letters and Applications* (Onitsha: A. Onwudiwe and Sons)	102
5.8	Back cover of Nathan O. Njoku's (n.dat.) *How to Read and Write Correct English, Better Compositions, Sentences, Proverbs, Office Routine, How to Pass Examinations and General Knowledge (For Schools and Colleges)* (Onitsha: Njoku and Sons Bookshop)	103
5.9	Back cover of Wilfred Onwuka's (1965) *How to Study,* showing an educated local man pasted into a scene with fashionable East Asian women (Onitsha: Gebo Brothers Bookshop)	104

5.10   Pages from Rev. Thomas Cooke's (1788) *The Universal Letter-Writer; or New Art of Polite Correspondence* (London: Osborne and Griffin), 58–9   106

7.1   Cover of Speedy Eric's (c.1964) *Mabel The Sweet Honey That Poured Away* (Onitsha: Onwudiwe)   137

8.1   Cover of Thomas Iguh's (1961) *The Last Days of Lumumba (The Late Lion of the Congo): A Drama* (Onitsha: Onwudiwe)   147

9.1   Cover of Shakespeare C. N. Nwachukwu's (1972) *The Tragedy of Civilian Major* (Onitsha: Nwachukwu Africana Books)   167

The author and publisher are grateful to all the institutions and individuals listed for permission to reproduce the materials to which they hold copyright. Every effort has been made to trace the copyright holders; apologies are offered for any omission, and the publisher will be pleased to add any necessary acknowledgement in subsequent editions.

Abbreviations

b.pag.	Back page
edn	Edition
GCL	*Gold Coast Leader*
n.dat.	No date
n.pag.	No page
n.pub.	No publisher
Supp.	Supplement
t.pag.	Title page

Note on Spelling

Authors' and compositors' original spellings, grammar and typos have been retained throughout this book and 'sic' has not been inserted into any quotations.

Acknowledgements

This book brings together nearly three decades of research and thinking. Numerous people have contributed to its intellectual formation along the way. Foremost among them is Karin Barber, whose work continues to inspire my research and whose generous feedback on the manuscript helped with the revisions. In Nigeria, Akachi Adimora-Ezeigbo has provided continuous encouragement and friendship since I first knocked on her office door as a PhD student in the late 1990s asking questions about Onitsha market literature and the Nigerian civil war. In the USA, Merve Fejzula, Marina Bilbija and Stephanie Bosch-Santana have been brilliant interlocutors in recent years, and the 'Connect Africa' research network has offered a friendly, receptive environment for ideas in formation. I am especially grateful to Eleni Coundouriotis for her warm friendship and perceptive feedback.

I am indebted to Kurt Thometz of Jumel Terrace Books, New York City, who generously allowed access to his collection of Onitsha pamphlets, and whose hospitality and anecdotes made for a memorable visit. In London, thanks go to staff at the British Library for access, over the years, to the many hundreds of Nigerian pamphlets held in their collections. Vital research assistance was provided by Adeola Gbolahan, Alexandra Galloway and Faith Vasquez.

The Leverhulme Trust made possible my visiting professorship to the University of Newcastle in 2019–20. I am indebted to Neelam Srivastava, James Procter and colleagues and postgraduate students in the School of English Literature, Language and Linguistics for their support and collegiality during the visit.

Chapter 1 contains extracts from two published essays: S. Newell (2020), 'Newsprint Worlds and Reading Publics in Colonial Contexts', *Itinerario: Journal of Imperial and Global Interactions*, 44(2), 435–45 and S. Newell (2022), 'Local Authors, Ephemeral Texts: Anglo-Scribes and Anglo-Literates in Early West African Newspapers', in Grace Musila (ed.), *Routledge Handbook of African Popular Culture* (London and New York: Routledge), 56–73. A shorter version of Chapter 4 was published as S. Newell (2021), 'The Work of Repetition in 1960s Nigerian Epistolary Pamphlets', *Journal of African Cultural Studies* 33: 3, 251–71.

Whenever you get a new book to read, first of all, read the contents page if it has one. Then read the preface or author's note, or the introduction, as the case may be. This will help you to grasp a little idea of what the book will teach you. Then you start to read the first paragraph in every chapter. Then you read the summary or conclusion page. This kind of reading is called 'SKIMMING.' It will help you in your reading for it helps to cool down the desire to know what the book is all about, which will not allow you for a concentrated reading.

Nathan O. Njoku (n.dat.: n.pag.)

Introduction

> The local that is at issue here is not the 'local' in any conventional or traditional sense, but a very contemporary 'local' that serves as a site for the working out of the most fundamental contradictions of the age.
>
> (Dirlik [1998] 2018: 85)

In the first half of the twentieth century, African newspapers were sites of intense literary activity in the colonies that made up British West Africa. Newspapers provided the chief – and in most cases the only – outlet for local creative writers and intellectuals to send short pieces for publication.[1] Newsprint gave diverse writers and readers access to spaces for imaginative expression alongside, but untethered to, the colonial education system, and local writers relished and exploited the platforms for creativity offered by the press. As a result, these newspaper archives contain a vast reservoir of original creative writing by local authors in genres ranging from serialised fiction to poetry and short stories, as well as other types of non-news text such as philosophical essays, articles on local history, travelogues, reviews, and prose forms that defy generic classification by today's literary standards.[2] These are surrounded on all sides by editorials, news reports, cinema listings, sports fixtures and shipping news, as well as advertisements for commodities and services from foreign and local businesses. These, in turn, sit cheek by jowl with creative materials from further afield, such as pan-Africanist essays and poems by African American intellectuals, as well as poetry and fiction by Europeans in West Africa and West Africans in Europe.

---

[1] For those with longer manuscripts, getting a book printed and bound at one of the many urban jobbing presses in British West Africa or in London was prohibitively expensive, even for relatively well established writers, whose struggles to raise subscriptions are often recounted in the press (Ajiṣafẹ 1934: 9, 11). Until the 1930s, most book authors – if they could afford it – sent manuscripts to printers and publishers in London.

[2] A digital repository of many African newspapers from the period before 1922 is available in the World Newspaper Archive administered by Readex and the Center for Research Libraries (CRL). Complete runs of many colonial-era African newspapers can be obtained on microfilm through the Cooperative Africana Microform Project (CAMP) administered by the CRL. The national archives of Ghana and Nigeria hold hard copies of many newspapers not available elsewhere.

This vibrant newsprint creativity, as it is termed in this book, forms a neglected corpus of West African literature that connects newspapers with the pamphlet literature of the 1950s and 1960s. *Newsprint Literature and Local Literary Creativity in West Africa* investigates the literary worlds constituted by newspapers and pamphlets written in English and printed on newsprint – the cheapest, lowest-quality paper – in the early to mid-twentieth century. The book asks how current approaches to anglophone African literature on the one hand, and African cultural history on the other hand, might be extended by the inclusion of this vast, unwieldy and under-studied archive of imaginative writing that falls outside contemporary transnational understandings of literary genres and anglophone world literatures. Combining a discussion of creative writing in African newspapers between the 1900s and 1940s with consideration of the Nigerian pamphlets known as 'Onitsha market literature' in the 1950s and 1960s, the book argues that it is necessary to make space in African literary history for newsprint creativity and, in so doing, to rethink some of the genres and chronologies through which African literature is interpreted in order to include material generally regarded as ephemeral.

The publications at the heart of this study yield a great deal of information about history, politics and society as, at different points in the twentieth century, local literati stepped into African newsprint spaces to define the aspirations of their social groups and assert claims to cultural and economic power. However, locally authored texts continuously exceed contextual explanations and should not be treated simply as a source of information. Their status as ephemera – a label that will be debated throughout the book and contested in the conclusion – should not cause this literature to be treated as any less generative of literary forms and styles than texts that are recognised within mainstream African literary studies. Debates about literary content and style permeated all aspects of West African print cultures in the first half of the twentieth century, shaping characters and producing plots, and occasionally causing fierce arguments in the press about what could, or should, be represented in print. In recognition of this potent textuality, this book regards newsprint literature as productive of aesthetic as well as social values, and shows how local writers relished the opportunities provided by print to exercise their imaginations and experiment with forms, using the medium of newsprint to offer educational, often moralising, stories that were inextricable from their lessons in literary style.

The movement of the book from colonial-era print cultures to 1960s literary production is not intended to suggest the organic emergence of the latter out of the former. A major objective of this study is to problematise linear explanations of anglophone African literary development as a story of emerging literatures leading inexorably to present-day classifications of textual form and style. African-owned newspapers provided platforms for all kinds of literary activities that did not in any developmental sense lead to or give rise to postcolonial literatures. The decades covered by this book were marked by the First World War, the Great Depression, the Italian invasion of Ethiopia, the Second World War, the Cold War, anticolonial nationalism, Independence, the assassination of Patrice Lumumba, the Nigerian Civil War, and many other periods of transformation in West Africa. Newsprint literature was produced by authors in the thick of political crises, at historical junctures when colonial, postcolonial and Cold War timelines converged in violent clashes and struggles for dominance (see Shringarpure 2019).

Newsprint provided a space where seismic political events could be creatively dramatised and deliberated as they happened, and distinctive literary innovations emerged in reaction to political crises as authors offered interpretations of recent history and produced their own understandings of time, place and history. Chapters 8 and 9 zoom in on two such political crises – the murder of Congolese leader Patrice Lumumba in 1961 and the Nigerian Civil War of 1967–70 – to show the ways in which local Nigerian authors responded to political emergencies and shifted the focus of newsprint creativity to include national and regional political events in the context of anticolonial nationalism and the Cold War.

In analysing the newsprint archive of the 1900s to 1960s, not as a precursor to postcolonial African literature but as a field in its own right with changing themes, technologies, styles, genres and temporalities, *Newsprint Literature* aims to introduce additional genealogies and forms to African literary and cultural studies. The book studies African printed literature in its most fleeting forms and asks how newsprint shaped readers' changing ideas about literature, writing, the English language and the creative imagination in the first half of the twentieth century. In particular, the book asks why so many authors chose to write in English rather than African languages when, as the example of the lively bilingual press discussed in Chapter 2 demonstrates, vernacular languages also offered platforms for creative writers.

Almost all of the English-language texts discussed in this book are characterised by a feature that differentiates them from vernacular printed literature, on the one hand, and twentieth-century African creative writing published in the Global North, on the other hand. English-language authors produced works containing thick layers of quotations from diverse anglophone literatures ranging from seventeenth- and eighteenth-century poetry and drama to nineteenth-century epistolary manuals and twentieth-century popular romances. Many university-educated anticolonial intellectuals in the 1960s believed that a century of missionary and colonial education on the continent had culturally 'bombed' local languages and systems of knowledge. For them, vernacular worlds had been replaced with 'mentally colonising' European languages imbued with anti-Black racism (Ngũgĩ 1986: 3). By contrast, local authors in West Africa treated the English language as a global resource and refused to connect it with the experience of imperial racism. Whether through references to Shakespeare and the English Romantic poets or through citations from Victorian and Edwardian bestselling romances, they hooked their imaginations into transnational discourses.

At one level, the explanation for the prevalence of quotations from English literature in local literatures is simple: a swift way to assert cultural prestige under British colonial rule was to exhibit a knowledge of reading and writing in English. An obvious way to demonstrate one's intellectual credentials was through an engagement with the canon of English literature circulating around colonial society. However, as the book will show, writers drew inspiration from anglophone texts in ways that were far more creative, complex and culturally specific than allowed for by models of British cultural hegemony and the mimicry it produced among local elites. Indeed, one influential Yoruba newsprint text from the late 1920s – I. B. Thomas's epistolary first-person account of a 'fallen woman' called Ṣẹgilọla – recurs throughout the book in different forms, helping to disconnect anglophone authors from their English literary sources and centring their practices in African-language aesthetic frameworks (Chapter 2).[3]

The majority of the authors featured in this book were products of British colonial and missionary schools on the continent: they had studied English literature on the secondary school curriculum and absorbed the works of the 'great' English authors, often in condensed forms like school primers and the Lambs' *Tales from Shakespeare*. As part of an expanding minority of West Africans educated to Standard VI in secondary school, they were able to read and write in English, a language that was not taught in elementary schools until the expansion of education in the period of decolonisation (Ofori-Attah 2006). With each new generation of authors and readers, English literacy brought promises of access to opportunities and social and professional hierarchies that were closed to the 'unlettered' masses. A history of social class in the colonies is thus uniquely embedded in anglophone West African newsprint cultures (see Chapters 3 and 4).

In turning to creative writing *in situ*, the term 'local' becomes a productive critical category in this book, marking the presence of creative agency that is more subtle than implied by the conventional usage of 'local' as a marker of lesser – narrower, more parochial – cultural concerns in opposition to global or cosmopolitan positions (Appiah 2007). In making space for the local in African literary history, the book seeks to appreciate literary tastes and values on the ground and insert jigsaw pieces into the picture we have inherited of anglophone African literatures in the first half of the twentieth century. In particular, printed matter that might otherwise be regarded as peripheral to world history because of its comparatively limited geographical circulation and readership regains relevance under the rubric of the local (see Primorac 2014). As the conclusion argues, a reconsideration of African newsprint culture opens up alternative

---

[3] For detailed analyses of Yoruba quoting techniques in Nigerian oral and print cultures, see Barber (1999, 2016, *forthcoming*).

genealogies and methods for understanding contemporary literary forms such as social media creativity.

Newsprint Literature offers close-ups of West African creative writing and readerships at different moments in the first half of the twentieth century, charting changes in literary tastes and transformations to genres and styles from within the literary contexts in which texts were produced. The book supports what the historian and anthropologist Insa Nolte describes as 'the importance of engaging with conceptual worlds which originate outside of academia's dominantly European-derived analytical categories to understand global phenomena' (2019: n.pag.). In adjusting our analytical categories to accommodate non-Eurocentric conceptual and aesthetic worlds, as Nolte proposes, Africanist scholars need to appreciate local authors' consciousness of time and place before thinking about how – as 'anglophone' literatures – these texts connect with globally circulating English literatures and international literary traditions.

Crucially, the newspapers and printing presses examined in this book remained in the hands of men who occupied public spaces as men, sought recognition as men and created new spaces of their own as men to participate in literary and political life. Men's perspectives on society and politics were reinforced by their access to printing presses, and much printed material was injected with male bias (see Chapters 6 and 7). In photographs and modes of address, local authors adopted visibly masculine positions as modern public intellectuals producing knowledge in print, and writing was filled with assumptions about the gender of authors: 'Why should we fill our libraries with love stories from abroad when we have young men who wish to try?' one young nationalist asked in an Independence-era Nigerian pamphlet, displacing, in the process, a bestselling global genre of women's writing in favour of local romances written by men (Asuzu 1960: n.pag; see Chapter 6). Popular authors adopted masculine pseudonyms such as 'Strong Man of the Pen' (pseud. Okenwa Olisah) and 'Speedy Eric' (pseud. A. N. Onwudiwe) and while their stories were aimed at (and filled with) women as well as men, they often represented knowledge in gendered terms without acknowledging the gendered hierarchies and exclusions produced by processes of acquiring literacy, especially English literacy (see Chapter 7). Thus wisdom itself was often construed as masculine: as Okenwa Olisah put it, 'You will doubtless be "Solomon the wise" after going through this wonderful booklet' (c.1963: n.pag.).

Many different social and literary values were articulated in anglophone print cultures in the colonial and immediate postcolonial periods, but this gendered assertion of identity superceded other affiliations. As Chapter 7 shows, tensions and ambiguities can nevertheless be found in the masculinist ideology underwriting newspaper fiction and pamphlets, opening up local print cultures to the presence of broader flows of knowledge and power that contradict the authority of writers and suggest the presence of alternative local centres of aesthetic and interpretive gravity. Indeed, the misogyny of the more extreme publications discussed in Chapter 7 can be interpreted as male authors' overreactions to women's and girls' independent desires and articulations of public opinion off the page, rather than a reflection of any kind of gender status quo in West African society.

Even as male authors displayed their intellectual capital by using the colonial language to assert male prestige to rival established elites and claim membership of emerging classes, they were often painfully aware that their publications had limited circulation and were excluded from competing local power structures (see Chapter 7). Writers asserted their status as an educated elite in cultural contexts where they were surrounded by other authority figures who had their own respected forms of expression. If writers exploited the opportunities offered by print to shape their class aspirations, they often did so uncomfortably and self-consciously, aware of the presence of these established elites, including women, who formed critical communities outside the purview of their newsprint cultures (1971: 3; see Chapters 7 and 9). Positioned in relation to residual, non-printed modes of knowledge production, West African print cultures should therefore be regarded as one particular representational space among several others.

Throughout the twentieth century, local writers took up positions as vanguard intellectuals who used the opportunities offered by print to shape the ideas and aspirations of their gender and class.[4] Numerous Nigerian pamphlets insisted, 'you are wise to read. And wiser after reading' and 'read and become wise, good advice is the best medicine of life' (Ogu c.1960: n.pag., Okonkwo c.1961: 4). 'Buy this book because Knowledge is Power', publishers urged, stating, on the covers of countless pamphlets, 'a word is enough for the wise' (Onwudiegwu 1965a: n.pag.). Representing themselves as modern intellectuals who could

---

[4] Gramsci's category of 'organic intellectuals' is not particularly useful in colonial contexts. Intended for western Europe, this model does not account for the social and political ruptures caused by colonialism, nor does it describe the complexities of class formation in colonial states where western models of governance combined with resilient structures of customary rule and robust forms of non-industrialised economic production. Nor does it explain the male domination of West African newsprint creativity in the colonial period. To view anglophone local authors by class alone, as petit bourgeois proponents of 'the dominant fundamental group' (Gramsci 1971: 5) – no matter how complex the layers of interconnection between social groups and the state – assumes an identifiable, dominant class ideology in colonial contexts that were characterised by multiple social systems and political affinities as well as fundamental gender differences between men and women in accessing colonial education and its rewards. In short, race and gender must be factored into the class identities of colonial West Africa's literati, with the addition, by the 1950s, of generation – or rather, youth – as fundamental to the self-assertion of the educated modern 'class' (see Chapter 4).

skilfully navigate the world of writing for the benefit of people less educationally fortunate than themselves, writers used print to assert their position at the top of the cultural ladder as presenters and interpreters of people's experiences. In this way, as Chapter 2 highlights, they endorsed literacy as a tool – if not *the* tool – for critique and opinion-formation in the public sphere.

Africanist scholars have come up with many different adjectives to describe the histories of intellectual activity on the continent. Emily Callaci describes producers of popular art forms in early to mid-twentieth-century Tanzania as 'popular intellectuals' who diagnosed and critiqued urban conditions by assembling the disparate cultural resources available on the streets (2017: 7–9). Historians of mass media on the continent have described the more politically engaged individuals among these groups as 'public intellectuals' – further subdivided into 'political', 'cultural', 'academic' and 'organic' public intellectuals (Reddy et al. 2020) – who stepped into public spaces as advocates for controversial social and political issues, and who entered public discourse as commentators, analysts, critics, opinion-makers and campaigners (Broodryk 2021). Perhaps most famously, Steven Feierman (1990) challenged conventional representations of African intellectual production as urban and elite with his study of 'peasant intellectuals' in Tanzania.

Karin Barber's provisional, far-reaching term 'local intellectuals' accurately describes the self-nominated shapers of public opinion who feature in this book with a variety of literary genres, political views and modes of engagement with African audiences throughout the colonial period. To recognise intellectuals as 'local' is not to set the local against the global in an oppositional relationship: rather, it is to recognise the public spaces claimed by an imprecise social group whose writings were 'published locally – or even remained unpublished – and reached a restricted audience' (Barber 2015: 569). 'Local intellectual' highlights the heterogeneous quality of this loose-knit social group and usefully encapsulates the homegrown quality of knowledge produced by all those mediators of public opinion who turned to print from the late nineteenth century onward (Ibid.). It is particularly appropriate when describing the Nigerian pamphleteers who feature in the second half of this book, who were not transnational like many of the editors and intellectuals writing for newspapers in the early twentieth century, but who, in a similar manner to earlier newspaper elites, used print to attract readers and shape cultural norms, consolidating local publishing infrastructures and defining local literary values in the process.

As 'thinkers who wrestled with issues in philosophy, politics, history and culture but who were not part of mainstream academic or cultural institutions', West African local intellectuals (and the groups they spoke for) deserve attention for their methods and modes of address (Ibid.). Whether publishing in newspapers or pamphlets, throughout the first half of the twentieth century they insisted that their role was to model good literacy skills for local readers.

Often with a touch of superiority, local intellectuals informed the public that the writer's special role was to mediate English language and form, and to teach good practices of writing and modern citizenship. In the introduction to his self-help booklet, *How to Speak in Public and Make Good Introductions* (1965: n.pag.), the popular pamphleteer J. C. Abiakam informed prospective readers that 'this book is very useful to house servants, regular travellers, motor Conductors, Drivers, Teachers, workers etc'. As H. O. Ogu stated in the preface to his comic novel, *Okeke and his Master's Girlfriend,* 'in preparing this book the author has tried his best to avoid some journalistic terms so that the mechanic, the farmer, and the labourer can as readily understand as one who has graduated with honours from our colleges and universities' (1960: n.pag.).

Literary production was not a democratic sphere of public participation open to all who could read and write, as colonial West African literary cultures have tended to be represented in print culture scholarship. Often in tension with their egalitarian ideas about democratising access to print, newsprint writers continuously asserted their superiority over less well-schooled readers, carefully role-modelling the power of literacy to those 'below' them in educational achievements, addressing readers as individuals who should both appreciate and benefit from their literary gifts, and offering advice on how readers could improve their writing styles through the emulation of the models authors provided. At strategic points in newsprint literatures, including editorials and prefaces, writers insisted that 'a lot of experience' was required to produce publishable English (Stephen c.1962a: n.pag.; see Chapter 3). If readers wished to become 'modern', authors emphasised, they should work hard on their English literacy skills to gain access to knowledge that was unavailable in other forms. In this way, through careful study of the knowledge contained in newspapers and pamphlets, readers could gain access to power, success and opportunities, and benefit from literacy in the same way as authors.

Whether they were the highly educated newspaper elites of the early twentieth century discussed in Chapter 1, or the secondary schooled pamphleteers of the 1950s and 1960s discussed in the second half of the book, local writers acted as gatekeepers of literature and literary values. From their elevated positions, published authors told readers, 'many a man has often asked that writers disclose to them the secret of their art and initiate them into the mysteries of it all, so that they too may worship with them in the sacred chambers of their literary Muse and pass as writers and journalists' (Nwangoro, *Comet* July 16 1938: 14). As the prolific pamphleteer Nathan O. Njoku put it, 'I hope strongly that with your careful reading of this work, you will in no distant date improve in your writing matters and become a famous "pen pusher" and get what you want' (Njoku 1962b: n.pag.).

From these platforms, local authors held readers continuously in view, addressing them directly and involving them in reading by inviting responses in the form of letters. Letters and letter-writing emerge as major topics in this book. A great deal of literary and critical activity in West Africa in the first half of the twentieth century took the form of correspondence. West African print cultures were hubs of epistolary activity. As different chapters of the book will show, letter-writing lent form to newspapers, inspired pamphlet literature, delivered particular forms of literary realism, shaped printed articulations of first-person subjectivity and provided spaces of public expression for many thousands of amateur correspondents who, if they carefully studied the rules of letter-writing laid out in newspaper editorials and epistolary self-help books, would be able to see their words appear in print. Moreover, literary genres and textual interpretations were debated in the letters pages of newspapers as readers patrolled each others' writings through letters to editors, eliciting – as shown in the case study of the Lagos poet discussed in Chapter 3 – fierce critiques if material appeared to overstep locally agreed generic boundaries.

Letters were also spaces where generic boundaries became slippery in local newsprint cultures. As shown in Chapter 2, letters often feature in West African fiction as simultaneously fictional and real, used by authors to connect printed narratives with the empirical world. To understand these slippages, and to see how local literary experiments with epistolarity were enabled in the faultlines, it is important to include newspaper correspondence pages and letter-writing manuals – ostensibly non-'literary' genres – in the study of literary aesthetics in West Africa. As suggested by the cases of I. B. Thomas and Amos Tutuola in Chapter 2, and as evidenced in the host of epistolary pamphlets from the 1950s and 1960s discussed in Chapters 5 and 6, letters provided both a bridge into print for correspondents and ways for creative writers to assert verisimilitude and deny the fictional status of their literary works. These chapters examine the uncertainties created by authors when letters from the outside world are treated as real in imaginary works, showing how epistolarity facilitated an intensely interactive aesthetic, placing readers in direct communication with authors in ways that elaborately ignored the printed status of texts.

The dense epistolary traffic in local newsprint genres highlights the presence of robust local reading cultures on the continent, but epistolarity remains a major underresearched area in African literary criticism. The proliferation of letters – both fictional and real – in West African newspapers and pamphlets demonstrates the omnipresence of readers as interlocutors in cultures where the audience's critical engagement was at the core of textual production. Whether in the form of letters to newspaper editors, model letters published in self-help pamphlets for readers to use as templates, or the intimate outpourings of eternal love found in epistolary romances, the exceptionally high volumes of letter-writing in West African print cultures offer valuable insights into how social class and cultural prestige, as well as the public expression of emotions, were negotiated in colonial society through acts of reading and writing.

Given the centrality of letters to the self-assertion of the educated classes, it is hardly surprising that letters drew attention to themselves in local literatures to the extent that they often outstripped their function as mediums of communication for people separated by time and space. Whether published on the correspondence pages of newspapers, with their weekly and – by the 1940s – daily tempo, or inside pamphlet literature, letters forged a space of direct communication between writers and readers, giving the impression of currency, offering timely interventions in ongoing situations, and demanding a judgment of some kind from the reader as addressee. Epistolarity also allowed local intellectuals to represent subjective interiority while displaying their mastery of the rules of letter-writing. As Barber argues for the Yoruba-language press in colonial Lagos, and as Chapter 2 indicates, printed letters in newspapers and pamphlets influenced how the 'real world' – and distinctive forms of literary realism – came to be shaped in locally published literatures (Barber 2012).

New types of literary representation imbued with the temporality of newspapers and letters emerged in local newsprint cultures. By the 1950s, when the popular pamphleteers who feature in the second half of this book emerged en masse in eastern Nigeria, local literary production was so heavily 'lettered' with the to and fro of correspondence that readers' letters can be regarded as intrinsic to the public space of print. This decades-long buzz of communication on the letters pages of newspapers and in epistolary pamphlets constitutes a vital interface between West African authors, publishers, editors, readers and correspondents, providing a distinctive archive for cultural historians and literary scholars with an interest in histories of reading and the formation of print genres and local aesthetics. Here is a printed archive that is uniquely attached to and dependent on its readers and historical contexts, but has remained largely neglected by scholars.

One key figure is missing from the epistolary activities described in this book: the public letter writer, who is nowhere to be seen in local publications. Newspaper correspondents may have used the services of amanuenses to pen letters to editors, but in the archives informing this book, stretching from the early 1900s to the late 1960s, their presence is rarely, if ever, acknowledged by authors. Admitting a need for the services of a professional amanuensis would, it seems, have risked alienating correspondents from the very class they claimed membership of as letter writers.[5] As becomes clear in this study, non-literate Africans were frequently regarded as the 'other' of lettered populations

---

[5] The case of a Lagosian poet accused of plagiarism in the late 1930s (see Chapter 3) comes closest to showing the role of remunerated third parties in helping corrrespondents to prepare material for publication in the press. The correspondent in question, F. Uzoma Anyiam, was publicly humiliated over several weeks in the *Comet* as a consequence of his dependence on a third party.

in twentieth-century newsprint cultures. People requiring the services of letter writers were positioned on the periphery of the intended readerships. At all costs, authors insisted, readers should read and study, and enter the folds of print culture (see Chapter 4).

In centring local writers and readers, and in asking questions about the changing ways people negotiated philosophies of reading and writing in the colonial period, this book seeks to enrich African literary history with past frameworks of literary creativity and interpretation and, in so doing, highlight local literary trajectories and provoke fresh conceptualisations of creativity and literary history outside dominant criteria for works of the imagination. Some of these negotiations, such as the verbose flights of fancy in the *Gold Coast Leader* discussed in Chapter 1, the debates about plagiarism discussed in Chapter 2, and the romances, epistolary manuals and political dramas discussed in later parts of the book, may seem anachronistic or overly derivative by contemporary standards of literary appreciation. This book aims to give them historicity within newsprint cultures dating back to the 1880s, asking about the reading practices and power relations they refracted and inspired. Other local literatures, such as the popular Nigerian pamphlets printed on cheap paper in the 1950s and 1960s, often regarded by critics as a spontaneous phenomenon, are compared with newspaper production of previous decades and given genealogies within newspaper history.

Newsprint provided a platform for local intellectuals to experiment with ideas and bring their creative imaginations to work on social and political issues. Local authors proposed solutions, offered forecasts, propelled ideas forward, and reflected on politics and morality in their writings. Their publications demand to be included in the discipline of African literary studies alongside works of oral literature as well as creative writing by transnational African intellectuals. Local intellectuals used newsprint to explore a panoply of social and political possibilities. The ephemeral, unbound spaces they occupied with their readers deserve to be reconnected with tightly bound textual forms such as books in order to make visible the differences and meeting points between local and global English-language literatures in the twentieth century, and to gain a fuller picture of the ways all those writers who were not published in the West produced influential timelines as well as new literary genres in an era of global political transformations.

Anglo-Scribes and Anglo-Literates in West African Newspaper History

English-language Newspapers in Colonial West Africa

In the decades between Europe's 'scramble for Africa' in the mid-1880s and the end of the Second World War, increasing numbers of educated professionals and local entrepreneurs secured investment and capital to import printing presses and newsprint into the territories that made up British West Africa.[1] Numerous English-language newspapers came into existence in this period, as well as bilingual and African-language titles (Omu 1978, Jones-Quartey 1975).[2] They were owned and edited by men who, at least in the earliest decades of newspaper production in the late nineteenth and early twentieth centuries, earned their main incomes as businessmen or lawyers and ran newspapers as a sideline.

West African newspapers in English date back much earlier to the Royal Gazettes in early nineteenth-century Sierra Leone and the Gold Coast, and missionary newspapers in mid-century Liberia and Nigeria (Jones-Quartey 1967, Burrowes 2004). These publications contained shipping and commercial news for European and African merchants, government and missionary reports and occasional poems and short stories, and they were read alongside British newspapers, Christian journals and trade journals in both Britain and West Africa.

By the mid-1880s, anglophone African newspapers were largely owned, managed and edited by African intellectuals and businessmen. Often belonging to migrant communities from towns along the West African coast, these elites articulated regional and global interests and, depending on their political persuasions, connected with British trading networks in Liverpool and London or pan-African networks in Europe, North America, Africa and the Caribbean, as well as with anticolonial movements further afield (Mann 1985, Gocking 1999). By the early 1900s, when the material selected for this chapter was published, West African newspapers had become hubs of political activism

---

[1] Difficulties in raising capital are described by many newspaper editors and managers. See, for example, Mustafa Abdelwahid (2011), *Dusé Mohamed Ali: The Autobiography of a Pioneer Pan African and Afro-Asian Activist* (Trenton NJ: Africa World Press) and Nnamdi Azikiwe (1970), *My Odyssey* (London: C. Hurst).

[2] In Nigeria alone, 51 newspapers were established between 1880 and 1937 (Omu 1978: 26).

and literary creativity. They were a significant part of the public life of educated West Africans as local professional elites and, in increasing numbers as the twentieth century progressed, newly educated sub-elites sought space for the expression of opinions and arguments.

From the earliest days of West African newspaper production, editors imagined the circulation and impact of their discourse in global terms. Often using the humanistic logic of anti-racism alongside the language of press freedom, newspapers demonstrated local elites' mastery of the logic of post-Enlightenment rationalism. Using European and indigenous languages to comment on social and political developments, African editors insisted on holding colonial authorities accountable for what Bodil Frederiksen, in her study of the colonial East African press, terms the 'deep contradiction of British colonial policy', whereby the state expressed a commitment to 'upholding the principle of freedom of speech' in contexts 'characterised by subjugation by force and [a] pervasive lack of rights' (2020: 406). Highly educated and politically engaged, early twentieth-century editors stood at the forefront of print cultures fed by a century of universalist standpoints – abolitionist, ecumenical, humanist and, by the 1890s, anticolonial – that connected them to international political and intellectual networks.

Through newsprint, colonial subjects in one location could address networks of political solidarity and support in other locations. Editors often conceptualised the communications networks made possible by newspapers as transcending the local. Even though life was neither egalitarian nor consensual for the majority of colonial subjects, and access to print constrained by multiple factors – not least income, gender and education – right up to the Second World War, editors and other media producers voiced utopian definitions of the capacity of newsprint to reach readerships of all classes, nations and languages beyond the specificities of place. One Nigerian editor in the late 1920s, I. B. Thomas, whose creative writing is discussed in the next chapter, repeatedly insisted that his newspaper, *Akede Eko*, 'reache[d] into all four corners of the world' (Barber 2012: 41). In practical terms, the impossibility of Thomas's vision is illustrated by its appearance in a bilingual Yoruba–English newspaper that could not feasibly lay claim to a global readership.

The imaginary world communities and multifarious subject-positions produced by local writers in colonial West African newspapers reveal how literate elites conceptualised communication in a world mediated by newsprint. Newspapers offered a medium that, on the one hand, could enter political spaces that would otherwise be closed to colonial subjects and, on the other hand, undermined the rationale of the imperial project by demonstrating the capacity of local people for literary self-expression, learning, expertise, independent critical thinking and, by implication, rational self-government of a type recognisable to the colonial powers.

With international networks being actively fostered through print, it is not surprising that literate locals in colonial contexts attracted loathing from government officials like no other category of colonial subject. Time and again, high-ranking colonial officials expressed venom towards local intellectuals as shapers of public opinion through which, in their view, vulnerable illiterate and semi-literate colonial subjects were made susceptible to incendiary printed media designed to inflame anticolonial emotions. In a report to the British Secretary of State for the Colonies in 1900, for example, the governor of Lagos Colony, Sir William MacGregor, described how the *Bale* (Yoruba traditional ruler) of Ayésan:

> complained loudly of the presence of a 'writer' that had settled in his village. This scribe is one of a class of young men that has been created by the educational establishments of Lagos. They take up their abode in native villages to write letters for people for hire, and to act as correspondents for the ill-informed and mendacious newspapers of Lagos. The *Bale* declares that the one then living in Aiyéssan was trying to stir up the people against him; that he would not come to the *Bale* when he sent for him; and would not obey him in any way. The *Bale* wished for advice, which I gave him to the effect that he should order the 'writer' to depart, and if he did not do so then to expel him by force. At certain other places I heard of people of this class thrusting their presence on native councils when sitting with the object of concocting contributions thereon for the Lagos Press. (CO 879/62/13, 20 July 1900)

MacGregor's draconian recommendation for the banishment of the derisively named 'writer' highlights the threat posed by 'people of this class', not only to colonial administrators but also to the customary authorities whose loyalty the British secured through power-sharing arrangements under the policy of indirect rule, backed by threats of forced removal if they became unmanageable. His report reveals how local print cultures and the readerships they generated created environments for circulating political opinions that challenged the tenets of European colonialism as well as the traditional structures of political authority through which the balance of power was maintained in the colonies. For the *Bale* of Ayésan, as much as for MacGregor, the danger of 'the "writer"' was his access, via Lagos, to a world of readers made possible by print. Contemptuous of locally negotiated processes of governance under colonial rule, such educated men asserted their destabilising presence: they were not legitimate political actors in the view of those in power but a new class whose opinions and utterances were always *en route* to print in 'the ill-informed and mendacious newspapers', and thence into a public space where their criticisms would 'stir up the people' against indigenous rulers and disrupt delicate imperial relationships between rulers and largely illiterate colonial populations.

Thirteen years later, in a memorandum on the topic of racial segregation to Lewis Harcourt, Secretary of State for the Colonies, Lord Lugard, the governor of Southern Nigeria, described the great insolence of the Lagos press towards Europeans, again revealing the centrality of educated local elites to any discussion of the relationship between print and public spheres in the colonial era:

> [Abeokuta's] 'educated' section is dominated by a fear of the Lagos Press, and I find opinions expressed in that Press to the effect that yellow fever is a disease to which Europeans are liable, but to which natives are immune, and that, if Europeans find that by residing in an African community they are liable to contract yellow fever, the remedy is that they should betake themselves elsewhere. (CO 879/112, 12 August 1913)

Lugard's appraisal of the Lagos press demonstrates how the expansion of African-owned newspapers in the early twentieth century was a reaction to British imperialism that, in turn, fuelled the hardening of imperial racism. It also reveals the reasonable indignation with which African editors rejected the racial pseudo-science driving public health and sanitation policies in British West Africa (see Newell 2020: 43–4). Brilliantly deploying sarcasm to convey antiracist rage, the 'Lagos Press' exposed how the need for racially segregated housing stemmed from imperial racism rather than African insanitary behaviour.[3] The logical solution, that Europeans 'should betake themselves elsewhere', showed that any failure of rationality lay in Harcourt's preposterous idea, mooted in 1913, to invest substantial amounts of local tax revenue in racially segregated housing for the small numbers of Europeans in Nigeria (Newell 2020).

MacGregor's and Lugard's comments draw attention to the potentially transformative impact of locally controlled print media on readers, illuminating opinions at the highest level of colonial government about the dangers of uncensored mass reading.[4] In the governors' views, indigenous newspapers amplified opinions that would reverberate through uncontrollable public spaces to come back, loaded with criticism, into their own political domains.

---

[3] Lugard is referring to Dr John Payne Jackson (1848–1915), anticolonial editor of the *Lagos Weekly Record* between 1891 and 1915, who was one of the many educated men to find themselves excluded from the expanding colonial infrastructure as a direct consequence of racial hierarchies in government services (Omu 1978, Sklar 1963, Sawada 2012).

[4] This echoed the anxieties of the bourgeoisie in Britain about the moral dangers of allowing working-class and women readers access to popular literature.

The steady increase in African-owned newspapers in the first half of the twentieth century caused the educated classes to be regarded as more 'troublesome' than ever by British colonial authorities. From the perspective of hardline colonial administrators, indigenous newspaper production posed a major threat to imperialist ideology. Simply by existing as vehicles to carry colonial subjects' commentaries on government to the rest of the world, newspapers had the potential to erode colonialism, either in the language of the dominant power or in indigenous languages. Men such as MacGregor and Lugard in the official sphere of government – where gazettes, reports and memoranda were written, circulated and archived – repeatedly noted the audacity of their interlocutors in the public sphere of the press, who produced printed commentaries that paralleled and rivalled material produced by the government.[5]

Colonial regimes developed strategies ranging from persuasion to punishment in a bid to control people's media consumption and extend European influence beyond the established elites. By 1913, for example, in reaction to the potential for African employees in the colonial medical service to publish newspaper articles critical of government that would be read internationally, including in London, British West African governments 'fell back upon the employment of Europeans in even minor posts … because they give less trouble' (PRO CO 879/112 No. 132a). In the face of an increasingly nationalist press that attracted large readerships in the 1920s, less overtly discriminatory strategies included the establishment of Nigeria's longest-standing daily, the *Daily Times* (est. 1926), as a government-backed moderate newspaper with African and European contributors to intervene in public debates, rebuff the anticolonial press, and provide readers with information and explanations about government policy. Meeting like with like, the *Daily Times* countered anticolonial newspapers such as the *Lagos Daily News* (est. 1925) with attacks on its credibility, describing it as a 'purveyor of fictitious sensational news' (October 21 1930, 4; see Adebanwi 2016). Softer measures to dilute the educated elite's dominance of public opinion included the expansion of primary and secondary education in the late 1920s and 1930s.

While they may not have created a public sphere in the Habermasian sense, African editors challenged political hierarchies by juxtaposing documents from the official sphere with the contributions of ordinary correspondents

---

[5] Africans employed directly by the government were prohibited from contributing to newspapers and could be dismissed or forced to resign if they published articles, or were suspected of writing under pseudonyms, in the local press. This was not simply a binary contest between white colonial officials and the 'native press', however, as conservative local newspapermen such as the editor of the *Nigerian Pioneer*, Sir Kitoyi Ajasa (1866–1937) and the editor of the *Nigerian Spectator,* Dr Richard Akiwande Savage (1874–1935), also regarded the 'great unofficial public' as open to exploitation by lettered Africans (see Newell 2020: 43–57).

and non-expert commentators.[6] Whatever their political persuasions, local newspapermen generated an 'unofficial sphere' with their printing presses, and created a field of influence to complement, if not rival, official efforts to produce governable colonial subjects. In form as much as content, newspapers flattened official discourse into a relationship of equivalence by juxtaposing contributions on the printed page. African newspapers published government ordinances, governors' speeches, court transcripts and other state-sanctioned statements side by side with their own correspondents' material, reducing the hierarchy between the colonial state and the public sphere to a set of dialogues and critiques. Editors nurtured shadow governments, shadow debates and shadow voters, printing the opinions and disagreements of local intellectuals as they jostled to shape public opinion and commented on one another's analyses of current affairs.

Newspapers were more than just spaces for the gathering of 'imagined communities', as Benedict Anderson ([1983] 2016) famously argued: they were training grounds for literary practices, offering forums where readers of diverse social and educational backgrounds could encounter one anothers' opinions and respond. Editors encouraged these encounters by inserting brief comments on the topics raised by correspondents. In so doing, they demonstrated their public engagement with individual correspondents and showed the value they placed on readers' opinions. Indeed, while they rarely admitted it, many editors of small local newspapers depended on letter-writers to generate copy, whether in the form of news from the regions or correspondence. As the British trader in Nigeria, J. M. Stuart-Young, pointed out in the early 1930s, 'Any enterprising newspaper proprietor out here could … fill his pages with nothing beyond letters to the Editor' (*Comet* 30 December 1933: 9; see Chapter 3).

African-owned newspapers were often small-scale and financially insecure, operating on tight budgets with little or no profit margin. Their dependence on unknown, amateur and occasional contributors was hazardous, not least because of the risk that correspondents might offend subscribers or, worse still, alienate advertisers whose revenue was often essential to keeping newspapers afloat. Careless, ill-informed, or malicious correspondents might also contravene colonial libel laws and propel editors into court.[7] At the very least, scurrilous or salacious material might jeopardise an editor's reputation for providing news

---

[6] For a full discussion of the differences between a Habermasian definition of the 'public sphere' and West African newspaper cultures in British West Africa, see Newell (2013: 29–43).

[7] Editors allowed correspondents to adopt pseudonyms but would not publish a letter if its author did not provide his or her name. While this was regarded as a goodwill gesture on the part of the correspondent to prevent malicious correspondence, British anti-sedition legislation, which was updated in 1934, required editors to obtain the names of pseudonymous contributors in case of litigation (see Newell 2013).

and attract accusations from rival editors that his title was airing gossip or 'dirty linen' in the public sphere (see Chapter 2).

The history of the English-language press in West Africa is filled with examples of editors offering guidance on the appropriate content and style for publication. Editors openly coached readers in the art of public writing, teaching them which grammar, emotions and topics were appropriate for publication and which were not. A column in the 1930s Lagos weekly, the *Comet*, detailed the problems editors faced. Having enthusiastically invited contributions from readers to keep his paper popular and current, a problem arose in every mailbag for editor Dusé Mohamed Ali:

> Each week this office receives bundles of unprintable manuscript which has to be returned to the writers or consigned to the waste paper basket because there budding authors have no concept of literary values. To be able to write passable English, or to copy some well known writer is hardly what is to be expected from West African graduates in English who must have had at least a bowing acquaintance with the classics. Youngmen, to develop a style of your own for high flown poetry or sensible articles, must digest, without imitating, literary styles of other men, as they must eat other animals or vegetables to build up their own bodies. (*Comet* 11 April 1936: 7)

Ali's prescription for these 'budding authors' was to sit down and study exemplary English books: in particular, they should read Thomas Carlyle's *Sartor Resartus* until they had built up an ability to write 'sensible articles' (Ibid.) Other authors recommended by Ali included Shakespeare and, in translation, Homer, Dante, Montaigne and Montesquieu (Ibid.).

The egalitarian gestures to be found in editorials, where readers were regularly invited to send in their opinions about particular topics, were curbed by this gatekeeping activity as editors and other readers patrolled literary standards, safeguarded their reputations, modelled how to pitch and phrase letters and exercised their authority as the guardians and spokesmen of local print cultures. As the case study of a fledgling Lagos poet in Chapter 3 will show, correspondents placed themselves in considerable danger of public humiliation by putting pen to paper in the genre of public writing. Despite the risks, with the expansion of secondary education in the late 1920s and the access it provided to English literacy, increasing numbers of non-elite men, and in fewer cases also women, made their opinions and tastes heard by writing articles and letters for submission to the English-language press.[8]

---

[8] Among elite, highly educated West Africans, Mabel Dove was the most notable woman to contribute articles and creative writing to the West African press in the 1930s. Several

While print must not be idealised or fetishised as an inherently democratising force, especially in colonial West African contexts where the acquisition of English literacy was largely limited to male elites, editors' requests for reader participation in West African newspapers display a democratising spirit that encouraged the participation of people who would not otherwise have put pen to paper. Newspaper editors and correspondents articulated a powerful sense of their connectedness with one another through print. Continuously quoting from globally circulating newspapers, engaging with one another through their own columns and reacting to articles in rival papers through letters to editors, educated West Africans used print to assert their belief that public opinion could circulate around a world rendered paper-flat by newsprint, entering political spaces that would otherwise be closed to Africans.

'A Banker', 'Dick Carnis' and 'B.B.'

Creative writing in West African newspapers is enmeshed in these political histories of reading and print. As described above, the editors and highly educated elites who produced and consumed creative writing in the early twentieth century existed in greater proximity to colonial regimes than many other sectors of West African society. They were in frequent contact with British officials through their professions and through their attendance at churches, racecourses, libraries, clubs and restaurants patronised by colonial officials (Mann 1985, Echeruo 1977). They also passed through colonial missionary and British private schools and their editorials and reports on current affairs demonstrated that they were as capable of writing English as any other person educated to their level. The florid literary style that characterises the creative writing of these West African elites therefore demands explanation.

The creative writers analysed below shared a style of writing that might be dismissed by current literary standards as turgid, sermonising, rhetorical, or simply too singular to be recognised as part of a genre or tradition. Three creative writers are considered here: 'A Banker', whose sonorous prose appeared weekly in the *Gold Coast Leader* for a period of six years from 1904 to 1910; the monogrammic 'B.B.', who published a three-part diary for the *Gold Coast Leader* in November and December 1904; and 'Dick Carnis', whose declamatory serialised narrative, 'Between Ourselves', was published in the *Gold Coast Leader* alongside the others in the early 1900s. Their literary styles collectively encapsulate a current of English writing that infuriated colonial officials in West Africa, especially educationists. 'Stand by! ye giddy wrestlers for the lustrous

---

other prominent elite women were regular newspaper correspondents, including the poet Gladys May Casely Hayford and her mother, Adelaide Casely Hayford (see Gadzekpo 2001).

Moon, stand by!' reads the first instalment of Dick Carnis's seven-part column, setting the rich tone for subsequent episodes:

> next to men by whom crude thoughts and past events in silken garb are clad – whose paeans erstwhile with lusty voice, in dulcet tones, we sang – lend us your ravished ears, all ye that thrive on Briefs; and ye worthy Leeches in numbers, least of all, – experts, men of science, hearken enrapt, enchained! (*Gold Coast Leader* 15 October 1904: 3)

High, bombastic language such as this typifies a mode of West African writing in which the sheer pleasure of the English language seems to stand at the forefront of texts, holding equal status to the communication of messages, or, more accurately, contributing fundamentally to the message to the extent that the content and form of these creative writings are coterminous. This literary style begs a question: in contexts of British colonial power, to what extent did local intellectuals' mastery of English literary discourse mediate their political relationships, helping them to gain access to transnational networks and stake claims to political power?

British officials regarded such wordiness as the worst outcome of the colonial education system in Africa, and by the 1920s and 1930s it was also regularly satirised by members of the African intelligentsia – the very class who printed this material in the early twentieth century – as a sign of failed mimicry of Englishness.[9] In W. E. G. Sekyi's Fante-English play, *The Blinkards* ([1915] 1974), for example, the 'bombastic' Mrs Borofosem gets her English grammar and British cultural references wrong, thus demonstrating Sekyi's derision for poorly educated Africans, especially women.[10] By contrast, the authors discussed in this chapter use impeccable English (and Latin) language and grammar, exemplifying what Sekyi's lower-class woman a decade later could never hope to achieve. Worse still, as the twentieth century progressed, high-falutin English was seen as a sign of sycophantic deference to a racist colonial culture, or, in the stark terms of Ngũgĩ wa Thiong'o in the mid-1980s, the colonisation of the mind by imperialist language (1986: 11, 18).[11]

---

[9] Many decades later, in his first novel, *Long Long Ago* (1957), the Onitsha pamphleteer Ogali A. Ogali parodied this 'high' intellectual manner, using hilarious fake Latin for Jack, a wastrel character who has plundered his illiterate parents' scarce resources to attend Oxford University, only to spend all the money on drink, returning within six months with no certificate in hand. Showing off his 'fluent' Latin to his uneducated family, Jack asks for a pen thus: 'giveabus meabus penabus' ([1957] 1980a: 17).

[10] Educated women were represented as 'henpeckers' from the earliest days of West African creative writing in English-language newspapers. See 'A Native' ([1886–8] 2002), *Marita: Or the Folly of Love*.

[11] Ngũgĩ's views on English are discussed in more detail in Chapter 4.

The writers discussed in this section might be regarded as exemplary mimics were it not for the fact that they displayed a distinctly decolonial relationship with canonical English literature, treating it as a resource to be tapped and absorbed into new genres. This was by no means a one-way relationship between English literature and colonial authors. In the creative writing discussed in this section, as in subsequent chapters, a strongly articulated credo shines through in which European civilisations are regarded as plural and relative. The imperialist belief that 'civilisation' – literary or otherwise – spreads outward from colonial centres in Europe is overturned in favour of different aesthetic models.

West African creative writing in early twentieth-century newspapers rarely yields empathetic characters, clearly structured plots, naturalistic scenes, or coherent themes and messages. Stylistically, authors like Dick Carnis operate so far outside the norms and traditions of realist prose that their work necessitates alternative forms of literary recognition and appreciation. A Banker, for example, is inspired by the Romantic poets in a thoroughly 'Romantic' manner whereby he seems to literally in-spire, or inhale, his models. There one finds Alfred Lord Tennyson mixing with Percy Bysshe Shelley, William Wordsworth and Lord Byron, sprinkled with quotations from other English Romantic poets and always re-purposed to Christian moral ends. In the manner of a preacher, A Banker de-personalises the intensely subjective Romantic lyric by replacing first-person perception with collective pronouns, through which he issues moral weather-warnings against conditions such as 'the icy clutches of a cold, callous wordliness' (*GCL* 15 October 1904: 3). Such 'wordly' anti-materialism may be surprising coming from an author who named himself after a profession associated with usury and greed by Jesus, whose presence he invokes in 90 separate articles published in the *Gold Coast Leader* between 1904 and 1910.

A Banker's short columns describe a Romantic view of the vastness of nature – where Nature stands for, or stands in for, God – but in the final paragraph of each narrative he floods this world with Christian symbolism and biblical morality, reclaiming Romantic meditational discourse for devotional ends. At the end of each article, the world he conjures up transcends earthly preoccupations and asserts universal connectivity: nature and history are removed from the material world and rendered channels towards the spiritual condition of redemption, where heaven is open to righteous souls and unspeakable consequences await the rest. This is an ecumenical vision that invites colonial readers into a belief system extending throughout the world, the universe and beyond into the hereafter. It is difficult to imagine a less local or material world than offered by this geography, nor a more universal vision of human subjectivity.

As it turns out, A Banker was an Englishman. In June 1910, the editor of the *Gold Coast Leader* informed readers that a 'regrettable inadvertence and oversight' had led to a seven-month delay between the delivery and the opening of a letter from a member of A Banker's family informing the editor of the death of the stalwart contributor on October 28, 1909 (25 June 1910: 3). Here readers discover that A Banker was Charles James Lacy Jnr, the grandson of Mr Benjamin W. Lacy of the bank Lacy, Hartland, Woodbridge, and Co., London (est. 1809). By the time he was circulating his Christian Romantic prose to newspapers in diverse corners of the British colonial world – including New South Wales (Australia), 'British East Africa' and Canada alongside colonial Ghana – Lacy had probably retired from his profession. 'Mr Lacy rendered us invaluable services during his lifetime, free of charge,' the editor wrote. 'His articles were most highly appreciated and immensely enjoyed by a wide circle of readers ... He preached the Gospel with a facile pen' (*GCL* 25 June 1910: 3).

A Banker's English identity is immensely useful in helping to clarify what is meant by 'Anglo' and 'local' in relation to the two other writers chosen for analysis, because the literary influences on Dick Carnis and B.B. are more eclectic and their content is more grounded in identifiable local settings. Dick Carnis's influences stretch back to Edmund Spenser's *The Faerie Queene* (1590) and John Milton's *Paradise Lost* (1667), through to the Romantic poets, particularly Shelley, and to mid-nineteenth-century Presbyterian psalms and hymns, including Charles Seymour Robinson's popular *Songs for the Sanctuary* (1865), with passing references to the titles of Shakespeare's plays. Unlike A Banker's one-way transports up to a heavenly destination, Dick Carnis knits these textual references together into dense, multi-layered blankets of prose that cryptically and metaphorically refer to specific local figures such as Fante chiefs and colonial governors, and to recent events such as the death of Queen Victoria alongside broader African political demands, including calls for enfranchisement. The 'universal' in Dick Carnis's work is humanist and this-worldly rather than transcendental: a general emphasis on existential freedom pervades every column.

Dick Carnis offers a promiscuous mash-up of the Victorian literature syllabus and produces cryptic matter that makes for very slow reading. Unlike A Banker's uprooted, anti-worldly writing, the bombastic language in Dick Carnis's work can be interpreted as offering critical commentaries on local political affairs as well as the general impact of the British presence in colonial Ghana. The exclamatory and symbolic language in the first instalment, for example, includes references to the recent death of Queen Victoria (via *The Faerie Queene*) and a commentary on political culture in its broadest sense.

From one perspective, overt protest and radicalism in 'Between Ourselves' are masked by the insubstantial, allusive content of the columns. From another perspective, however, this tone produces and gives substance to the serial's political critique. Dick Carnis's citations are multi-layered, working outwards from the empirical to the allusive through layers of quotation. Interestingly, when one turns to his Romantic influences, the poet who takes precedence above the others is Shelley, whose visionary language is duplicated in the column.[12] A typical paragraph from 'Between Ourselves' reads:

> We have Kings to the right and Chiefs to the left in plenty, but who like sorry steeds no longer sport the shaggy mane, nor strong to prance, nor swift for the unequal race. Cheer them, in their saddest plight; keep watch and ward – not for loaves nor for fishes but with joy that shakes the spheres, and for strenuous love that moves the wheels of whirling orbs. (*GCL* 15 October 1904: 3)

This paragraph unbinds material from *Prometheus Unbound* by extracting and reusing individual words from Shelley's poem. Lines such as 'Vast beams like spokes of some invisible wheel / Which whirl as the orb whirls, swifter than thought' (Shelley [1820] 1847: 122) are made present without being actually cited in an attributable manner. Through this quoting mode, Dick Carnis demonstrates the tonal and stylistic influence of a poet who, of all the English Romantics, offered the most potential for social and political critique, influencing Mahatma Gandhi (1869–1948) as a model for nonviolent resistance while, in his own time, formulating an early human rights discourse invested in universal humanism that singled him out as one of the most radical poets of his generation (Stroup 2000: 91–127).[13]

Without any direct reference either to the Gold Coast, West Africa, or British imperialism, Dick Carnis portrays traditional African authority in the Gold Coast as weak, vulnerable and anachronistic, incapable of achieving an equal footing with British imperial power. A passing reference to Shakespeare cloaks a general complaint about political progress: 'There's much ado about nothing grand and high: much stir but no certain sign of sure advance' (*GCL* 15 October 1904: 3). This is the same message offered by B.B., discussed below, and in numerous editorials in the *Gold Coast Leader*, indicating that B.B., Dick Carnis and the editor may have been one and the same person. The political frustrations harnessed to English literary quotations convey this author's – or these authors' – intellectual and political readiness to take the reins as educated Africans who could creatively fuse colonial and African traditions.

---

[12] My guarded acceptance of the gender pronoun indicated by this pseudonym is no indication that this author was in fact a man. While historians have identified few, if any, female columnists for the West African press at this time, authors' use of pseudonyms demands that readers keep open the diversity of possibilities for gendered authorship and attribution (see Newell 2013).

[13] Alongside Shelley, the other poet accompanying Dick Carnis on his literary journey is John Milton, another writer renowned for his advocacy of freedom of speech and the right to self-determination for oppressed people (Schwartz 2012).

Unlike A Banker, who always explains the moral of each symbolic episode in the final paragraph, transforming allegory into parable in the process, Dick Carnis uses his English literary sources in the manner of local oral practitioners, creating new environments for his quotations and relying on them to produce morals to be extrapolated by readers. The ebullient style of his writing displays his artistic authority and skill as an innovator, while readers carry out the work of interpretation. Combining metaphorical language and quotation, he leans on Akan oral traditions in which an expert in the use of proverbs will cite the familiar line, embellish it artistically, and shape it to fit a particular circumstance without commenting directly on the situation under scrutiny: the listener completes the work by applying the proverb and drawing out its lessons (Yankah [1989] 2012). In this manner, Dick Carnis remains outside the incendiary political implications carried by the quotation he has chosen in its dialogue with readers, while drawing from the English literary canon for an additional reservoir of materials.

'Between Ourselves' achieves its political critique through this densely woven network of English literary references, rendered with complete linguistic and grammatical control. In a similar manner to James Joyce's *Ulysses* (1918–20) and, decades later, Derek Walcott's *Omeros* (1990), the author's free-ranging quotations can be regarded as ways to translate West African 'national' life into epic terms, pressing local events and characters into a high heroic frame and, in the process, generating august, neo-classical status for the Gold Coast and its inhabitants. Perhaps paradoxically, Dick Carnis's emulative English prose is put into the service of a West African national – or cultural nationalist – politics. Importantly, his profoundly patriotic assertion of the capacity of local people to occupy heroic worlds and rule themselves occurs through the literary production of delocalised worlds that are articulated through canonical English literatures. *Contra* Ngũgĩ, Dick Carnis asserts a global and cosmopolitan relationship with English literature in which the latter is flattened out and treated as mobile, available for transnational 'nationalist' uptake.

If Dick Carnis inscribes heroic references into local public spaces by emulating Spenser, Milton and Shelley, B.B's three-part narrative, 'A Poor Man's Diary', has a more ambivalent relationship to its sources. The column is narrated in the first person by a young man named Boves Bones (Latin: Cows Bones), whose name circles playfully back to the author's pen name, which at first sight might be regarded as the least pseudonymous of all markers of authorship, a monogram being the lightest disguise of identity. Boves Bones recalls paying regular visits to his 'mentor,' Fidus Achates (Latin: Faithful Achates), also known as 'the Old Man', who lives at the Bunyanesque address, 'All Fool's Paradise, Blunderment House, Circumlocution Office, Humburg Street' until his death. The column comprises extracts from Fidus's journals, which contained versions of the senior man's political oratories of the 1880s and early 1890s, bequeathed to B.B. and entitled 'De Omnibus Rebus' (Latin: With Regard to Everything; On All Kinds of Matters).

At first glance, the characters' Latin names and satirical addresses indicate that the author will choose to adopt a traditional mock-heroic style to criticise senior political figures in the Gold Coast without naming (or libelling) his targets. With blunders, humbug and foolishness inscribed into Fidus's address, readers might expect the youthful narrator to outshine the senior man, and for B.B. to satirically appropriate and expose the original 'fidus Achates', Aeneas's faithful companion in Virgil's *Aeneid*, in a colonial setting. While the senior man's eccentricity is constantly on display – his habits include chain-smoking cigar butts from an overfull ashtray and constantly repeating his tagline, 'If I were a millionaire, if' – the mock-heroic rapidly collapses as the column proceeds, and the classical framework loosens into lucid political commentaries on colonial rule in West Africa. 'The wealth of each town, village and hamlet in the Protectorate is … entirely and absolutely in the wrong hands', reads the first extract from Fidus's diary (*GCL* 12 November 1904: Supp. I). 'Think of the potentialities of and the undoubted possibilities of our youths', the diary continues, contrasting these with the 'illiterate nobodies' currently in power, 'who have not a scintilla of imagination, who know nothing of the Promethean Fire, nor any notion of the Social and Political exigencies of the Protectorate' (Ibid.). The bias against unschooled Africans is unequivocal in this sentence, illustrating the sense of intellectual superiority asserted by educated elites in their support for 'modern' educated youths against 'illiterate chiefs', an ideology that continued in Nigerian pamphlet literature well into the 1960s (see Chapter 4).

'A Poor Man's Diary' demands to be situated in its immediate local environment for its fragments of commentary and ambivalent satire to make sense. Episodes cover topics ranging from agricultural experiments with cassava, potatoes and other crops to the Latin syllabus in Gold Coast secondary schools. Of all the columns discussed so far, B.B's is the least oblique, and the most realist, in its outward orientation to colonial Ghanaian society. Fidus's initial positioning as a mock-heroic target using Latin and classical literary references rapidly becomes a critique of these very sources. Ultimately, the most quoted writer is the West African diarist himself who, after 'five academic years fighting with … our own chief Euclid' at one of the colony's two secondary schools, and after being made to learn Latin, concludes that 'the Declensions and Conjugations of Dead Verbs' alongside 'Problems and Theorems, Riders and Corollaries have profited me NOTHING' (*GCL* 26 November 1904: 5; emphasis retained). Instead he calls for 'Practice, Practice, Practice!' and an appreciation of the beauty and productive potential of the 'cross-grained, matter-of-fact world' (Ibid.). Translated into aesthetic terms, this Gradgrind-like utilitarianism sounds like a call for realism to puncture and deflate the tendency among educated West Africans to emulate classical and Romantic sources.

B.B. hides twice-over from political answerability, first in his use of a pseudonym, and second in his adoption of the ruse of a journal written by an eccentric dead genius that contains a host of 'utopian schemes and other impracticable projects' in agriculture and industry (and in so doing, he distances himself from the practical achievability of Fidus's 'matter-of-fact world') (Ibid.). The narrator quotes Fidus's lengthy speculations 'regarding the Colony, the World in General, the Government and the People of his day' while continuously reiterating the gap between the past and the present and between Fidus and himself (Ibid.; 12 November 1904: Supp. I).

For all its simplicity, B.B's narrative contains a complex and politicised temporality: allegedly composed in the 1880s before Fidus's death in the early 1890s, and published by B.B. as a historical document, the diary offers optimistic projections for the future of the Gold Coast in the forthcoming century. 'In the democratic age of the Twentieth Century, Home Rule shall become an accomplished fact', the diarist predicts (*GCL* 26 November 1904: 5). As a present-day narrator who occupies the time anticipated by his mentor, Boves Bones comments without political aggression on the extent to which his mentor's ideals have – or have not – been achieved. For example, in one annotation to Fidus's call for rapid expansion to the education system in the Gold Coast, he writes, 'N.B: In this year of grace 1904, the Government has 7 Schools in the Colony and Protectorate, 3 for Boys, 2 for Girls; 1 for the Fanti Police and 1 for the Hausa Force. We are moving on!' (26 November 1904: 5). The cleverness of the column lies in the way the voice of the diarist reverberates through the decades behind Bones, predicting self-rule and mass education that were further-off in 1904 than they were in the 1880s as a consequence of the new imperialism that swept from Britain across the colonies in the 1890s.

The 'Pleasure of Influence'

In different ways, A Banker, Dick Carnis and B.B. all need to be understood through the combined impact of English poetry, the classics and colonial Christian education at the end of the nineteenth century. Learning by rote and recitation were accepted teaching techniques in British as well as West African schools well into the twentieth century, and emulation was a highly rated and respectable literary endeavour in Europe until the rise of the mass-produced novel, existing in parallel with it as a separate literary trajectory and, as Chapter 5 discusses in more detail, often considered to be an act of homage (or satirical doubling) rather than dependency or plagiarism (see Winter 2011, Ofori-Attah 2006, Gazda 2002).

The derivativeness of A Banker's, Dick Carnis's and B.B's prose is impossible to ignore, but as the ebullience of their writing demonstrates, these authors were anything but colonial mimics. Their richly emulative prose would have challenged readers to identify the chains of literary reference while also – particularly in the case of Dick Carnis – inviting local readers to relish the explosive pleasure of deciphering the local referents behind the metaphors and symbols. These authors' work exhibits so little 'anxiety of influence,' to use Harold Bloom's ([1973] 1997) influential explanation for how poets' sources exist in unbearable tension with their desire for a unique vision, that alternative models of appreciation to mimicry become necessary in relation to the literary expressions of these English-language authors (see also Chapter 5).

All three writers exhibit confidence and pleasure in their influences and pay homage to their diverse literary mentors in the best Victorian sense of emulation as role-modelling. What connects these authors is the way they de-verse poetry, stripping out rhyme and metre, rendering their sources into prose and, in the process, freely borrowing individual words and distinctive phrases from the poets to add beauty and erudition to their own chosen topics. Notably absent from the repertoire of these writers is the novel – realist, romantic, picaresque, or otherwise. For all its seriousness of tone, their writing can be regarded as less anxious and more playful than allowed for by notions of mimicry, either in its subservient sense as emulation or in its politically subversive sense as parody and satire. These authors seem to relish and exploit the disembodied quality of writing that characterises newsprint, as articulated by newspaper editors in their sense of the global reach of print, and as theorised by Anderson in his classic account of newspaper readerships. This writing is ludic, playful with English language and literature while also carrying symbolic and moral messages about readers' capacity to inhabit a world made available by print.

A Banker, Dick Carnis and B.B. make sense if read through popular literary genres in the late nineteenth century, including homilies and psalms; they can also be understood through educational techniques such as recitation and copying out, as well as in relation to local West African aesthetic cultures in which the use of quotation simultaneously enabled creative innovation and political critique (see Chapters 5 and 9). Creative writers in the *Gold Coast Leader* thus show that to write well may have been to write 'in the style of' canonical authors, and in so doing they showcased their erudition and intellectual leadership.

These writers produced postcolonial utopias, imagining universal spaces inhabited by humans unmarked by hierarchies of class, gender and race. Dick Carnis defined his audience as 'all [who] may read': 'no flowery legends these, but actual facts in golden letters wrought that all may read, e'en they who run' (*GCL* 15 October 1904: 3; citing *The Book of Habakkak* 2:2). Given its dense, verbose literary style, many readers might have wished to run from the full serialisation of 'Between Ourselves', but the world Dick Carnis addressed included all Anglo-literates: all can freely access his 'actual facts in golden letters' because they appear in the medium of newsprint. Moreover, these authors' pseudonymity gave them status as print-mediated subjects that took away the pressure either to mimic or to innovate and rendered any dichotomies between originals and copies irrelevant: why would a pseudonymous author be anxious about his or her influences, given that accusations of derivation (and acknowledgements of originality) require the existence of a named author as a legal entity who wishes to assert ownership over a text for posterity?

Their work illustrates the importance of activating the category of 'local' as an adjective and as a noun. English-language creative writing in colonial West African newspapers is not equivalent to anglophone literatures from other parts of the English-speaking world. Whatever the geographical origin of an author, it is necessary to think about how English-language writing, as printed locally in colonial settings, is entangled with the social histories of reading and print in those places. Given the crucial mediating role of print in English-language writing in the British Empire, anglophone might usefully be pulled into two parts, the prefix retained and the suffix discarded. In disconnecting the '-phone,' with its emphasis on spoken language and sound, it becomes possible to think about authors and readers in British colonial contexts as 'Anglo-scribes' and 'Anglo-literates'. These were people who were mediated by and saturated in print, whose textual 'voices' were produced by and in print and not prior to it, and who were firmly situated in local print cultures where – in British West Africa at least – mastery of English facilitated political relationships between local and transregional elites and sub-elites and also helped a person to gain access to transnational networks.

The newspaper creative writing discussed in this chapter reveals local editors and authors projecting the existence of an egalitarian world produced in and by print, populated by disembodied print-subjects (separated from their 'selves' by pseudonymity and print), who had access to the English language, who existed in and because of newsprint, and whose works had the potential to circulate globally. Their shared belief in the capacity of print to carry messages across the world, and their sense of the free availability of English-language literature, the Bible and the classics for their own use, was anything but a watery universalist vision of 'imagined communities' or a call for visibility from peripheral cultures. Rather, to borrow Edward W. Said's (2001) terms in his essay on Fanon and Lukacs, 'the fiery core' of the borrowed material was 'reignited', and a postcolonial humanist affiliation was asserted worldwide (452). Said's argument works well to describe Anglo-literate print communities for whom the borrowing of poetry across global spaces exemplified a utopian humanism made possible by print, a universalism that was locally situated in the political specificities of authors' times and places.

Nevertheless, Dick Carnis and B.B. remained 'local' – or located – in a way that A Banker was not, using English poetry to host political critiques of Gold Coast institutions. The pleasure of influence and confidence shown by Dick

Carnis and B.B. exhibit a form of local cosmopolitanism in which, as Anglo-literates, they asserted the right to cite freely from, and to globalise, the English literary canon. This is the flip side of the nineteenth-century vision of English literary superiority, infamously pressed into the service of imperial expansion in India by Thomas Babington Macaulay in his 'Minute on Indian Education' (1835). Quoted copiously and indignantly the world over by postcolonial critics, Macaulay insisted that the global superiority of English literature gave cultural legitimacy to the British right to rule. Against this nationalist insularity was the universalist idea of English literature espoused by West Africa's local literary elites in the *Gold Coast Leader* at the beginning of the twentieth century.

The Time of Letters: Epistolarity and Nigerian Newsprint Cultures

2

> Here comes a letter from a man who wants to ask a question and the reply given to him.
>
> (Nnadozie c.1962: 24)

Towards the end of Amos Tutuola's *The Palm-Wine Drinkard* (1952), the first-person narrator is called upon by the chief of 'mixed town' to judge two complex court cases. The first involves so many complications that he adjourns the judgement for a year. Eight months pass and the chief calls on him to judge another equally impenetrable case, on which he also postpones judgement for a year. Utterly stumped by the complexity of both cases and under pressure as time passes, the narrator and his wife decide to leave mixed town and return home. But waiting for them at home are 'more than four letters' which have overtaken the travellers en route. In them, the narrator is begged by the people of mixed town 'to come and judge the two cases because both were still pending or waiting' (115). Under this epistolary pressure, as 'pending or waiting' time catches up with him, the narrator breaks the fourth wall of fiction and turns outward with an urgent appeal: 'I shall be very much grateful if anyone who reads this story-book can judge one or both cases and send the judgement to me as early as possible' (Ibid.).

While the letters from the people of mixed town arrive inside the narrative envelope of Tutuola's story, if judged by chronological standards, no correspondence, early or otherwise, is possible between the narrator and the reader as called for above. The narrator attempts to use letter-writing to transcend the limits of his story, but the reader's advice can never arrive in time. No reader's 'now' can synchronise with the narrator's present. The narrator's appeal for correspondence would only be feasible in a newspaper or another type of serialised genre in which a subsequent issue could carry readers' replies: without that, 'as early as possible' will always be too late because of the narrator's and the reader's incommensurability.

The narrator's appeal for correspondence in *The Palm-Wine Drinkard* draws from a neglected tradition of West African writing in which writers used real and fictional letters to assert authenticity, heighten truth-claims, secure readers' involvement in moral judgements of scenarios, mark periods of anticipation within narratives, play with the 'dear reader' convention in which readers are magically sucked in from the wide world beyond the covers of the book and parody or exploit all of these processes. Tutuola's call marks a literary moment with a long history and future in West African literature, up to and including social media creativity.[1] Whether fictional or real, in the first half of the twentieth century many thousands of letters filled West African printed texts with networks of mediation, interaction, invitation, critique and readerly involvement, suggesting an untapped history for contemporary epistolary forms.

Local elites used public letters to claim cultural prestige: in displaying their mastery of the rules of different epistolary sub-genres – from letters to editors to fictional love letters in romantic novellas – they furnished evidence of their status as intellectuals and society's spokesmen, a cut above ordinary readers. As this chapter will argue, letters represent a vital strand of textual productivity in West Africa in the first half of the twentieth century, fundamentally shaping local print cultures and serving as mouthpieces for literate classes, helping to define how subjectivity could be conveyed in print.

By the early 1950s, when Tutuola wrote *The Palm-Wine Drinkard*, letters had dominated local newspapers for more than 50 years as vehicles for public commentary on moral, social and political issues. Epistolarity also infused the earliest locally published self-help pamphlets as well as the eastern Nigerian dramas and novels that came after Tutuola's novel in the 1950s and 1960s (studied in Chapter 4), in which authors made use of letters to develop plots and give protagonists emotional vocabularies. Through the publication of letters in diverse West African print media, members of the educated classes honed a genre through which they could authenticate their opinions and feelings as well as satirise western romantic discourse (see Chapter 5). In literary twists to the 'real' correspondence published in newspapers, they also made use of Tutuola's 'dear reader' convention, incorporating the veracity, sincerity and faithfulness of letters into their creative projects.

As indicated in the introduction to this book, and as this and subsequent chapters will show, newspaper consumption was heavily 'lettered' in the first half of the twentieth century. The correspondence pages of English-language newspapers provided important entry points for local readers to express themselves in a colonial world language. Readers with diverse levels of literacy were inspired by what they read in the press to write letters to editors, and debates between letter-writers sometimes extended across several weeks and across different newspapers as correspondents had spats with fellow letter-writers

[1] Online epistolary forms include Chimamanda Ngozi Adichie's epistolary manifesto posted on Facebook, 'Dear Ijeawele, or a Feminist Manifesto in Fifteen Suggestions', which combines the device of the letter with literary discourse (see Edoro-Glines 2022).

about issues raised in articles. Often using pseudonyms, letter-writers applauded or condemned particular articles, praised editors and columnists for their erudition, critiqued the opinions of other correspondents and exercised their agency as subjects-in-print.

Letter-writing was a crucial marker of a person's membership of the educated class and the letters pages of newspapers provided a public training ground for writing by amateur contributors, helping reading communities to coalesce around their chosen newspapers. Yet while these letters pages offered a bridge into print for amateur authors and journalists, they were by no means a training ground for local writers destined to be authors or journalists with the support of editors. In fact, editors were often dismissive of correspondents who appeared to be in poor control of English grammar: '(Sorry! Ask me another? Editor)' Ali wrote rudely in bold print after publishing a letter from a correspondent in Jos who clearly struggled with English expression (*Comet* 7 May 1938: 2). Clearly, the *Comet* did not offer carte blanche to readers who fancied themselves as aspiring local writers. He was unequivocal in his view that readers should study the 'literary values' promoted in his weekly columns and work to improve their writing styles before setting themselves up as contributors to his journal.

One local letter-writer recalled the painful lesson of his failed transition from correspondent to author under Ali's tutelage. Filled with ambition after his letter had been published in Ali's *African Times and Orient Review* in the early twentieth century, 'Lans, the African' recalls sending a short manuscript to Ali for publication: 'Do you remember having the painful but very pleasing duty to return my Mss. with an advice that I should try again?' he asked, in a letter published in the *Comet* in 1933, adding humbly, 'unfortunately, twenty years hard study and practice fail to cure my defect and here I am to-day and ever since been content to lie low preferring to profit by the wisdom of efficient writers than attempting the impossible' (23 December 1933: 17). This aspiring West African writer – like many others forced to 'lie low' by local literary gatekeepers – had his literary ambitions crushed rather than nurtured by the press.

Adopting a more confrontational tone, another contributor to the *Comet*, 'J.O.A.' upbraided Ali and other West African editors for their failure to encourage local talent or provide opportunities for nascent authors. Using creative prose that modelled the artistry lost to editors, he wrote: 'We beginners; we noise makers; we pecksniffian charlatans; we vampires; we literary pedants submit to you, you Editors in West Africa (particularly here in Nigeria) with due deference that you have not been fair to us: because you do not give us a chance; because you do not encourage us' (*Comet* 19 June 1937: 19). Rather than encouraging local literary creativity, Ali and his peers put 'literary aspirants' back in their places, mocking their linguistic choices and concluding that, as one elite commentator put it, 'West Africa has … a long way yet to go before it can claim a literary culture and tradition of its own' (*Comet* 30 December 1933: 9).

Readers had access to the wide array of newspapers circulating in their towns, evidenced by the number of times correspondents cross-referenced local and international publications in their letters or included quotations from other journals in support of their arguments. Editors often showcased letters that praised their publication or defended their journals against criticism in rival newspapers. Sometimes they generated correspondence by engineering debates around particular topics, and on several occasions they may have inserted fabricated letters into their columns. However, editors typically faced a surfeit of genuine readers' communications, especially at times of heightened political crisis or moral controversy, when the influx of letters threatened to overwhelm the letters pages, causing editors to apologise for the lack of space and plead with correspondents for brevity. 'You need not ransack tomes of dictionaries for words to suffocate your readers with', advised the editor of the *Gold Coast Leader* in an early twentieth-century editorial inviting 'all classes to write' (5 July 1902: 4).

By 1934 readers had been warned so frequently and aggressively to avoid submitting poorly worded missives that, when Ali encountered examples of it in his correspondence bag in the *Comet*, he issued an exasperated reprimand to readers about wasting editorial time:

> We know that many of our correspondents glory in the excellence and prolixity of their literary effusions and much ink and paper is wasted over what is intended to be brilliant descriptive writing. But although there is the usual avalanche of words, it is necessary for us to either waste valuable time wading through such inconsequent communications in order to arrive at the intended object, or cut the preliminary cackle and read the contribution backwards in our frantic endeavours to discover the intention of the writer. Each correspondent, believing his communication to be epoch-making, becomes highly incensed when it does not appear. This shows scant consideration for editorial difficulties and an absence of appreciating the limited space at our disposal. (7 July 1934: 5, 9).

The short-tempered tone of Ali's intervention indicates that readers who could not write well in English, or who could not control their personal feelings in correspondence, were expected to remain on the margins of the printed page, studying the models provided by their weekly newspaper until they were capable of written self-expression that was suitable for the medium of print.

As a consequence of all these interventions, in addition to providing newsworthy content, the West African press is full of what Rachael Scarborough King, in her study of seventeenth- and eighteenth-century English letters, terms 'epistolary meta-commentary' (2018: 28). King shows how editors, columnists and letter-writers in early English newspapers continuously debated 'the act of writing and receiving letters' and, in the process, shaped wider public perceptions about reading, writing and print, including the aesthetic values that gave rise to early English novels that were largely epistolary (Ibid.). Similarly, over a period of more than 50 years on the letters pages of English-language West African newspapers, correspondents and editors shaped how subjective experience could – and should – be expressed in print in West Africa. The sustained character of their 'meta-commentary' about the rules and styles of letter-writing gives insights into how local writing practices were negotiated in this period, and how readers' access to print was mediated and patrolled by newspaper-owning elites.[2]

In King's account of epistolarity, letters had a definitive role in the form and pace of early English newspapers as flows of handwritten correspondence from the regions were assembled as daily or weekly printed news, submitted through private messengers or through the fledgling postal system that delivered letters and newspapers back out to the regions (2018: 25). The correspondence pages of newspapers 'bridged written and printed media and brought readers into a new world of printed news', she writes (Ibid: 23). Out of this 'new world' arose genres that mixed personal utterance with public opinion and set the terms for written expressions of selfhood outside the pages of the press as letters became vehicles for time itself, influencing how verisimilitude was established in early English novels.

In West Africa, the continuity and regularity of the weekly newspaper perfectly suited the epistolary relationship as new, sometimes hesitant, first-person subjects found space for expression on the letters pages, often apologising profusely for errors in their style. The flow of correspondence onto letters pages, the publication of readers' opinions and the appearance (or not) of responses to letters in subsequent issues all helped to attract subscribers to a newspaper and produced a particular tempo – as well as genres – though which topics could be raised and readerly anticipation and involvement nurtured. In becoming letter-writers, readers entered into the pace of newsprint with its reflections on the reader's own time and locale. The temporality of letters matched the temporality of printed newspapers: both were defined by pauses (as readers waited for replies to letters or for the next issue of a journal),

---

[2] There is considerable scope for further research into letters and letter-writing in English and Yoruba newspapers in colonial Nigeria. As Barber points out in her work on Yoruba and bilingual newspapers in the early twentieth century, a great deal of Yoruba newspaper content, including regular columns, took the form of letters to the editor or open letters to individuals in positions of power, to the extent that epistolarity was the '"default mode" of contributions to the paper' (Barber 2012: 50; see also *forthcoming*).

by immediacy (as letters conveyed the letter-writer's current position and newspapers reported recent events), and by specificity (as letters addressed precise topics and newspapers detailed the exact locations of occurrences). In short, newspapers and letters shared the same pulse. The unique space of newspaper letters pages, where the two genres coincided, thus generated powerful new conceptions of time and reality.

Alongside the English-language press in West Africa, letters also shaped the content and form of bilingual newspapers to the extent that one of the few Africanist scholars to have given serious attention to epistolarity, Barber, describes letters as 'the key to the whole Yoruba-language 1920s press' (personal comm., 5 April 2020). Barber's observation relates to Yoruba discursive practices such as proverbial modes of address and the intensely fluid, colloquial language of letters as written Yoruba took shape in newspapers (2012: 5). Yoruba newspapers did not have separate letters pages. As a consequence, a distinctive, epistolary Yoruba print culture emerged in columns that was different from the formal prose expected of letter-writers in the English-language press (Barber, *forthcoming*).

Given the intensity and duration of West African editors', columnists' and correspondents' epistolary meta-commentaries, it is unsurprising that one of Nigeria's most sensational early novels, *Itan Igbesi-Aiye Emi Segilola*, is a serialised epistolary narrative published in a newspaper. In 33 weekly letters, the confessions of a repentant prostitute using the pseudonym 'Segilola of the Fascinating Eyes' were printed in Yoruba by I. B. Thomas in the bilingual Yoruba-English newspaper *Akede Eko* between July 1929 and March 1930 (Barber 2012). In the letters, Segilola – a decrepit, disease-ridden woman in her forties – vividly narrates her fall from youthful virtue into sexual promiscuity and sin. Motivated by a love of money and consumer goods, she describes how she used her staggering natural beauty to seduce and exploit countless men, some of whom truly loved her while others only wanted sex. Now unloved and reduced to rags, she reflects on how her morals were corrupted in Lagos, warning readers continuously against adopting the same ruinous lifestyle.

To describe these letters as a 'novel' is misleading, however; as Barber points out, at no point did Thomas, as *Akede Eko*'s editor, admit to his authorship of the letters (2012: 7).[3] For the duration of the series, readers were encouraged to believe the letters were direct communications from a living correspondent. This was no serialised memoir in the manner of J. G. Mullen's thrilling account of his escape from the German Cameroons, published in the *Gold Coast Leader*

---

3   Thomas only admitted to their authorship obliquely in defending his literary style against accusations of indecency from the editor of the Nigerian *Daily Times* (Barber 2012: 341).

in 1916 and 1917 (Newell 2008); nor was it a fictional first-person autobiography like 'The Adventures of the Black Girl in her Search for Mr Shaw' by Marjorie Mensah (pseud. Mabel Dove), published in the *Times of West Africa* in 1933, in which an ebullient, intellectually gifted girl outwits European missionaries and colonialists before travelling to England to meet her hero, George Bernard Shaw, to interrogate him about questions of race and Christianity raised in his own satirical critique of mission Christianity, *The Adventures of the Black Girl in her Search for God* (1932) (Newell and Gadzekpo 2004). Mullen's and Dove's prose narratives could be interrrupted or extended by editors as column inches allowed without negatively impacting the continuity of the story; they did not comment on the medium of their publication or their genre of expression; nor did they depend on both their medium and their genre for evidence of their authenticity. Ṣẹgilọla, by contrast, submits one complete letter each week to *Akede Eko* with all the necessary epistolary trimmings such as a date, a salutation, direct comments to Thomas, a complimentary sign-off and her name. As Barber notes, these generic epistolary markers combine with references to well-known popular songs, recent historical events, fashion trends, local businesses, imported commodities, births, marriages and deaths to conjure up the impression of a person living and breathing in the reader's own Lagos (2012: 10).

Thomas covered his creative tracks at every turn with evidence of the protagonist's authenticity. He used every available resource in the newspaper's epistolary repertoire to construct his correspondent as a real woman nervously narrating her shameful life story from behind the mask of pseudonymity. In a note accompanying the first instalment, for example, he secures for Ṣẹgilọla a place in the present time of newsprint: 'This woman sought us out to plead with a sorrowful heart that she wanted to share her life story in Yoruba in our newspaper every week' (2012: 263). For the duration of the confessions, he used editorials, commentaries, and (pseudo-)readers' letters to assert the veracity of Ṣẹgilọla's account, simultaneously reinforcing and exploiting the relationship of trust between the newspaper editor and the reading public.

Within the letters, Ṣẹgilọla presents herself as a regular reader of *Akede Eko*, fully participating in the temporality of the newspaper. She comments on readers' responses to her letters and self-consciously thanks the editor for publishing her correspondence each week, assuring him that future letters will continue to be despatched if he continues to respect her anonymity. In this way, Thomas brilliantly controls readers' anticipation and manages their (im)patience by synchronising Ṣẹgilọla's voice with the production schedule of the paper. Ṣẹgilọla is co-terminous with the readers of *Akede Eko*. The 'letters looked real', Barber writes, because they were 'hooked into real time', offering 'a wealth of detail' while fulfilling the West African newspaper's established relationship with readers by 'demanding attention and response' (2012: 5). Always on the point of death during the period of her correspondence, Ṣẹgilọla conveniently vanishes into anonymity after the publication of her final letter and fails to die, relieving Thomas of any commitment to disclose her real name or publish photographs upon confirmation of her demise (Barber 2012: 11, 351–3). Meanwhile, Thomas continued to print authenticating materials for several weeks after the appearance of the final letter, culminating in the publication of the letters as a bound volume in Yoruba under the pseudonym of Ṣẹgilọla (7 [n.2]).

Thomas's deployment of all these strategies makes the narrative hyperrealist as much as it is realist. The letters read like a handbook of methods for achieving epistolarity in print. Above all, they reveal how epistolarity can be a particularly powerful vehicle for first-person subjectivity in creative writing. This first West African epistolary novel provides an extended commentary on the literary resources required to produce, and sustain, a fascinating 'I' in both fiction and non-fiction. Thomas brilliantly exploits the realism produced by epistolarity on the one hand and newsprint temporality on the other hand, to create a personal, intimate voice that conveys moral lessons about unchecked female sexuality.

Ṣẹgilọla's life story in Yoruba was a wholly new intervention in West African newspapers because the 'personal' was at the forefront of her correspondence. Her lively language was not duplicated in the English-language press until well after the mid-1930s, which saw the arrival of Nnamdi Azikiwe and a new brand of colloquial popular journalism (Omu 1978). The closest parallel with Ṣẹgilọla's letters is the sometimes cheeky, often gossipy 'Woman's Corner' in the *Times of West Africa* between 1931 and 1934, where the pseudonymous 'Marjorie Mensah' (Mabel Dove) used playful English filled with references to popular films, fashion, food, music and literature, and included frequent references to the sexual promiscuity of modern, urban Gold Coast youths, including a play, *Woman in Jade*.[4] What connects and characterises both pseudonymous women is the linguistic license their gender confers. In West African newspapers, where the 'personal' was off-limits, the 'feminine' voice could be adopted to release print from the strictures of public writing and give access to intimate, domestic, personal topics such as marital infidelity, good parenting, romantic love and leisure.

Ṣẹgilọla's many references to crying, to heart palpitations and to being emotionally overwrought during the act of writing are all staples of socalled

---

4 Given that she had her own column in the *Times of West Africa*, Mabel Dove rarely contributed to the letters pages of newspapers, although she made use of the epistolary form, including a notoriously flirtatious open letter to the Gold Coast governor, Sir Shenton Thomas, taking him to task for the Sedition Bill of 1934, which included a clause requiring the disclosure of pseudonymous authors in the event of legal action against a newspaper by the authorities.

'feminine' sentiment in English epistolary fiction dating back to Samuel Richardson's *Pamela; or Virtue Rewarded* (1740) and *Clarissa; or the History of a Young Lady: Comprehending the Most Important Concerns of Private Life. And Particularly Shewing, the Distresses that May Attend the Misconduct Both of Parents and Children, In Relation to Marriage* (1747). When she writes 'tears of regret are falling thick and fast from my eyes as I write these words' (87), 'Woe! woe! woe! ... [tears] do not allow me to continue at present' (Barber 2012: 93), 'great sobs are shaking me' (123) and 'Now, editor of *Akede Eko,* my heart is very full and tears of sorrow are gushing from my eyes, so I will stop here and resume next week' (103), she invokes textual strategies for feminine subjectivity dating back 200 years in Europe and carried over into epistolary novels by West African authors. As Chapter 6 will show in more detail, the stiff upper lips and dry eyes that characterise English romantic heroes in the British literary tradition are, however, largely absent from the Nigerian canon. Male-authored Nigerian romances frequently depict men weeping and swooning as signs of their capacity for elevated self-expression. Indeed, in Nigerian romances the absence of physical signs of emotion in a male character tend to signify the presence of a baddie who is intent on exploiting his gullible lover rather than a stoical hero taking emotional punches on the chin.[5]

If Thomas's opening of newspaper writing to the emotions created a space for locally published literature where sex and betrayal – and an entire field of personal experience hitherto prohibited under the rules of public letter-writing – could find expression, one section of Nigerian society was scandalised by the letters, especially when they became available as a bound book. On acquiring the volume in September 1930, the editor of the English-language *Daily Times* condemned the story on grounds of public morality (Barber: 333). This editorial did not challenge the authenticity of Ṣẹgilọla's letters: rather, it accused Thomas of impropriety for printing such material, and rudely turned Thomas's transgression into a critique of the Yoruba press as a whole for its 'filthy' vernacular (Ibid.). The *Times*' editor took offense at Thomas for reprinting 'a series of muck … in the Columns of a so-called bilingual newspaper. That the article should ever have been accepted or got up for publication was bad taste enough, but that they should have been reprinted in "book" form and sold to, or eagerly bought and read by people *is worse still*' (Barber 2012: 333; emphasis retained). The authenticity of the letters was

---

[5] Barber observes that Thomas frequently referred to himself as overcome with emotions using the same stylistic devices to mark the outpouring of feeling as he did for his heroine: 'tears come into my eyes when I remember my dear friend, the late George Debayọ Agbebi, CE, BSc. A! Alas! What a pity! Hi! Hi! Hi! Hi! Hun!!! Alas!!!' (cited in Barber 2012: 45–6).

secondary to Ṣẹgilọla's vulgar and shameful language, exposed for all to read in the public space of print.

For *Akede Eko* to carry – and carry off – such a story suggests that the genre of letter-writing in Yoruba print culture followed rather different rules about permissible content than those of the English-language press described in this book. Few of the sentiments expressed in Ṣẹgilọla's letters – from her sexual adventures to her domestic arrangements – would have been deemed printable on the letters pages of the English-language press. Few anglophone editors in the late 1920s or early 1930s would have allowed a correspondent to describe losing her virginity, as Ṣẹgilọla does. Moreover, Ṣẹgilọla's feisty Yoruba breaks the rules of correspondence set by the English-language press in previous decades. As Barber points out, the letters are 'written in a fluent, colloquial, conversational style – often repetitious and sometimes verging on incoherence' (2012: 5). On the letters pages of the English-language press, by contrast, as editors such as Ali and his predecessors made abundantly clear, informal wording was forbidden and repetition and rambling were taboo. The formal prose of the English-language press at this time, with its roots in the stiff, grammatical English of the educated elites described in Chapter 1, rendered Ṣẹgilọla's mode of expression unprintable. In short, Thomas's correspondent broke all the rules of public letter-writing in English. Yet in *Akede Eko* there is no editorial admonishment, either of the intimate nature of her non-'news' material or of her style of expression.

Ṣẹgilọla's letters beg an alternative consideration. Perhaps Thomas had no intention of deceiving readers with – and perhaps readers were not in the least bit deceived by – the textual tricks he deployed. For Yoruba readers of *Akede Eko*, the letters may not have been regarded as either as 'real' or as comprising a 'novel.' In his editorial at the start of the series, Thomas describes how Ṣẹgilọla wished her confessions to be published 'in order to serve as a warning to everyone, both men and women, who revel in loose living and promiscuity in their lives' (263). As such, the story may have been accepted from the outset as a moral parable whose hyperrealist narrative devices and claims of legitimacy contributed to the 'higher' (than the world of news) moral truth about female promiscuity as sinful behaviour. As one reader put it in a letter to the editor, 'We don't know whether Ṣẹgilọla's story is true or not, but it teaches us what the English call Moral Instructions' (2012: 12, 357; emphasis retained). Thomas's innovative literary style brought to life the popular parabolic figure of the sexually self-determining woman in a conservative moral tale depicting the social death earned by such people.

One should not overstate the differences between Yoruba and English-language newspapers, however, especially given the overlap between Yoruba and anglophone print cultures and the status of *Akede Eko* as a bilingual newspaper. Readers of newspapers and books in both languages would have been familiar with the genre of the Christian confessional in which epistolarity played an important role. They would have listened to stories about 'fallen women' delivered from the pulpit, and been confronted by the same in early English novels and Victorian popular literature and newspapers (Wendelin 2010; Rosenthal 2015).[6] Recurring across the centuries in Christian moral discourse, and featuring in eighteenth- and nineteenth-century libertine and reformist novels, as well as starring in West African popular and literary fiction well into the twentieth century, prostitutes are parabolic figures who appear so frequently in male-authored literature that they stand in for, and stand over, women's (mis)behaviour (Rosenthal 2015). Situated in the newspaper, Sẹgilọla's confessions could be deemed accurate and informative as well as imaginative and fictional. Readers were conscious of, comfortable with, and entertained and impressed by the editorial ruse of having a 'fallen woman' write letters to the press. 'When your story first began to appear', reads a letter from 'D.A.L.', 'I thought that the editor of the *Akede Eko* newspaper was just joking or was on a fool's errand, but when I began to pay attention to the names, neighbourhoods, times and all kinds of other things, this banished all my doubts, and I became convinced that all of it is true' (Barber 2012: 279).

The 'truth' of Sẹgilọla's account may not have required her reality as a living person. If one regards Sẹgilọla as parabolically (rather than empirically) plausible, and her letters as scandalous 'factual fictions' made possible by print, Thomas's narrative can be viewed as a brilliant moral lesson in the form of a cautionary life story. Sẹgilọla invites this reading in her continuous self-objectification as a moral deterrent to readers, drawing lessons from her autobiography in the manner of a reader or omniscient narrator: as she repeats from start to finish, 'Anyone who is wise, whether male or female, will take this sad story of the life of me, Sẹgilọla, as a lesson about promiscuous behaviour and loose living' (Barber: 123).

Thomas showed how epistolary fiction could bring intimacy and emotions into public print, allowing authors access to hitherto unpublishable subjects, especially in the realm of interior self-expression. Yoruba readers snapped up the letters in book form, published by popular demand shortly after the conclusion of the series, while English readers enjoyed the serial as a translation in *Akede Eko* (Barber 2012). In the process of purchasing the volume, Yoruba

---

[6] A letter from an ex-prostitute enclosing money for Sẹgilọla may have been genuine, but it also duplicates the Victorian Christian fund-raising tradition in Britain, where letters from, or about, prostitutes were published in the press to elicit sympathy and raise donations for hostels and reformatories for 'fallen women' (Wendelin 2010). Prostitutes' confessions had filled volumes of English literature since the eighteenth century, some from a libertine perspective, others from a reformist perspective, and all of them authored by men (Rosenthal 2015).

readers further separated the story from the currency of the newspaper and facilitated its movement towards the genre of the novel.

It took another 25 years for local English-language authors to wriggle loose of the grammatical formality and strictures on content imposed by anglophone newspaper editors and burst into epistolary life with racy moral stories about 'harlots' and good-time girls whose letters propelled female characters onto the page of local anglophone literature, and who, like Sẹgilọla, remained firmly present in the reader's world at the end of stories, 'doomed. Doomed to death ... And she is living somehow. You can always see her in one of the Lagos hotels. She is now a Harlot. But she is never happy ... If she had known she should have been contented with Jerry, she should have been a house wife now instead of being a HARLOT' (Obiaga n.dat.: 34).

'Shameless Thefts' vs Local Literatures: Dusé Mohamed Ali's *Comet*

In December 1938, a reader in Jos using the pseudonym 'Literature' wrote to the editor of the *Comet* in Lagos to point out that a poem entitled 'Thus Success Comes' sent in by F. Uzoma Anyiam of Lagos and printed on 29 October, was 'letter by letter, word by word, position by position, the same as a poem by Edwin Carlile Litsey' (3 December 1938: 2). After citing Litsey's poem and showing that only two words had been changed in the local version, Literature added, carefully avoiding any defamation of Anyiam while exposing the duplication, 'while I do not intend to imply plagiarism or literary piracy on the part of one or the other, I wish to register my wonderment at so striking a coincidence or carbon-copy likeness' (Ibid.).

Rather than capping his pen in shame, Anyiam defended the poem as his own original work, explaining that the coincidence was entirely reasonable given that both verses contemplated the common human experience of success. In his reply to Literature, printed in the following week's *Comet*, Anyiam wrote:

> It was an unfortunate coincidence that my poem tallied with that of Mr. Litsey which I did not read, and I can assure 'Literature' that I had never read any of Mr. Litsey's writings. I wrote mine to encourage myself and some other youngmen who have not been fortunate in life. Perhaps Mr. Liisey and I have suffered equally to have an identical view of 'Success'. (10 December 1938: 2)

Towards the end of Anyiam's reply, a truth comes out that is riveting for what it reveals about literary creativity among newspaper correspondents in 1930s Nigeria: 'I gave the MSS to a sound poet in Lagos who edited it before I sent it to the "Comet"', he confesses, 'and if Mr. Literature is not satisfied I would mention the name to him' (Ibid.). In defending what at first sight appears to be indefensible, Anyiam's letter reveals some of the behind-the-scenes collaborations that made creative self-expression possible for new writers seeking access to newsprint in Lagos. Even as responsibility for the problem is displaced sideways onto a third party, the collaborative quality of literary creativity among writers in Nigeria is revealed in Anyiam's reply, while still asserting authorship and claiming the poem as 'my honest endeavour', in spite of its 'edits' (Ibid.).

One regular contributor to the *Comet* was having none of it. In a letter entitled 'A Shameless Theft' published in the *Comet* on 24 December 1938, 'Odeziaku' of Onitsha described Anyiam as 'guilty of most deliberate piracy' (2). 'Odeziaku,' or John Moray Stuart-Young (1881–1939), was a Manchester-born British palm oil trader and Onitsha resident who produced many thousands of poems and numerous essays and memoirs for publication in the West African press between the early 1900s and his death in May 1939, as well as novels and lyrics for publication in Britain (see Newell 2006). Although he was ignored or derided by the metropolitan literary establishment, by the time Ali established the *Comet* in 1933 Stuart-Young had become not only a prolific contributor to the English-language press in the region but also a West African celebrity, hailed as 'West Africa's poet laureate' and 'West Africa's Rudyard Kipling' for his songs and poems.[1] As this chapter will show, he used the *Comet* to define – and in some cases dictate – the parameters of anglophone literary taste to the aspiring African writers for whom the *Comet* was intended to provide a weekly source of literary inspiration.

It is not suprising that Stuart-Young chose the *Comet* as his chief platform for publication in West Africa. Ali's weekly journal was reminiscent of an earlier era of local newspaper production, when editors printed miscellaneous material and encouraged readers to write responses and engage in debates, exemplified by Ali's London periodical, the *African Times and Orient Review* (1912–18). By the early 1930s in West Africa, this tradition of critical engagement had given way to a fiercely adversarial press, drawing observations from less polemical readers to the effect that:

> One cannot escape the feeling that we contribute articles to the papers most often out of sheer contentious spirit ... the old 'debate-motif' is still too much with us ... Writers too often take sides which they really do not accept in sincerity ... The readers themselves add to our confusion by absorbing uncritically everything which filters through. (*Comet* 7 September 1935: 18)

In Lagos, editors like Herbert Macaulay, Ernest S. Ikoli and, by the mid-1930s, Nnamdi Azikiwe were using newspapers as flagships for new political movements, making use of the printing press to promote their own visions and goals for Nigerian nationalism (Omu 1978, Adebanwi 2016). These were the newspapermen whose printed vitriol Ali and his contributors wished the *Comet* to dilute. 'Our object is to deal with the larger issues affecting West Africa rather

---

[1] Stuart-Young's writings were published in British journals such as *John O'London's Weekly* and the *Westminster Review*. His volumes of poetry were published by various London presses. His essays on spiritualism were published in *The Two Worlds, Light, The Occult Review* and *The Science of Thought Review*.

than the minor issues of Nigerian politics', Ali responded patronisingly when correspondents complained about his political non-aligment and accused him of refusing to show the public leadership expected of Nigerian editors (*Comet* 7 October 1933: 3; see also Christmas Number 1933: 6).

Ali printed English-language material from a global community of intellectuals, including British contributors such as Stuart-Young, and he continued the old newspaper tradition of cutting and pasting articles and stories from diverse international sources (see Newell 2013). Loyal letter-writers praised the *Comet*'s 'long visions' for being 'only possible if we judge the questions of the hour by standards that are beyond the hour, beyond the time, eternal standards' (*Comet* 4 August 1934: 1). Other commentators, however, including prominent medic and politician Dr Moses da Rocha, warned, 'it really needs a skilful pilot to keep his barque afloat in the turgid waters of Lagos Politics' (Christmas Number 1933: 17).

Rather than adopting the bold nationalism of Azikiwe and other radical anticolonial editors in the 1930s, Ali's editorial project in Nigeria was to cultivate the exchange of ideas, in English, between people on a global scale while recognising the degeneration of 'civilisation' in Europe and the regenerative political energy and intellectual vitality to be found among local intellectuals in the colonies.[2] To this end, Stuart-Young, whose columns promoted a particular form of poetry as the singular ideal, was one of his celebrity contributors.

The greatest verse was lyrical, pastoral and sentimental, the Englishman insisted. Inspired by the most syrupy Edwardian poetry, Stuart-Young's lyrics and lullabies depicted children and maidens prancing around in bucolic settings:

> Gee-up, my little horse, gee-up again, sir!
> Here we go galloping o'er mystic miles:
> Dada and Sonny-Boy tasting life's honey joy,
> Shouting with laughter or melting in smiles. (*Comet* 15 February 1936: 14).

Another typical example is:

> Somebody's tired! – Come, climb my knee:
> Birdies are sleeping in every tree;
> The rose had its pale gold petals furled,
> And peace, sweet peace, fills the dreaming world. (*Comet* 17 September 1938: 15).

The titles of Stuart-Young's lyrics – 'Lonely Road to Home', 'Mist on The Moon', 'Sunshine in the Garden of my Heart' and 'Dainty Maids of Dorset' (18 August

---

[2] Ali's position is hardly surprising given that he was a migrant intellectual and pan-Africanist rather than a Nigerian-born activist at this time of party political nationalisms (see Duffield 1976).

1934: 14, 17 August 1935: 9, 11 April 1936: 13, 13 February 1937: 15) – indicate their whimsical contents, which appealed to Edwardian popular taste in Britain, with some being set to music and recorded. Regarding himself as the scion of English-language verse in West Africa, and convinced that the European 'moderns' were morally dangerous for their experiments with form, not to mention their general decadence, in his many essays on aesthetics for the West African press Stuart-Young argued that rhyme was the vehicle of beauty and simplicity was the essence of poetic decency. Through 'lilting little lyrics', he implemented his mission to protect African newspaper readers from modernity and modernism on the one hand and from what he regarded as the 'primitive' currents of the African environment on the other hand (*Comet* 5 March 1938: 10; see 3 March 1934: 13).

Under the guise of showing local readers how to improve their writing, Stuart-Young put standards in place that often actually excluded Africans from the lyrical forms he promoted. 'This', he wrote scathingly in one literary commentary, 'was recently written by an African', going on to quote the offending piece:

> The beautiful leavy trees, the flourishing fields, and the vast lawns of green grass starred over with myriads of flowers of greater or smaller size. There the birds sing and build their nests; the meandering streams flow with fresh water; and the happy peasants, toiling afar from the multitude of town-life, purify the human wishes from any personal stain. (*Comet* 3 March 1934: 12)

Such an attempt at pastoral writing, he wrote contemptuously, 'is sheer unadulterated moonshine' (Ibid.). The writer's effort was ethnically impossible 'inasmuch as the normal African knows as little of "happy peasants" as he knows of "vast lawns of green grass starred over with flowers"' (Ibid.). In this way, Stuart-Young used the *Comet* to assert the inherent Englishness of pastoral lyrics while policing his own literary territory to keep out African interlopers and obstruct local poets from developing their own poetic responses to the African landscape.[3]

For this particular Englishman, Anyiam's 'Success' threatened a cardinal principle of authorial integrity. The local man's 'theft' was laid bare by its starkness in print. 'That the lines are by the Canadian versifier Edwin Carlisle Litsey can be proved by reference to any popular book of quotations', Stuart-Young railed: 'I stand amazed at the temerity of Mr. F. Uzoma Anyiam (of Lagos)

---

[3] After Stuart-Young's death in May 1939, Nigerian poems in free verse and non-lyrical forms started to be published in the *Comet*. Politically uplifting poems by new writers such as 'Mose of Owerri' also started to appear in the *Comet* (see, for example, 11 November 1939: 15, 18 November 1939: 15).

in daring to set up a claim to that supreme polish of style and masterly skill of technique which Mr. Litsey's verses always reveal' (*Comet* 24 December 1938: 2).[4] He added sarcastically, 'had the poem on Success actually come from the brain and heart of Mr. F. Uzoma Anyiam we should have been fain to kneel at his feet and acclaim him the first African Henry Wadsworth Longfellow, the first and earliest trousered Ella Wheeler Wilcox of the Coast' (Ibid.). On and on Stuart-Young's letter ran, shaming Anyiam in the most categorical terms:

> this sort of theft, the picking of a live man's brains, disenchants me so terribly ... For every one or two ... honest and earnest souls, how many thousands of others there are who think (or like to make themselves believe) that the writing of rhyme is a 'gift' and demands no study. (Ibid.)

In Stuart-Young's opinion, this plagiarism was audacious and inexcusable. In conclusion, he condemned 'the wicked folly of any Mr. F. Uzorma Anyiam stealing a better man's crown of bays!' (Ibid.).

By the time 'Success' was reproduced under Anyiam's name in the *Comet*, however, the Nigerian poet's claim that he had not 'read any of Mr. Litsey's writing' would probably have been accurate. Originally published in 1903 in the *Era*, a Philadelphia magazine, Litsey's poem was reprinted in unattributed or pseudonymous forms so many times, and in so many different American popular journals, that by the time it surfaced in the *Comet* 35 years later, in every likelihood it had become untethered from its source and placed into free circulation in the public domain as part of popular discourse (*The Era* January 1903: 24). In the months after its publication in the United States, for example, 'Success' was printed in *Our Paper* (1903: 142), *The Summary* (1903: 8), *The Saint Paul Globe* (Minnesota) (1903: 11), *The Tiller and Toiler* (Kansas) (1905: 3), *The Fairfield Evening Journal* (1905: 7), the *Arkansas City Daily Traveler* (1905: 7) and many other journals. Each time, it was attributed not to Litsey but to *The Era*. Litsey's poem was thus probably in the air in Nigerian schools and offices in the first decades of the twentieth century, circulating between speakers as a public maxim in verse.

As a freely broadcast poem, detached from its author and containing an extended maxim, 'Success' was the precisely type of text to be taken up for quotation in popular West African discourse, either in full or through the extraction of proverbial phrases to add depth and sagacity to ordinary conversation (see Yankah 2012). If one reads Anyiam's letter against the grain of the stark opposition put in place by Stuart-Young, the exchange is therefore

---

4   Litsey was not Canadian: he was known as 'poet laureate of Kentucky.' Stuart-Young was perhaps confusing Litsey with the Candian poet Robert Service, who he also admired.

revealing for how, as his efforts to clear up the misunderstanding indicate, for Anyiam there was no obvious contradiction between creative innovation, transcription and collaboration.

Anyiam's poem was not an isolated case of literary 'theft' in the West African press. Even if one allows for disingenuity as he tried to wriggle free from blame, the local poet's non-differentiation between his own original words, Litsey's poem and his Lagos collaborator's insertions indicate the existence of a creative logic in which authorship and attribution were regarded differently from the binary of 'original' and 'duplicate' that motivated Stuart-Young's critique. Examples of similar practices can be found throughout the English-language press in West Africa in the first three decades of the twentieth century, as already indicated by the citations of Romantic poets discussed in Chapter 1.[5] In the Christmas 1933 issue of *Comet*, for example, a poem entitled 'Conscience' by Olabode Pinheiro of Lafiaji, Lagos, condensed and duplicated 'A Good Conscience', which appeared in the Victorian children's prayer book, *The Sunday School Gift: A Help to Early Prayer and Praise* by Rev. Charles Bullock (1870: 128). Bullock was not the original author of 'Conscience', however: the poem can be found in the 1860s in *Bob, The Crossing Sweeper* (1864), creating a citational 'hall of mirrors' that will be discussed in detail in Chapter 5. As with Anyiam's 'Success', 'A Good Conscience' was probably known off by heart by Christian-schooled local readers. Their recognition of its beauty would have included this cumulative, recited quality as Pinheiro re-worked it from available resources, making a maxim of it in the same way that other contributors to the press heaped up aphorisms for readers to recognise, implement, quote and interpret.

Similar aphoristic quoting practices are stark and recurrent across the decades, defining Nigerian pamphlet literature of the 1950s and 1960s as much as early twentieth-century creative writing (see Chapter 5). A typical example of this writing style can be found in the appropriately titled 'Too Many Cooks', published in the *Comet* in 1938, in which the author Adebesin Dosunmu-Ainnah tells readers:

> A word is enough for the wise. Too many cooks spoil the soup; too many of any good thing, causes the goodness to vanish. It is irrefut-

---

5   The editor of the *Comet* was himself widely discredited in Britain when his extensive plagiarism of sections of W. S. Blunt's *Secret History of the English Occupation of Egypt*, T. A. Roshtein's *Egypt's Ruin* and the Earl of Cromer's *Modern Egypt* in his book, *In the Land of the Pharoahs* (1911), was exposed (Duffield 1976: 163). In West Africa 25 years later, Ali boasted about the success of this book in 'crystalising public opinion and in opening the eyes of the thinkers of the English-speaking world to the enormity of Egypt's betrayal', blaming its negative reception on the 'jealousy' of others rather than the copyright case that led the book to be withdrawn from circulation by its publisher, Stanley Paul (*Comet* 22 August 1936: 7).

ably true that vague imaginings breed ill will far more than honest differences of opinion on points of principle; when we cannot find repose in ourselves it is useless to seek it elsewhere. (2 April 1938: 17)

As this short extract from the longer article shows, well-known sayings are packed into the free-standing article as the author stews his wisdom in the juices of oral lore.

An article on 'native plays' by the Yoruba historian E. Ita describes the collective pleasure of this assimilative creative practice, celebrating the ways in which archives of well-known vernacular stories connect performers and audiences in 'thrilling' scenes of recognition. 'The plays themselves have no playwrights', Ita explains: 'They are part of our social birthright. They have been deposited in us from childhood and we carry them in us as internal treasures' (*Comet* 21 November 1936: 6). Shared between authors and audiences, such a collective internal treasury has the effect of 'enabling every one to enter into the "spirit of the play" and share the thrill of the creators and the actors; it keeps our art pregnant with the universality which no great art can afford to lack' (Ibid.). As Ita makes clear, collective ownership of creative texts in the form of repeated material produces the pleasure of recognition as creators and actors innovate with the familiar archive.

The vehemence of Stuart-Young's response exposes a tension between the Englishman's declared aesthetic protocols, drawn from a combination of Romantic aesthetics and British copyright law, and collaborative notions of literary inspiration articulated by local creative writers. This is not to suggest that copyright was irrelevant to West African authors, nor that the idea of original writing was somehow absent from local literary value systems. Barber (2016) shows how copyright was selectively asserted in the Lagos press of the 1900s, and with reference to South Africa, Isabel Hofmeyr (2021) points out that copyright assertions by Black writers were a vital part of citizenship claims in the colonial state. However, in Stuart-Young's model of authorship, literary inspiration had to take shape within a poet's intensely subjective consciousness, from where it would be attached to a poetic genre and crafted into shape. For Anyiam, Pinheiro and the other Lagos poets who engaged in the citational practices described above, by contrast, verbatim duplication of a work was remarkable but not impossible, and it was admirable if executed with style.

In the local literary culture from which Anyiam and his fellow poets drew inspiration, an individual's poetic integrity was not automatically compromised by the summoning of multiple authors to help with the improvement of a work. Cumulative compositional processes went into works intended for publication. However, the controversy of 1938 introduced anxieties about collaborative authorship into the creative process. In an anonymous letter published in the *Comet* shortly after the Anyiam affair, one correspondent described how his history of Ogwashi-Ukwu began with oral history sources within his family and underwent numerous revisions in response to the suggestions of colonial education officers before, in 1933, being submitted to the District Officer and Obi of Ogwashi-Ukwu for approval. When the manuscript was rejected by the Superintendent of Education, the author rewrote it again and passed it to another reader, Mr Odiwanor of Benin. Cautious about the prospect of this collaborative labour being mistaken by members of the 'literate class' for a failure to credit co-authors, and in a nod to the controversy in the *Comet*, the writer wisely noted, 'I had thought that when publishing this History in question I would mention all those who had assisted in the task of gathering informations and perfecting the writing. If I did so I felt I would not have been cast out from the number of literate class' (15 April 1939: 3).

It should be noted that Stuart-Young benefited enormously from West African practices of re-attribution arising in cultural spaces that were not subject to European copyright law or judgments about plagiarism. By his own admission, he frequently 'polished and embellished' and 'improved upon' other poets' published works, arguing that 'rather than the harsh word plagiarism, that of collaboration might appropriately be used' (*Comet* 16 April 1938: 11–20). In one blatant example of copyright violation and identity theft, he audaciously claimed co-authorship of two songs with 'Mrs Stuart-Young' (*Comet* 1 September 1934: 14). The words of the first song, 'Absent', duplicate a popular song written by Catherine Young Glen – who was never Stuart-Young's spouse – performed by Margaret Romaine with music by John W. Metcalf.[6] The second song co-attributed to Glen, 'Love's Golden Hour', is not listed in the archives and was probably penned by Stuart-Young. Its lyrics closely resemble the quotations appearing under 'dew' in Samuel Johnson's *A Dictionary of the English Language*: 'Give your heart, as the rose, dew wet/ Entices the honey-bee', the lyric reads, as Stuart-Young peels off phrases from Johnson's examples from Shakespeare, Milton and Dryden. In publishing the pair of songs together, Stuart-Young attached his second lyric to Glen's well-known popular song, and in scandalously claiming Glen as his matrimonial 'other half' and renaming her 'Mrs Stuart-Young', he deleted her identity and appropriated her song while hiding the fact that his own lyric had not been recorded at all.

Another example of this practice can be found in February 1936 when, in place of his usual poem, Stuart-Young sent Ali an English translation from French of a witty Arabic maxim:

> There is the man who knows not, and knows not that he knows not. He is a fool – avoid him!

[6] This song is listed in the music archives as Victor 60124, 26 August 1914 (first published 1899). The sheet music became available in 1927, which is probably how Stuart-Young came to access it.

There is the man who knows not, and knows that he knows not. He is open to instruction – teach him!
There is the man who knows, and knows not that he knows. He is asleep – wake him up!
There is the man who knows, and knows that he knows. He is a wise man – follow him! (*Comet* 8 February 1936: 15)

'He who knows' spread like wildfire, becoming immensely popular throughout West Africa. It was – and still is – attributed to Stuart-Young, who 'originated' it by putting it into circulation. By 1938, Stuart-Young was happy to take full credit for inventing the wise saying as he continuously forged, borrowed, re-worked and claimed others' material as his own. Indeed, everything about him, including his autobiographical essays, was ripe with fabrications. 'Although I may be omitted by the anthologies', he declared defensively in his autobiographical essays, the *Comet*'s readers should know some facts about him: that he had given lectures at exclusive clubs attended by British royalty (*Comet* 5 March 1938: 11, 16 January 1936: 10); that his distinguished family members included Edward Young, author of *Night Thoughts* (1742), and Sir Edward Hilton Young (1879–1960); and that he cherished lifelong friendships with Oscar Wilde, Roger Casement, Lord Alfred Douglas, Arnold Bennett, Rupert Brooke, Rudyard Kipling, W. T. Stead, George Bernard Shaw, D. H. Lawrence, William Watson, and countless other famous (and infamous) literary figures (*Comet* 3 November 1934: 14, 9 February 1935: 11, 20 October 1934: 11–15). These distinguished networks extended through his patrilineage, conferring additional pedigree on the Englishman: his father, he claimed, was an acquaintance of 'Carlyle, Darwin, Stuart-Blackie, the Brownings, Thomas Huxley', and his grandfather 'met on terms of equality with men as far apart as Russel Wallace and Leslie Stephen, W. E. H. Lecky and Herbert Spenser' (*Comet* 20 October 1934: 13).

Nigerian readers were fully aware of Stuart-Young's habits of borrowing and embellishment. Even in eulogistic commentaries on his work, some of his 'lovelist poems' were described as 'well-known though not strictly original' (Williams, *Comet* 13 August 1938: 10). Yet what makes Stuart-Young's Nigerian cultural interventions relevant in the context of this book is the increasingly proactive role of local readers in critiquing his literary gatekeeping activities. With the rise of a 'renascent' African consciousness in the 1930s, inspired by Azikiwe, whose self-confident nationalism and intellectual brilliance made him literate Africans' brightest star on his return to Nigeria from colonial Ghana in 1936, Stuart-Young's paternalistic commentaries on African self-improvement in the *Comet* became increasingly intolerable to local newspaper readers.

In the mid-1930s, Stuart-Young boldly stepped out of the literary role for which he was widely recognised in West Africa and tried to make recommendations about colonial politics and the pace of decolonisation. By this time, African readers had come to regard him with suspicion as a 'strange man' filled with 'weirdness' and were quick to send him back to his designated literary zone (*Comet* 13 August 1938: 10). One reader described Stuart-Young's fiction as 'damned good stuff – but at the same time it is utter baulz' (13 July 1935: 1). 'Sir – Odeziaku, the Poet Laureate of Onitsha is out again to caricature the African', wrote another reader, 'Rambler', in a furious response to Stuart-Young's long article, 'The Simple Life', in which Africans were described as naturally lazy and work-shy, lacking the white man's 'energy … efficiency and zeal' (*Comet* 5 February 1938: 10–11, 17–18). 'This is not the first time that Odeziaku has taken advantage of his pen on the poor African', Rambler complained, for 'his "Black Man's Cradle" serialised in the issues of the "COMET" is still fresh in our minds' (12 March 1938: 2). 'As a poetic and miscellaneous writer, we admire Odeziaku', Rambler concluded, 'but as a moralist we loathe to think of him' among Africans for nearly 40 years: 'From those that would kill us under the pretence to save us, good Lord deliver us!' (12 March 1938: 2).

The novel to which Rambler refers, *Black Man's Cradle,* was set in an eastern Nigerian market town closely resembling Onitsha and serialised in the *Comet* between March 1935 and August 1935. In theme and content it so closely resembles Stuart-Young's creative writing from earlier in the century that it may well have been composed in the early 1900s.[7] The story merits discussion, not for its unpalatable contents but for the strong response it elicited from Nigerian letter-writers to the *Comet*. In it, a working-class British trader with a love of books and an aversion to sex, who bears an idealised resemblance to Stuart-Young, witnesses the corruption of Tazie, a 'half-caste' girl, as she is passed from one white trader to another as a sexual plaything in town. The erotic content is hinted at through unintentionally comic lines such as 'Tazie could feel his unconsciously amorous knees against her own' (16 March 1935: 13). Meanwhile, white female characters are allowed to be openly expressive of their passion, even when it occurs in the form of an extramarital affair: '"Dick, Dick", she cried: "Oh! never cease to love me, or I shall die!" / On the instant she slipped from the settee to the floor, helplessly grasping his feet… unconscious' (17 August 1935: 12).

Stuart-Young's fiction condemned the consequences of inter-racial love and rejected cosmopolitanism, seeking instead to situate Africans in an unsullied pre-lapsarian world outside history, beyond literacy and far away from colonial

---

[7] From his first West African novel, *Merely A Negress* (1904), Stuart-Young made interracial relationships his vehicle for depicting the disasters of colonial contact in West Africa, reiterating popular European discourses about miscegenation and racial degeneration. This placed him ahead of popular novels about racial mixing published in the west, such as Ida Vera Simonton's *Hell's Playground* (1912) and Sarah Gertrude Millin's *God's Stepchildren* (1924). Stuart-Young had an abhorrence of sexual intercourse in general. Again and again in his many novels and poems, he defined moral purity in terms of sexual abstinence (see Newell 2006).

towns: 'our vaunted Civilization is ... spoiling the African's true nature', he complained repeatedly (*Comet* 5 February 1938: 17). With intellectual roots in an Enlightenment tradition of romanticised 'noble savages' untouched by 'civilisation', he continuously berated 'the European who superimposes an alien Culture upon Nature's raw material' and lamented 'the tragedy, implicit always behind miscegenacious marriages, which accrued to the offspring' (*Comet* 3 March 1934: 12, 16 March 1935: 13). His loathing for the influence of decadent European civilisation on healthy African cultures led to repeated statements in the press against racial mixing, which he believed to cause degeneration and moral disaster in 'half-caste' Africans arising from their toxic mixture of 'blood' (see Ray 2015, Baptiste 2014). True to form, in *Black Man's Cradle* the hero condemns the pollution of the purity of Africans by his fellow white residents in town and proselytises against the education of Africans: 'not more than one Black man in a hundred thousand can ever hope to receive any good out of a literary education', the white hero states, warning, 'the more the African knows, the more dangerous and antagonistic to the White man he becomes ... Look at India, as an example ready to our hands' (*Comet* 11 May 1935: 15).

Stuart-Young was not alone in producing pseudo-scientific discourses about racial degeneration in the African-owned press. The *Comet* carried occasional articles on miscegenation as part of the editor's project to generate 'complete citizenship for the African in the broadest sense of the term' by encouraging critical engagement with 'eye-opening', uncensored articles (29 July 1933: 3, 11 June 1938: 2). To this end, a piece by Rev. Fr. J. Ward in the Christmas 1933 issue described cross-racial relationships as involving 'intermarriage with slaves and vassals' who are naturally 'of a weaker race than their masters', causing 'the blood of the conquering race' to become 'debased' (*Comet* Christmas Number: 23).

Although the cosmopolitan editor of the *Comet* held a lifelong belief that 'peoples of mixed blood are invariably progressive' (17 August 1935: 8), he frequently published items like this to stimulate correspondence from readers.[8] Even the most offensive material conveyed 'the considered views of a thinking mortal', he insisted, flagging up controversial items in editorial spoilers, while urging readers, as empathetic humanists, to 'get to the core of the writer's thoughts and observations' (*Comet* 14 May 1938: 10). In order to stir up critical debate, he even printed apologies for Nazism, such as Ernst Hanfstaengl's justification of Hitler's efforts to reclaim Germany from 'apathy and loss of spirit,' republished from the *Sunday Chronicle* (London) (*Comet* 11 May 1935: 8). A similarly anti-Semitic contribution by 'The Growler' in 1933 was accompanied by an editor's note warning that while 'his views are

---

[8] Ali modelled racial intermarriage in Lagos with his wife, the American actress Gertrude La Page.

not necessarily our views ... he has a right to be heard and, even as we have opened up our columns to the prosecution, we shall be delighted to accord a like privilege to the defence' (*Comet* 16 December 1933: 2).

At a time when 'race purity' had been popularised by fascists in America and Europe, and by racists in South Africa and other African settler colonies, racist printed material had dangerous overtones. Indeed, when Italy added Ethiopia to its strategically important cluster of east African colonies in 1935, Mussolini justified his murderous invasion in terms of racist colonialism rather than fascism as a necessary European intervention to pacificy the 'savages' and civilise the 'unspeakable barbarians' (cited in *Comet* 19 September 1936: 5). As many scholars have shown, the myths of racial purity (and degeneration) that inspired white nationalist ideologies in the 1930s grew out of decades of colonialist constructions of Africans as 'primitive' in scientific, anthropological and historical writing as well as in creative writing, implicating an expansive array of written materials in the perpetuation of racist ideologies.

Ali's publication of racist and Nazi material under the banner of freedom of expression was controversial, even in this age of extremes.[9] In a similar manner to the Gold Coast intellectuals discussed in Chapter 1, he believed that civilisations were plural and equal, requiring comparison and not hierarchisation. All civilisations were subject to colonial invasions, in his view, in spite of, and not because of, the strength and sophistication of their indigenous cultures: 'Did not the Spaniards discover in Mexico and Peru a more advanced civilization than their own?' he asked: 'Yet they were conquered in the interest of Christianity and progress even as Spain was subsequently conquered by our Muslim brothers in the interest of Islam and progress' (*Comet* 7 September 1935: 8). World civilisations were impure by nature, he reiterated, and the intermingling of people should be a source of celebration not hatred: 'pride of race is arrant humbug because there are few pure blooded unmixed races on this plant' (*Comet* 22 February 1936: 7).

Ali vehemently and repeatedly condemned the degeneration of the Global North into 'madness' and 'savagery' in the 1930s. While these terms were also used by western leaders to describe the looming war, references to European barbarism took on new anti-colonial connotations when used in the African press. 'Europe of today', Ali wrote, is 'a boiling cauldron or a habitation for

---

[9] In an example of the critical consciousness advocated by Ali, a work of propaganda by Amedeo Tosti entitled *The Greatest Colonial Enterprise in the World* in which the 1935 Italian invasion of Ethiopia was condoned, was brilliantly read against its grain by regular contributor S. O. Nwangoro in 1937. Nwangoro ironised the book at every turn and exposed it as a work of fascist propaganda that deserved to be read and studied as an exemplar of 'false imperialism' (*Comet* 14 August 1937: 14).

maniacs' (*Comet* 17 March 1934: 3; see also 24 August 1935: 5).[10] 'Reports from Continental Europe suggest a return to that condition of savagery for which it was noted in the Dark Ages', he wrote in another editorial, adding that warmongering has 'transformed the reputedly civilized to the level of brute' (*Comet* 4 August 1934: 8; see also 9 December 1939: 5). Again and again, African editors made the same point in the 1930s, but Ali was foremost among them, and the most repetitive: 'We have frequently stated in these pages that Europe has gone mad' (18 July 1936: 5); 'What is wrong with "Civilisation"? Western civilisation appears to be gradually reverting to a condition of barbarism' (1 May 1937: 5); 'Western civilisation … is on the way to self-extermination' (2 September 1939: 5).

Yet so completely did Stuart-Young believe in the genetic source of moral pollution in his 'mixed race' fictional creations in the mid-1930s that, in a long article entitled 'Black and White – Or Brown', he used the characters from *Black Man's Cradle* as evidence for a case study of 'Negro psychology' in which he supported the new South African law criminalising interracial marriage and insisted that the races 'should be kept as widely apart as possible' to avoid 'social conflict' and sexual profligacy (*Comet* 4 January 1936: 7). Mixed-race women in particular, he argued, were licentious by nature and 'breed degenerates, or highly-strung neurotics, simply because their passions know no restaint – once they have been loosed' (Ibid.: 9). Mixing anecdotes from his own creative writing with observations about alcoholism, promiscuity, deformity and insanity among 'half-castes' in Onitsha, whose immorality and illness were the outcome of heredity in his view, the essay concluded with a warning and a curse: 'ostracism and disdain must ever be the lot of those who so far forget their racial pride as to enter into a miscegenacious union' (Ibid.: 9–10, 18).

Readers of the *Comet* had tolerated *Black Man's Cradle* without complaining to the editor, but they responded immediately to the claims made by Stuart-Young in his self-declaredly 'scientific' article.[11] The controversy far exceeded

[10] In 1933, British Prime Minister Stanley Baldwin described Europe as 'living in a madhouse', referring to Hitler and Mussolini as 'lunatics' (Pick 2012: 97).

[11] Readers had previously castigated Stuart-Young for his condemnations of Liberia as being filled with the 'moral leprosy' of 'opportunist and degenerate descendents of American slaves' (*Comet* 29 December 1934: 15, 5 January 1935: 11). In response, the letters pages of the *Comet* of 26 January 1935 were filled with protests. However, it must be noted that many local readers admired Stuart-Young's poetry: in August 1938, the creative writer and journalist Adisa Williams wrote a glowing tribute to Stuart-Young in the 'Book of the Week' section of the *Comet*, praising the 'beauty' and 'truth' of the Englishman's lyrics and taking an unnamed British 'gentleman' to task for suggesting to Stuart-Young, in one of the latter's reminiscences, that African readers were not sufficiently sophisticated to appreciate the aesthetic qualities of English poetry (13 August 1938: 10). Replete with appreciative commentary and examples, Williams's long essay celebrates Stuart-Young as a humanist whose verse communicates a 'genuine

the pages of the *Comet*, with condemnations appearing throughout the Nigerian press. These readers' responses are important, demonstrating the extent to which articles printed in one newspaper were read and critiqued in others, as well as the way correspondents reprimanded the Englishman for stepping out of his designated position as a creative writer in order to dabble in science. 'When Mr. Young writes Poetry or Fiction, custom permits him licenses which he is entitled to exercise; no one has a right to dispute with him, then, no matter how misleading or fantastic his views are', the British Medical Superintendent Dr Vivian Renwick commented in the *Comet*: 'But when on the other hand Mr Young essays an entry into the realms of Science one naturally expects that he will discipline his mind and conform to the laws and practise of science' (11 January 1936: 12).

In every letter of protest about Stuart-Young's views, racial prejudice rather than genetics was identified as the source of the social problems the Englishman described. 'Let us advocate the brotherhood of man and, the brown man would have his full share under the sun', correspondents advised (*Comet* 25 January 1936: 24). Under pressure, Ali vacated his position as open-minded cosmopolitan giving space to all political perspectives and took a position against his stalwart contributor, criticising the Englishman's 'unchaste effusion' and offering a wealth of counter-examples of mixed-race success stories ranging from ancient Roman military leaders to his own observations of vibrant mixed communities during his travels through South America and the West Indies (Ibid.: 7).[12]

Letters to editors provide insights into West African reading cultures. Whereas British colonial censorship in the mid-1930s was premised on assumptions about Africans' tendencies to regard even the most sensational fictions as factual and 'real', readers of the *Comet* clearly recognised how fictional scenarios could be manipulated and repackaged for ideological ends. From the perspective of a literary historian, what is interesting about all these letters to the editor is how readers accepted *Black Man's Cradle* as a work of the creative imagination, permitting its status as fiction – albeit flawed in its realism, offensive in its

---

love of Mankind' without any 'glorification of the imperial spirit' (Ibid.: 10). Passing references in Onitsha pamphlet literature of the 1950s also indicate the lingering influence of Stuart-Young over writers in his adopted town. In Ogali A. Ogali's *Eddy the Coal-City Boy,* for example, the repentant protagonist describes his location as, 'my little room of many regrets', an explicit reference to the name of Stuart-Young's famous Onitsha residence, 'The Little House of No Regrets' ([1958] 1980c: 97). Williams was a regular contributor to Azikiwe's *West African Pilot,* and several of his book reviews and short stories were published in the *Comet* in 1938 and 1939.

[12] One wonders if the printer of the *Comet* was taking revenge on Stuart-Young several months later when he introduced the typographical error 'Vox Pox' for a 'Vox Pop' column containing a long tirade from the Englishman against church marriage for Africans (1 August 1936: 2).

representations and removed from life on the ground – but when Stuart-Young extracted a racist ideology from the novel and promoted it as science, readers identified the transformation of prejudice into propagada. They further scoffed at the author's claim that a film of *Black Man's Cradle* 'would go far toward solving the great race problem of the hour' (*Comet* 8 February 1936: 12). Such a belief was completely 'fatuous', readers stated, demonstrating nothing more than the Englishman's 'foolishness and peevishness' (Ibid.).

In a hurt letter of response to the condemnations, Stuart-Young retreated from science into the emotions, explaining that his article was inspired by 'a pang, whenever I see … half-caste children' (*Comet* 25 January 1936: 14). Attempting to draw a line under his article, he dissembled, 'For me, there's an end! I cannot take sides' (Ibid.). The controversy ran on for many more weeks in the Lagos press, however, and clearly still rankling after the correspondence had died down, Stuart-Young conveniently claimed to have received a letter from none other than George Bernard Shaw with the message, 'Note: on miscegenation and a Brown New World, I believe JMSY' (*Comet* 16 May 1936: 24).[13]

Stuart-Young's contributions to the anglophone press and the responses they aroused from local readers illustrate the vitality of the West African critical tradition that is at the centre of this book, in which printed literature stimulated correspondence from readers, and readers contributed to the formation of printed genres. In the case of Stuart-Young's racist contributions, local readers' reimposition of disciplinary boundaries around fiction and science showed an astute consciousness of the capacity of ideologies to permeate different genres of writing. In other words, in an era of increasing fascist propaganda in Europe and southern Africa, the *Comet*'s readers recognised the capacity of print to incite racism and violence. The exchanges between Stuart-Young and the *Comet*'s contributors and readers demonstrate how the freedom of expression enjoyed by writers for the *Comet* was matched by the critical engagement of readers as they monitored generic boundaries, tolerating opinions in one genre that were deemed unacceptable in another. They also reveal how West African newspapers were not simply free spaces for the emergence of local literary genres: they were patrolled by educated elites, often full of bias, who acted as literary gatekeepers and sometimes discouraged nascent authors from pursuing their dreams.

---

[13] In a second serialised novel, *Not All a Dream* (1937), Stuart-Young carefully avoided controversy: this novel featured a magnetically attractive mixed-race boy called Yo-Yo, gifted with such musical genius that he halts a race riot in Liverpool simply through the hypnotic beauty of his whistling. Readers politely ignored this serialisation; however, they complained again about his intrusion into fact with a short story on the topic of Igbo man-leopard transformations, published in 1937 (11 September 1937: 2).

The *Comet* contains an archive of literature and literary criticism in which contributors set forth aesthetic values on behalf of readers, intervened in the formation of tastes, described critical practices and guided readers' interpretations with their own evaluations. Ali combined a global humanist perspective with creative writing by local authors to make the *Comet* a literary journal that sought to emancipate readers' imaginations from the limits of local politics as well as the precriptions of British colonial culture. His philosophy was to 'let the rich variety in human nature be respected … and add interest to life and speech and thought' (*Comet* 28 May 1938: 9). When selecting what to print, he was interested less in anticolonial activism than in works that drew readers' creative imaginations into global anglophone intellectual culture, exposing them to a diversity of literatures and opinions in order to emancipate their critical faculties. As with the creative writers discussed in Chapter 1, he universalised English literature and laid claim to it, disconnecting it from colonial cultural hierarchies while setting expectations in place for the genres and styles of future local productions.

Ali wished to produce critical readers of all the world's citizens, not just those with privileged access to secondary and higher education. In his view, only when such a level playing field had been created could world leaders be fairly identified and inferiors disqualified (*Comet* 13 February 1937: 7). For all his romantic idealism, however, Ali's global cosmopolitan vision and commitment to the power of print produced a major blindspot. He believed that individuals without English-language newspapers and works of English literature in their hands lacked the tools required for modern citizenship. The possibility that local populations had their own established genres for record-keeping and political critique, or had the capacity to engage in communications, global trade, literary activities and politics without requiring western education, seemed to lie beyond Ali's expansive imagination. 'We have frequently witnessed many worth-while native plays which were done in the vernacular and which, although possessed of undoubted merit, were devoid of general appeal', he commented dismissively in August 1934, calling for 'native drama done in English' to replace vernacular literature (18 August 1934: 4).[14]

A general bias toward print in general and English print in particular permeated the *Comet*. In a celebration of the 'noble art' of printing in the first Christmas issue, for example, I. W. Oshilaja, manager of the Ife-Olu printing works where the *Comet* was produced, hailed the role of print 'in the world's progress' (*Comet* Christmas Number 1933: 55). The printing press 'has played a great part in the civilisation of the world; it has contributed much to the

---

[14] This may have been a reference to the 'wholly African' vernacular plays with all-African casts produced in Lagos in previous years by Dr O. Sapara (*Comet* 29 December 1934: 29).

Figure 3.1 Photograph of the manager and staff at I. W. Oshilaja's Ife-Olu Printing Works, Lagos, where the *Comet* was produced (*Comet* Christmas Number 1933, 54).

Figure 3.2 The composing room at I. W. Oshilaja's Printing Works (*Comet* Christmas Number 1933, 39).

spread of knowledge and its aid to business of every description cannot be overestimated' (Ibid.).

Print enables knowledge from the past to be communicated to present generations, Oshilaja insisted, ignoring the many oral and mnemonic modes of storing knowledge in favour of the idealistic view that the democratising power of print has 'opened the land of fair opportunity to countless peoples ... [bringing] more happiness, wider enlightement and truer liberty than ... with the preceding crude ages' (Ibid.: 55–6).[15] Other correspondents called for 'a paper-reading civilization' in Nigeria (*Comet* 7 September 1935: 18). The regular columnist S. O. Nwangoro stated that anglophone reading would cultivate habits of critical reasoning and eliminate popular prejudice as well as helping local people to realise their intellectual dreams: for Nwangoro, 'no ambition is higher than the acquisition of a high standard of writing and speaking in English' (*Comet* 16 July 1938: 14).[16]

Only reading in English would deliver the rational consciousness required for postcolonial independence in the view of Ali and his regular contributors: literacy in English was the weapon for intellectual liberation. From their residence in Broad Street, in the heart of the colonial old town, Ali and La Page promoted this ethos through their participation in dramatic societies, musical groups, reading circles and study groups for the circulation of English-language material.[17] Ali directed plays for the Lagos Players, the Lagos Shakespearean

---

[15] In a letter to the editor the following year, he reiterated this view – hardly surprising given his trade – that 'the printed word ... fosters the world's progress' (28 July 1934: 1). Oshilaja was from a family of printers: his brother worked for the government printer.

[16] In an article on 'Why I Read Novels', Nwangoro offered a strong vote of support for the gatekeeping activity of book reviewers, stating, 'I vote for novels ... that have passed the censorship of the Press and carry the unanimous approval of the literary "elites"' (*Comet* 28 April 1934: 12). Interestingly, however, of the three novelists recommended by Nwangoro in this article – Edgar Wallace, 'Sapper' (H. C. McNeile) and Oliver Goldsmith – the first two were generally regarded in Britain as 'escapist' rather than 'literary.' In comments that echoed Victorian and Edwardian notions of reading to prevent 'idle and mischievous' temptations among the working classes in their leisure time, such as drinking, gambling, and visiting (or working in) brothels, Nwangoro endorsed these writers for precisely their escapism, recommending them for the 'recreative pleasure and delight' they provided: their high entertainment value would, he argued, prevent any 'idle or mischievous' thoughts from entering readers' minds after a day at work (*Comet* 28 April 1934: 12).

[17] In a weekly column between 1933 and 1936, Ali's wife, Gertrude La Page, amassed a large readership for her essays on Rosicrucianism and other esoteric philosophies. La Page's column explained the complexities of 'soul science', 'magnetism', 'spiritual alchemy' and astral projection, and she encouraged readers to find their own special gifts (see, for example, 24 February 1934: 8, 21 December 1935: 9).

Society, the Little Garden Theatre and the Lagos Dramatic and Musical Society.[18] All these literary entertainments were intended 'to broaden the artistic outlook of the population of Lagos', whom Ali considered to be culturally insular (*Comet* 18 August 1934: 5).

Underlying this bias was a prejudice against 'unlettered' populations whose access to oral, vernacular archives placed them beyond the reach of modern knowledge in the view of the anglo-literate class. In fiction and letters in the *Comet*'s weekly columns, contributors repeatedly condemned 'the illiterate' for believing in 'juju – black magic … the greatest drawback for the progress of this country', while others promoted the acquisition of print-knowledge above oral learning, advising traditional elites to develop 'knowledge and understanding in place of his ignorance and superstition' in order for the individual to 'reap the full benefits of his life by the enjoyment of a higher political, economic and social status' (*Comet* 19 July 1935: 7, 20 October 1934: 17). 'In no country has the march of Civilization begun if the Newspaper and the printed word are neglected', wrote Nwangoro in 1938, highlighting the formative role of the press in people's 'conscious awakening':

> the Newspaper is, at once, the strongest mouthpiece of the people. It collects their opinions: it sifts their views, it interprets their deepest motives and so sets them on the highway that leads to political, religious and moral advancement. Intellectually too, the Newspaper educates since it places in the hands of its readers the most up-to-date events of the world, and enables them comparatively to measure themselves with others in other parts. Hence the spread of the Press in Nigeria is a true indication of the internal march of civilization in it. (*Comet* 12 February 1938: 23)

As subsequent chapters will show, this view persisted in Nigeria well into the 1960s: 'illitracy is a disease,' local writers declared in their publications, arguing that without printed 'history book[s] for the generations yet to come … a country can never be remembered or recorded in the world history' (Okeke 1964: 25,

---

[18] Lagos's several amateur dramatics societies performed American and British plays that included *Hobson's Choice* (Brighouse 1916) as well as locally authored material such as Dr J. C. Vaughan's 'drama on native life', with locally composed incidental music (18 August 1933: 5). The Little Garden Theatre was owned by Mr Candido da Rocha (29 December 1934: 30); Glover Memorial Hall was the other main venue for entertainments in Lagos, hosting travelling troupes such as the Coast Optimists from Ghana (8 August 1936). Plays were also regularly staged at Kings College, Lagos, where, in May 1934, the Lagos Shakespeare Society performed *The Taming of the Shrew* (19 May 1934: 3). In December 1934, the Lagos Shakespeare Society performed extracts from *The Merchant of Venice* 'interspersed with dialogues, songs and recitation' at the Native Court Hall with an all-Nigerian cast (29 December 1934: 1).

Abiakam c.1973: n.pag.). Clearly, 'civilisation' was interpreted to mean informed public opinion, and informed public opinion could not be oral in the views of these lettered African elites. Ali, Nwangoro, Oshilaja and the other writers cited above echoed the elitism of previous generations of West African newspaper editors, joining their broad project to produce 'lettered' citizens from the 'unlettered' masses by connecting English with modernity and modernity with print.

The structural impact of this bias on local African literatures can be seen in an article complaining about the difficulties of fundraising for research and publication by the distinguished Yoruba historian and transcriber of songs, A. K. Ajiṣafẹ. Describing his struggles in an article in the *Comet*, Ajiṣafẹ recalled how a public appeal published in West African journals, including the British-based *West Africa*, yielded just four pounds toward the publication of a book on the Yoruba language, and he failed to raise funds for future research and publications (20 January 1934: 8).[19]

The *Comet* was a literary magazine in English, addressing a gap that was widely recognised in British West Africa. Regular contributors to the *Comet* lamented that 'African authors are wanted badly ... We need more authors in Nigeria!', while government and missionary publishers often published appeals for 'manuscripts of African writers with a native background' (*Comet* 5 February 1938: 18, 1 October 1938). As the editor of the Liverpool-based *West African Review* noted, 'talented writers' in the region 'pour out their literature upon political questions and none enter the realm of lighter or didactic literature' (cited in *Comet* 30 May 1936: 13). Ali's paper was intended to remedy this problem, and his many contented readers hailed the journal for hosting the 'contributions of so many intellectuals of literary eminence', relishing the 'literary beauty' of its regular columns (*Comet* 8 September 1934: 1, 2 May 1936: 2).

The *Comet* diluted British cultural hierarchies and disengaged readers from elite tastes in the metropolis while holding firmly on to English literary culture. Ali stripped literacy of racism with his cosmopolitan approach to world literatures, inspiring local readers to think imaginatively and comparatively across global cultures and belief systems, encouraging them always to be situated critically – as critics – at one remove from the material before them. With his global frame of reference and universalist mindset, he flattened cultural hierarchies in a similar manner to Dick Carnis and B.B. and shared their universalism, locating the *Comet* and its readers outside colonial 'centres' as critical observers looking in to see how capital and power functioned in Europe and the colonies, comparing and juxtaposing colonial formations with alternative possibilities drawn from elsewhere while demonstrating a thoroughly British literary consciousness. This, however, came at the expense of support for African-language literatures.

[19] In a token gesture towards Yoruba print, Ali published a short-lived Yoruba page by L. Lincoln Glick in early issues of the *Comet* (see 29 July 1933: 19).

Meanwhile, for local readers without resources for international travel or easy access to libraries, the *Comet* was an educational hub that provided a mass of metropolitan and international publications in English. 'The Nigerian youths have been in need of a Literary Magazine for the past years and the *Comet* is undoubtedly a fulfilment of their desire', wrote one satisfied reader a few months after the inaugural issue was published (11 November 1933: 17). 'We entreat you to … be very far from Political Paper Controversies', another reader wrote in warm appreciation of the editor's politically disengaged approach (28 October 1933: 17). Even so, as demonstrated by Stuart-Young's attempted takeover of the *Comet's* literary aesthetic, when Ali allowed a migrant writer of a less cosmopolitan mindset than himself to adopt the role of maestro and claim space for weekly expression in the *Comet*, the cultural blindspots this produced had direct and negative consequences for aspiring African writers.

Onitsha Pamphlets: Youth Literature for the Modern World

4

> This is an African booklet, written by an African, for Africans and other interested readers.
> (Stephen 1964: n.pag.)

'Onitsha market literature' has been described by literary critics as an extraordinary phenomenon: it started in the early 1950s with the sporadic publication of locally authored romances and how-to pamphlets in the eastern Nigerian market town of Onitsha, commissioned by local printers who wished to generate income and keep their staff busy in the quiet months when the rush for school textbooks subsided after the start of the academic year (Dodson 1974). With the publication in 1956 of Ogali A. Ogali's runaway bestseller, *Veronica My Daughter: A Drama*, which sold an estimated 80,0000 copies in its first year, these generative spores mushroomed into a full-scale local publishing industry in Onitsha and surrounding cities (Dodson 1973: 174).[1] Printers and publishers – who were often also authors and booksellers – started to produce pamphlets by the hundreds, largely in English, in genres ranging from adventure stories to 'how-to' books, popular romances, dramas, epistolary manuals, travel narratives, poetry collections, fictional autobiographies and commentaries on current affairs.[2]

Known locally as 'little books' and 'small books', Onitsha market literature contained 'a distinctive, African colour' and was filled with 'the familiar people we see around us', providing advice about life alongside 'funs and amusements to one and thousands of Nigerians' (Madu, n.dat.: n.pag.; 'Speedy Eric' 1964, n.pag.; Ogu 1960: n.pag.). For the first time in British West Africa, large-scale local book publishing broke its tethers to colonial and missionary institutions and independent authors did not have to take financial responsibility for printing and marketing their books.[3]

---

[1] *Veronica My Daughter* was in fact first published by Zik's Press in Enugu, with subsequent editions published in Onitsha.
[2] Many pamphlets were also published in Igbo: these focused on proverbs, songs, rhymes and folklore, and did not include 'how-to' books, plays or works of fiction. Igbo pamphlets were generally marketed as language study guides.
[3] West African newspapers contain many stories of the difficulties faced by local authors in raising subscriptions for book publications. Authors with resources sent manuscripts

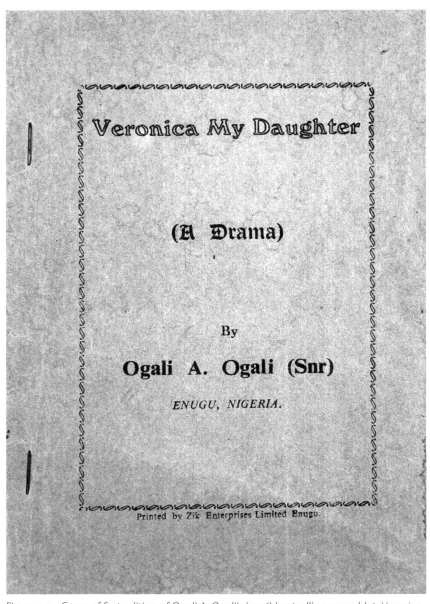

Figure 4.1 Cover of first edition of Ogali A. Ogali's (1956) bestselling pamphlet, *Veronica My Daughter* (Enugu: Zik Enterprises).

This chapter offers a bridge between the colonial-era newspapers discussed in previous chapters and Independence-era pamphlets produced on local presses in Nigeria.[4] Turning towards new genres, a later historical period, and a noticable change in the social class of authors, the chapter nevertheless highlights continuities across these literatures as examples of English-language newsprint creativity. Primary among these is the way pamphleteers turned to newspapers for sources of information and instruction as well as literary models. Responding rapidly to news stories, Nigerian pamphleteers competed to be the first to dramatise momentous political events such as the assassination of Congolese prime minister, Patrice Lumumba, in January 1961, or the imprisonment of Obafemi Awolowo for treason in 1963 (see Chapter 8). The most inventive authors embellished sensational recent news stories in their pamphlets: Nathan O. Njoku's *How to Write Love Letters* includes a fictionalisation of the murder by Ada Ocha Ntu (aka Esther Johnson) of her white lover, Mark Hall, in 1953.[5] The life-story of Daniel Onwubuta, whose gigantism was widely covered in the Nigerian press at his death in 1959 but has since been forgotten, was fictionalised immediately by 'Highbred Maxwell' (pseud.) in *The Gentle Giant 'Alakuku'* (1959). Also inspired by the news, in the aftermath of the Nigerian Civil War several pamphleteers dramatised the exploits – and public executions – of armed robbers in eastern Nigeria as crime levels soared and law and order broke down.

As well as providing material for plots and characters, newspapers featured at the core of pamphlet literature in other ways. Creative writing was often presented in the form of 'news' and 'reports'; pamphlets were given headline-like titles such as *The Lady Who Robbed her Mother to Defend her Husband* (Aroye and Aliche 1964) or they carried leaders announcing 'Life News in Brief' (Olisah 1960: 14) or 'Counterfeit Policeman Runs Away' (Nnadozie c.1962: 26). Some included periodical-style columns such as 'Short Advice for Men about Love and Marriage', 'The Work of a Woman in the House' and 'Short Story about Marriage' (Abiakam 1960: 7, 9–11). In at least one romance, the denouement is facilitated by a newspaper headline announcing the death of the obstructive old suitor in a car crash, releasing the heroine to marry her beloved boyfriend (Kamalu 1960: 48).

---

to Arthur H. Stockwell, a British publisher established in 1898, who placed adverts in newspapers throughout the British empire and attracted large numbers of new authors from almost every region under the British flag with affordable rates and publication packages. Stockwell filled a vital gap in the local publishing sector throughout the decades of colonialism, printing books and pamphlets in the UK and dispatching them for authors to sell at home. The many thousands of books he produced provide a rich bibliography of unofficial literary production by authors throughout the anglophone world.

4   For a study of locally published Ghanaian pamphlets in the 1950s and 1960s, see Newell (2000).
5   In 1956, Ntu's death sentence was commuted to life imprisonment; she was pardoned and released by Nnamdi Azikiwe in 1961 (Lindsay 2005).

In other pamphlets, characters refer to newspapers as part of their regular reading matter. 'I prayed for a reliable [boyfriend...] because many a time have I read in novels, newspapers and magazines about boys who make all sorts of promises to girls only for the purpose of gratifying their wicked impulses,' narrates one tragic heroine who is about to be cursed by the storyline she dreads (Nwosu 1960: 14). Additionally, many pamphleteers were – or went on to be – journalists, naming newspapers among their literary influences: 'I developed the sense of dramas by daily attendance of film shows and by reading novels, booklets and daily newspapers', stated Alexander Obiorah Okeke in the preface to *I'll Rather Break My Sword and Die* (1964: n.pag.).[6]

All these examples demonstrate that whilst Onitsha market literature was unprecedented, it did not appear out of nowhere. Pamphlet production was not the result of a spontaneous literary upsurge in eastern Nigerian towns, as critics often suppose. In content and form, these pamphlets were shaped by nearly a century of African newspaper production. Local authors, in turn, inserted themselves into newspaper cultures, sharing the medium of newsprint, sometimes making use of newspaper printing presses and contributing to locally agreed aesthetic values about authorship and reading in the manner of earlier print cultures.[7]

For a period of approximately twenty years, from the early 1950s until the early 1970s, local jobbing presses in eastern Nigeria were engaged by local bookseller-publishers, or took the initiative themselves, to produce cheap pamphlets in vast quantities for the local leisure-reading market. Authors were often booksellers and booksellers were often publishers, and publishers were often also the managers of jobbing presses.[8] 'Try us by sending us your Pamphlets, Invoice, Letter-headings, Hand-bills, Complements-cards, Wedding-cards, and all printable books', adverts

---

[6] At least twelve pamphlet authors in the 1960s were journalists or described themselves as freelance journalists.

[7] Pamphleteers' claims to newspaper-like currency were, however, continuously imperilled by the amount of time it took for pamphlets, as bound small books, to reach readers. In the second edition of *A Dictionary of Current Affairs and Army Take Over* (1966) by 'The Young Dynamic Author' (pseud. A. N. Onwudiwe), a 'public information' notice was inserted in red letters into the first page describing how the pamphlet 'had been completely delivered from the Press ready for distribution when the news of the new regime [of Major General Ironsi] reached us. It was therefore impossible to scrap the already compiled copies delivered in view of the heavy losses this would entail as well as delay' (1966, n.pag.). In desperation, Onwudiwe (the author-publisher) says that he has made 'the whole work current by adding a few chapters on the recent situation' at the end of the volume (Ibid.). Once printed, pamphlets could not easily be superseded by their next edition in the manner of a newspaper: as The Young Dynamic Author sadly admitted, 'all political offices printed in this second edition no longer apply' (Ibid.).

[8] Given that printing, publishing, authorship and bookselling were so intertwined, 'pamphleteer' is more accurate than 'author' to describe the collaborative production processes for this genre of literature.

declared in their pages, wrapping pamphlet literature into other commercially printed products aimed at Nigeria's expanding educated class (Olisah 1963c: 19). Authorship was actively encouraged. 'I welcome manuscripts by both new and well-known Authors,' the Port Harcourt pamphleteer V. C. Okeanu wrote in a section headed 'Boon to Authors' on the final page of *The Surprise Packet*: 'I am looking particularly for fast-moving novels with plenty of action that will appeal to the Nigerian readers. I shall be very pleased to hear from Would-be-AUTHORS *and to give them encouragement and advice*' (1960: v; capitalisation in original; emphasis added).

Intended readers came from a wide variety of backgrounds and included houseboys, fishermen, tailors, rubber tappers, mechanics, brick layers, drivers, electricians and textiles workers alongside better-educated white-collar workers such as teachers, clerks and nursing assistants, all of whom had benefited from the expansion of education in West Africa after the Second World War (Dodson 1974: 187–8). Such readers would have had some schooling, and were keen to maintain their literacy skills by studying English-language pamphlets that promised moral and practical advice alongside entertaining stories in local settings. 'This pamphlet is worth owning', front covers promised: 'It arms the buyer against hard-ship and generates in him the courage to deal wisely with world-difficulties – Advice a friend to buy one' (Olisah n.dat.: fp).

Pamphlets were bound into an intensely competitive market economy where the principle of usefulness was vital to boost sales. Usefulness and literariness were not counterposed: the serious business of self-improvement co-existed with art and entertainment. And at every turn, pamphleteers emphasised the pleasures alongside the benefits to be gained from reading literature. Pamphlets, they informed readers, offered 'a searchlight which will obviate the painful difficulty they would have experienced if the book had not been written' (Young Dynamic Author 1966: n.pag.).

Pamphlets placed the personal and emotional at centre stage, filling the gaps left by English-language newspapers' avoidance of intimate and domestic matters, as discussed in Chapter 2. Authors addressed readers' personal lives and carved out a space for love, desire, fantasy and sexual relationships, often in the form of sensational romantic stories that addressed readers' domestic and professional concerns. Action-packed dramas and entertaining romances using local characters in familiar urban settings were simultaneously 'exciting, lecturing, instructional and educative', boasted authors, who were engaged in a project of personal self-betterment on behalf of readers and had declared 'wordy war' on social evils such as 'harlotry' (Aroye and Aliche 1964: n.pag.). Writers seized upon popular plots and innovative formats each time a new bestseller appeared, borrowing and reworking its contents and form, tweaking storylines and adding flourishes of their own to the blueprint. This process of accelerated genre formation, made possible by the close proximity of authors, printers and booksellers, and the high

Figure 4.2 Cover of Nathan O. Njoku's (n.dat.) *How to Read and Write Correct English, Better Compositions, Sentences, Proverbs, Office Routine, How to Pass Examinations and General Knowledge (For Schools and Colleges)* (Onitsha: Njoku and Sons Bookshop).

Figure 4.3 Cover of J. Kenddys Onwudiegwu's (1965) *English: The Language of the Modern World. How to Write Good Letters, Better Compositions, Agreements, Good Business Letters, Applications and Teach Your Self How to Speak and Write Good English* (Onitsha: Gebo Brothers Bookshop).

numbers of local readers with sufficient spare cash to purchase cheap reading matter in the 1950s and 1960s, gave Onitsha unique status as a crucible of local literary production.[9]

The booksellers and publishers who compiled pamphlets and purchased manuscripts directly from authors were conscious of the need to capture readers' attention and turn browsers into eager purchasers. To this end, the covers and first pages of publications are crammed with eye-catching slogans, woodcuts, promises and photographs, all to boost sales in the competitive marketplace (see Figs 4.2 and 4.3). Nathan O. Njoku, the successful 1960s bookseller whose productions are the focal point of the next chapter, excelled in these practices. His preface to *How to Marry a Good Girl and Live in Peace with Her* (c.1960) reveals the extent to which he had mastered the art of attracting readers through marketing ploys: 'Hip Hip Hurrah! Hip Hip Hurrah! Hip Hip Hurrah! That's okay you have warmed yourself up now. Well then, get every ready to go through this book, particularly originated to guide you and make you have fun out of reading' (4).

These opening words exaggerate and parody the typical 1950s pamphlet preface, demonstrating the extent to which the 'how-to' market had become saturated with competing publications by the early 1960s, when this pamphlet was printed. Other pamphlets, such as *Why Harlots Hate Married Men and Love Bachelors* (Moneyhard [pseud. C. N. Onuoha, also listed as C. N. Obioha] c.1955), went into multiple further editions within weeks of publication, by which time it had to compete with numerous imitations published in its wake. Self-help pamphlets such as *How to Speak to Girls and Win Their Love* by Abiakam (1965b) and *How To Make Friends With Girls* (Okonkwo c.1963) remained on sale in Onitsha well into the 1990s, sold as cheap classics alongside schoolbooks on stalls in the heart of Onitsha market.

In her study of the North American self-help tradition, Micki McGee (2005) points out that how-to literature has a special relationship with the reader's own lifestory, involving a continuous forward projection out of the present time of reading (16–17). A distinctive temporality is invoked in self-help literature. Reading is equated with the reshaping of futures: self-help literature involves the deliberate losing or loosening of ties to the past as authors inscribe readers into new lives where a successful, self-created self exists in a happier state (Ibid.). Past and present are thus reconfigured through the activity of reading.

Given this relationship with time, self-help literature is particularly well suited to decolonising contexts with their concerted transcendence of ideologies about Europeans' right to rule and Africans' place in racial hierarchies. It perfectly suits the forward-looking mentality of the young men who formed the majority of authors using pen-names such as 'The Teenager With Knowledge' (J. Kenddys

---

[9] Pamphleteers were active in many Nigerian cities at this time, from Port Harcourt, Calabar and Aba to Lagos and Ibadan.

Onwudiegwu) and 'The Young, Dynamic Author' (A. N. Onwudiwe). These authors had everything ahead of them. They filled the moment of decolonisation with a plethora of 'how-to' pamphlets and entertaining moral stories reiterating core messages that insisted on recognising readers' potential for learning and self-transformation. Through self-help, drama and fiction – often combined innovatively within the same text – pamphleteers promised readers who felt unable to realise their economic and social ambitions, but had the determination to continuously improve their minds through reading and study, that they could harness English, erase historical inequalities and empower themselves for fulfilled futures.

Pamphleteers adopted an array of revealing pseudonyms and nicknames that highlighted the gendered power of authorship and their credentials as local intellectuals: examples include 'The Strong Man of the Pen' (Sunday Okenwa Olisah; also used by Wilfred Onwuka), 'Master of Pen' (Wilfred Onwuka), 'Master of English' (Nathan O. Njoku), 'Master of Life' (Sunday Okenwa Olisah), 'Ralph O. Ability', 'Speedy Eric' (A. N. Onwudiwe) and many more. Some pen-names projected the writer's class and status, such as 'Highbred Maxwell' (who also published under 'Master of Life') or 'Moneyhard' (C. N. Onuoha or C. N. Obioha). 'Money hard' is the opening of a popular Nigerian maxim, 'money hard to get but easy to spend', and appears to contradict other authors' emphasis on masculine success and power. As a pseudonym, however, 'Moneyhard' refers to having control over money rather than being in hardship, as the following autobiographical boast from the author demonstrates: 'I am Mr. C. N. O. Money-hard, the money commander, master of money and small man with great value' (c.1955: 5).

Veteran authors such as Ogali and Olisah were local celebrities, hailed by their pen-names on the streets of Onitsha: 'Every place I go "People shout the strong man of the pen"', Olisah wrote in the preface to one of his pamphlets: 'I very much appreciate this type of popularity and I am encouraged more to push my pen with all the advisable words at my disposal' ('Strong Man of the Pen' [pseud. Okenwa Olisah] c.1964). In spite of his literary fame, however, Olisah was plagued by financial hardship, and his pamphlets complain bitterly about the difficulties of accumulating wealth when men are faced with 'money-monger' women, false friends and bad luck. By the early 1960s he was using the back page of his bestsellers to advertise his willingness to sell their copyright to 'any publisher who may wish to make an offer' (Olisah c.1963a: 54).[10]

In a similar manner to the local newspaper editors described in previous chapters, pamphleteers displayed their self-positioning as members of the

---

[10] The Okenwa Correspondence College in Onitsha may have sapped Olisah's income. While no details could be found about how long this enterprise survived, Onitsha produced at least two other rival colleges at this time, teaching secretarial skills, book-keeping and typing to local students (Aririguzo 1960: n.pag.).

educated elite.[11] Many texts included photographs of young men in suits and ties brandishing fountain-pens, standing or sitting at solid writing desks surrounded by books and paperwork in striking displays of successful white-collar modernity (Figs 4.4 to 4.8). These portraits function as creative and aspirational advertisements for the contents of pamphlets, illustrating the future selves that, pamphlets promise, a mastery of English will deliver if readers are astute and receptive. Forming part and parcel of the literary experience, these photographs illustrate how purchasing the pamphlet will open up pathways to success for those readers who choose to heed their advice.

If such photographs invite a suspension of the present in favour of a new futurity in accordance with the self-help tradition, they signal far more than the projected fantasy life of individual writers and readers. Many images are rich with imaginative references to heroic types of masculinity from American cinema and popular culture (see Gondola 2016). In one striking photograph, the author poses as the hypermasculine frontier figure of the American cowboy (Fig 4.9). In other pamphlets, readers encounter 'the Bad Boys of Tinubu Square, the Wild Takwa Bar-Beach Boys and the jayi-jayi addicts of Idi-Oro suburb' who ride by taxi (rather than horse) from bar to bar in Lagos, tote pistols, drink hard liquor with fellow members of their gangs, smoke Lucky Strikes, have trouble with 'dames', and communicate in innovative local versions of Wild West slang where '[we] rocked and crooked the suburbs of old Lagos; all the time dodging the law and the blue guys and the deals' (Anyichie c.1962: n.pag.).[12]

Nigerian pamphleteers played competitive intertextual games with one another, attracting readers by swapping names, metaphors and maxims with bestselling rivals and borrowing titles from international popular novels: thus the American self-help classic, *The Game of Life and How to Play It* (Shinn 1925) is echoed in Abiakam's *The Game of Love* (1960), *How to Play Love* by Felix N. Stephen (c.1962b) and 'The Sea of Life and How to Swim It', a section of *Experience In Life, is Key To Success*, (Stephen c.1962a: 36). Similarly, Marius U. E. Nkwoh's *The Sorrows of Man* (1963) references, and brings down to earth, Marie Corelli's sensational novel, *The Sorrows of Satan* (1895).

Each new pamphlet tried to eclipse its predecessor with promises of additional novelty and fresh material. Many Nigerian pamphlets were collaboratively authored by writers and publishers in a similar manner to the collaborations

---

[11] Some pamphleteers, like Ogali and Thomas Iguh, used the proceeds of their bestsellers to fund their studies at university (Dodson 1974: 248).

[12] At least one pamphleteer – the journalist Charles U. Uwanaka – called for the prohibition of 'morally bad' books, cowboy films, boxing films and crime and detective stories, supporting Nkrumah's censorship of cinema in Ghana in 1960: 'in Nigeria today we have local cowboys', Uwanaka wrote: 'no doubt, they got the idea of what they are doing now from films at the cinema' (Uwanaka 1964: 12, 29).

Figure 4.4 Back cover of Nathan O. Njoku's (1963) *The Complete Letter Writing Made Easy for Ladies and Gentlemen* (Onitsha: Njoku and Sons).

Figure 4.5   A. Onwudiwe, Managing Director of Onwudiwe and Sons, flyleaf of *The Bitterness of Politics and Awolowo's Last Appeal* (1964) by Mazi Raphael D. A. Nwankwo (Onitsha: A. Onwudiwe and Sons).

Figure 4.6 The author Raph Oguanobi, flyleaf of *Two Friends in the Romance of Runaway Lover* (c.1960) (Onitsha: Obi Brothers Bookshop).

Figure 4.7   S. Aw. Emedolu, Manager of Treasure Press, Aba, pictured on the final page of H. O. Ogu's *Rose Only Loved my Money* (1950), with the caption, 'Hints: African authors are cordially invited to send in Manuscripts to us. We allow negotiation'.

Figure 4.8 Portrait of F. B. Joe, front cover of *The General Guide in English: Complete Compositions, Business Letters and 95 Modern Questions and Answers Made Easy for Elem. Schools and Colleges* (c.1965) (Onitsha-Fegge: United Brothers Bookshop).

Figure 4.9 C. N. O. Moneyhard in cowboy's dress on final page of *Why Harlots Hate Married Men and Love Bachelors* (c.1955) (Port Harcourt: C. N. O. Moneyhard).

described in Chapter 2, where aspiring writers received assistance from others in preparing work for newsprint publication. The schoolboy author, Nathaniel O. Madu, who was a Standard IV student when he wrote *Miss Rosy in the Romance of True Love* (n.dat.), opens with an expression of 'indebtedness to various authors whose compositions I have persued with delight, and from whom consequently I borrowed a pattern, this being my first attempt' (3). Madu goes on to lift material verbatim from a contemporary pamphlet, Cletus Gibson Nwosu's *Miss Cordelia in the Romance of Destiny* (1960), which is itself heavily dependent on David Hogan's *The New Universal Letter Writer* ([1813] 1839) (see Chapter 5). Meanwhile, Nathan O. Njoku jumped at the opportunity to purchase Olisah's 'famous pamphlet[s]', which the author advertised for sale in the early 1960s, incorporating them into new publications under his own name. 'I cannot claim that I alone originated all the contents in this little work', Njoku wrote in the preface to *How to Succeed in Life*: 'Generally authors gave me their contributions and I am thankful to them, especially Mr. Okenwa Olisah a native of Nnewi, who wrote the famous pamphlet "No Condition is Permanent"' (1960: n.pag.).[13] In turn, after the Nigerian Civil War, Njoku sold the copyright of his list to J. C. Anorue (see Chapter 9).

Njoku's open acknowledgement of Olisah enhanced, rather than diminished, the appeal of his publications and served as a guarantee of local literary value. Many other pamphlets were similarly 'revised and enlarged' after authors submitted (and sold) manuscripts to professional pamphleteers, and numerous pamphlets were compiled in their entirety by bookseller-publishers, who updated older publications with new cover images, deleted old publication dates and inserted new authors' names to avoid obsolescence.[14] As a consequence of this constant change of names and hands, pamphlets are notoriously difficult to date.

At the same time as pamphlets poured into eastern Nigerian bookstores and markets in the 1950s and 1960s, West African literary heavyweights such as Chinua Achebe, Wole Soyinka, Ama Ata Aidoo and Ayi Kwei Armah were earning global recognition with English-language novels and plays about the cultural and psychological damage suffered by Africans in British colonial history. These international, university educated authors engaged in a

---

[13] Judging by their joint announcement in 1960 of a plan to go on 'a tour of some African Countries' together 'in order to study their MARRIAGE SYSTEM', this relationship with Olisah appeared to be friendly and productive (Njoku c.1960a; emphasis retained). The plan may not have come to fruition, however, as no publication arising from this trip can be found.

[14] While the love letters in J. Abiakam's *How to Speak to a Girl about Marriage* (c.1987) have not changed in content since the pamphlet was first published as *How to Speak to Girls and Win Their Love* in the mid-1960s, the dates at the top of each letter in the edition circulating in the mid-1990s have been changed to the mid-1980s, reflecting the most recent reprint of the classic pamphlet.

sustained decolonial project to re-inscribe African systems of knowledge into their narratives, pressing for alternative histories to the racial subordination experienced under British imperial rule. As Ngũgĩ (1986, 1993) famously and repeatedly insisted, English literature and the English language were vehicles for British cultural nationalism and colonial racism, loaded with descriptions that erased the value of cultural production in vernacular languages in the colonies.[15]

By the early 1960s, Nigerian pamphleteers were well aware of the international upsurge in African literary production, positioning themselves as part of the new anglophone world literary order. Authors declared a national spirit behind their publications: pamphlets were offered as 'gifts to the young stars of Nigeria Republic' and 'Specially Dedicated to Republic of Nigeria' (Okeke 1964: n.pag., Kamalu 1960: n.pag.). Authors were praised in blurbs for their 'great service to humanity in Producing this book' or confidently celebrated their own capacity, as Speedy Eric put it, to 'impress most readers all over the parts of the world' (Egbusunwa 1964: n.pag.; 'Speedy Eric' 1964: n.pag.).[16] The Port Harcourt publisher V. C. Okeanu summed up pamphleteers' collective spirit in his preface to Sigis Kamalu's novel, *The Surprise Packet*: 'by aiding African literature books and novels, the African Authority shall have a place under the Sun' (Okeanu 1960: iii).

Writers were keenly aware of international African authors' impact and ideas, and Onitsha pamphlets are peppered with references to Igboland's most distinguished creative writer, Chinua Achebe, whose *Things Fall Apart* is often named in model letters showing readers how to place orders for books with international suppliers. While Achebe's famous first novel drew the world's attention to the British dismantling of precolonial Igbo civilisation and the rise to power of new local elites composed of messengers and clerks in the very towns inhabited by Nigerian pamphleteers, it was too expensive for the majority of local readers to afford. As Kamalu complained, most African literature was 'produced abroad where the authors have gone for higher learning' and 'because of their expensive printing and high quality paper are far beyond the pocket of the average Nigerian reader to possess' (Kamalu 1960: n.pag.). Pamphlets, by contrast, were printed on newsprint with affordable prices ranging from two to four shillings. They filled a vital gap in the leisure-reading market in the 1950s and 1960s and provided an

---

[15] With their interest in social themes rather than colonial politics and nationalism, Nigerian authors Flora Nwapa, Cyprian Ekwensi and Amos Tutuola are closer in content and style to locally published pamphlets than the African nationalist writers of the 1960s.
[16] Not all authors were as confident as this: first-time authors entering field of writing often offered apologies for their errors and humbly invited constructive criticism from readers.

'original cast of African back-ground, style and idea[s] ... that will meet the pocket of the average reader' (Ibid.).

Pamphleteers emphasised that they wrote for the benefit of ordinary people (Dodson 1974: 188). Nkwoh expresses this orientation toward the ordinary in his pamphlet, *The Sorrows of Man*: 'Art (education if you choose) should take account of the ordinary life, the humble people. This is why, dear reader, I have been doing literary works' (Nkwoh 1963: n.pag.). 'Life is always helped by the reading of booklets', writes Stephen in *The Temple of Love,* in one of many reflections on the usefulness of pamphlets: books give 'courage in dismay serve as watch dogs or signal bells, when something strange is likely to happen' (Stephen 1964: n.pag.).

Local authors endorsed the practical worldliness of the English language, stripping it of political specificity as an instrument of colonial control. In many respects, they reversed Ngũgĩ's political warnings against the English language, promoting the alternative view that the social and economic constraints arising from British imperialism could be overturned through mastery of English as a world language. As the barrister V. E. Eze wrote in his foreword to Ralph O. Ability's pamphlet, *A New Guide to Good English and Correct Letter Writing*, 'both good English and Letter-Writing are a sine qua non in the business world of English-speaking peoples generally, and in Nigeria where as yet there is no vernacular lingua franca' (1964: n.pag). In place of colonial control, individuals who could demonstrate their capacity to write in English using genres they had learnt in school and from reading local literatures would, pamphlets promised, be able to access higher incomes as well as the opportunities and social and professional hierarchies that had hitherto been closed-off to the masses. In the optimistic spirit of self-help, readers were urged to put their literacy to good use and 'help yourself more by reading different novels *especially local ones*, news papers and other story books' (Eleonu c.1976: 7; emphasis added). In fact, according to this author, 'there are so many ways of learning how to read and write whether you schooled or not. You can do so by frequent reading of any book or any written piece of paper that you come across' (5–6).

English literacy was regarded as more than a useful technology of self-expression in Nigeria. Authors sought to democratise English as a world language and give readers equal access to global networks of printed knowledge in hitherto inaccessible centres of power. In *English: The Language of the Modern World*, Onwudiegwu expands this vision of a world free of 'discrimination' in a manner reminiscent of Ali's anglocentric cosmopolitanism in the 1930s:

> All of us today are speaking English. Those who have not known it are burning with intense desire to know how to speak and write English Language. But many of us bluntly fail to understand why we are speaking English – a foreign language ... [A]s England has

> the greater part of the world government, it is a must that the whole world should understand its language – English Language … time shall come when the whole world shall be speaking English and there will be no more discrimination throughout the entire people in the whole world. (1965: 4–5)

In spite of their optimism and patriotic loyalty, however, the authors of some pamphlets – letter-writing manuals in particular – initially appear to manifest the very 'mental colonisation' identified by Ngũgĩ in his condemnation of the psychological effects of imperial racist ideology on Africans (1986: 11, 18). The large numbers of wholly derivative pamphlets produced locally in the 1950s and 1960s create the paradox of a locally published self-help literature that plagiarised English texts and promoted the etiquette of the British bourgeoisie during decolonisation and Nigeria's first decade of Independence while, at the same time, a locally unaffordable nationalist literature by authors published in the Global North promoted African epistemologies and decried eurocentrism.

As the next chapter will discuss in more detail, local pamphleteers' borrowings from nineteenth-century publications, their rejection of 'illiterates' and their self-projections as genteel 'men of letters' appear to endorse anachronistic models of English bourgeois manners so wholeheartedly as to not only illustrate Ngũgĩ's devastating observations about (neo)colonial Africa, but also to exemplify the problem with exogenous – and colonising – languages that stifle a creative engagement with local expressive cultures. From a cultural nationalist perspective, it is hardly surprising that some critics positioned Onitsha pamphlets as a happily brief moment in the emergence of a truly Nigerian (or African) literature, necessarily surpassed by later, 'more sophisticated' authors rather than possessing expressive integrity in their own right (Obiechina 1975: 13, 108, 177). One early critic, Donatus Nwoga, expressed literary scholars' reservations succinctly: 'much Onitsha market literature is below the standard of even its own audience', he wrote, adding that even the 'best of its examples do not attain a high literary standard' (1965: 33). The next chapter will contest such dismissive chronologies and offer an alternative framework for assessing one of the most reader-oriented, dialogical pamphlet genres that was also the most 'plagiaristic': epistolary manuals.

The Work of Repetition in Nigerian Epistolary Pamphlets

> 'Novels and English Literature ...
> haunt my brain.'
> (Oguanobi n.dat.: n.pag.)

In 1964, an Onitsha author using the pseudonym 'Ralph O. Ability' published a pamphlet entitled *A New Guide to Good English and Correct Letter-Writing* that went into circulation in eastern Nigeria alongside numerous similar letter-writing guides by local authors, feeding the prodigious local demand for affordable self-help literature. From its title page onwards, however, this 'entirely new and up to date handy compilation of good English and correct letters on current topics of current interest' reproduced extensive portions verbatim from three nineteenth-century publications: *The New Universal Letter-Writer, or New Art of Polite Correspondence*, an influential, popular volume by the Rev. Thomas Cooke first published in England in 1788 and republished with additions by David Hogan in Philadelphia throughout the first half of the 1800s; the bestselling *Classical English Letter-Writer* by Elizabeth Frank, published in Britain in 1814 and America in 1816, with numerous revised editions in subsequent decades; and *The American Letter-Writer: A Complete Guide to Correspondence on All Subjects of Every-day Life*, a popular volume published by George Brumder in Milwaukee in 1888. Large sections of *Pitman's Office Desk-Book*, an office manual first published in 1906 and revised and reissued throughout the remainder of the century, were also included verbatim at the end of the pamphlet.

A long nineteenth century of English epistolary manuals was condensed into this pamphlet, rendering it anything but 'entirely new' or 'current'. In a letter of condolence offered as a model to readers, for example, Ralph O. Ability writes, 'Dear Mr Okeke, I hardly like to intrude upon you in your great sorrow, but I cannot resist telling you how much my husband and I sympathised with you' (1964: 93). 'Dear Friend,' opens the same letter in the 1888 edition of George Brumder's *The American Letter-Writer: A Guide to Correspondence*: 'I hardly like to intrude upon your great sorrow, but I cannot resist telling you how much my husband and myself sympathize with you' (77). Death and empathy, this duplication shows, are universal and repeatable across different social times and spaces. In another rather more disruptive and revealing duplication, a Nigerian schoolgirl informs her boyfriend that she cannot consider his marriage proposal until another time

Figure 5.1   Photograph of 'Ralph O. Ability' (probably the publisher, R. O. Egbusunwa) as a smartly dressed 'man of letters' from the pamphlet, *A New Guide to Good English and Correct Letter Writing* (1964: 29) (Onitsha: R. Egbusumh and Bros).

because 'My worthy guardian, Mr. Ralphsco is now at this seat near Ofenwafo' (54). With small modifications for geography and local sense, this echoes a letter in David Hogan's *The New Universal Letter-Writer* where a young woman explains to her suitor that 'My worthy guardian, Mr. Melville, is now at his seat near Bristol' (1839: 59). In this case, the author's playful, ventriloquistic projection as 'Mr. Ralphsco' – a bourgeois (if not aristocratic) propertied gentleman – conveys a specific message to local readers about the author's social status as a 'man of letters', a class apart from unschooled Africans and a cut above the reader whose personal lives he assists on the pages of this epistolary manual (see Fig 5.1).

Sometimes slightly localised but often left in their original condition, multiple quotations of this type form clearly distinguishable layers as Ralph O.

Ability turns the pages of his source texts and extracts the examples of English epistolary culture he considers best suited to local Nigerian contexts.[1]

Were this a one-off instance of unattributed copying among the multitude of texts published in eastern Nigeria between the late 1950s and early 1970s, Ralph O. Ability might have been accused of plagiarism – in the manner of the Lagos poet, F. Uzoma Anyiam, whose humiliation in the *Comet* was discussed in Chapter 3 – and dismissed as the least interesting type of Onitsha pamphleteer in a rich literary marketplace of 'little books' (Ogu 1960: n.pag.). However, Ralph O. Ability was not alone in his writing method; nor were he and his contemporaries deliberately hiding their sources from gullible local book-buyers and disappearing behind cloaks of pseudonymity for fear of discovery. As with the material discussed in Chapter 3, an entirely different critical framework is required if we are to appreciate the aesthetic choices of 'plagiaristic' pamphleteers.

Countless epistolary 'how-to' manuals by local authors – including well-known names such as Sunday Okenwa Olisah (aka 'The Strong Man of the Pen' and 'The Master of Life') and one-off pseudonymous writers like Ralph O. Ability – circulated around eastern Nigerian bookshops and markets in the early 1960s. All were packed with previously published letters for readers to emulate, ranging across different categories of correspondence from love letters to business letters and 'public letters' to the press.[2] Bearing similar titles and covers to Ralph O. Ability's pamphlet, these included, to take a small sample, *English: The Language of the Modern World: How to Write Good Letters Better Compositions, Agreements, Good Business Letters, Applications and Teach Your Self How to Speak and Write Good English* by Onwudiegwu, *How to Write Love*

---

[1] Another example of this practice can be found in Onwudiegwu's (1965a) *English: The Language of the Modern World: How to Write Good Letters Better Compositions, Agreements, Good Business Letters, Applications and Teach Your Self How to Speak and Write Good English*. Here the author cuts and pastes letters from foreign sources and exchanges foreign for local place names, inserting his own name in the letters. A model letter between friends in this pamphlet is sent from 'Kenddys College of Technology, Bridgway Street, London, KC2' and signed by 'Boy Negro Kenddys' (1965a: 12): in it, the writer describes how 'my entire countenance was transported to joy when I received your letter' and how 'in the field of sport we have long established ourselves as being formidable particularly in football. In boxing, table tennis and basketball, we have also distinguished ourselves' (Ibid.). In spite of its claims to come from London, this model letter combines material from a number of sources, including Indian epistolary pamphlets and English and American letter-writing manuals from the nineteenth century. Readers familiar with *The Arabian Nights' Entertainments* will also recognise the Prince of Persia's answer to Schemselnihar's letter: '[your letter] inspired me with joy, which immediately appeared in my eyes and countenance' (Townsend 1896: 459).

[2] Besides letter-writing manuals, other epistolary genres circulated in eastern Nigeria in the 1950s and 1960s such as pamphlets offering emotional and professional advice in response to readers' letters.

Letters, Toasts and Business Letters by Speedy Eric, *How to Write Good Letters and Applications* by Olisah and *How to Write Better Letters, Applications, Business Letters and English Grammar* by the prolific publisher-bookseller Nathan O. Njoku, whose epistolary manuals dominated the Onitsha book market in the 1960s.[3] In them, mothers tell daughters, 'Daddy and I do hope that you will bear [boarding-school lessons...] bravely and not give way to naughtiness and laziness' (Njoku 1964: 20); employers are informed, 'I attended evening classes in millinery and dressmaking, at the Kensigngton Gore Evening Institute' (31); and best friends are told, 'Well, Francis, you are none the worse minus the appendix. Cheer up, old boy, we shall yet plan another, grand holiday next May' (37).

How could these bourgeois English voices be offered as models of self-help to Nigerian readers in the era of decolonisation? How could authors ignore the social and historical specificities of their sources and suggest, instead, that 'polite' English correspondence of this type was universal, timeless and available for cross-cultural epistolary uptake? As Ralph O. Ability correctly, if paradoxically, observes in the elevated voice of a nineteenth-century English author, 'no elegance in the choice of words would compensate for want of ease and grace in forming them into phrases' (1964: 27). Numerous model letters featured bourgeois subjects such as these, whose grammatically correct letter-writing style was so formal as to appear out of place in postcolonial Nigeria with its distinctive English dialects. As such, the pamphlets appear to be an extreme example of the processes identified by analysts of global cultural flows in which the unevenness of societies on the so-called peripheries of economic and political power are manifested through locals' mimicry of anachronistic western genres, always 'coming after' – both energetically chasing through space and lagging behind in time – dominant western cultures and economies (see, for example, Appadurai 1996). Yet local Nigerian readers seemed to be delighted with the manuals: 'Readers write me congratulatory letters almost every day', boasted Olisah, 'The Strong Man of the Pen', in the preface to one of his many pamphlets, demonstrating one of the first uses to which readers put the skills he imparted (c.1964: n.pag.). Likewise, Speedy Eric, in the highly derivative *How to Write Love Letters and Toasts and Business Letters*, described how he regularly 'received letters of congratulation from different parts of the region' (1963: n.pag.). 'We cannot all hope to become writers of good books', he stated in another publication, adding encouragingly, 'yet most people can ... become very nice letter writers' (1964: n.pag.).

Contemporary literary scholars reading *A New Guide to Good English* and the many other local epistolary pamphlets of its type might be tempted to home in

---

[3] Up to the Nigerian Civil War of 1967, when he sold the rights to his works to J. C. Anorue, Njoku was an aggressively entrepreneurial publisher. He purchased the rights to many bestselling pamphlets. Together with Sunday Okenwa Olisah (whose rights he also bought) as his co-author and co-editor, Njoku fed and encouraged the expanding demand for epistolary how-to books in eastern Nigeria.

on the 'original' letters to be found in their pages over and above the 'plagiarised' material, not least because the local material offers contemporary mini-narratives about ordinary people's daily lives in cities and contains details of social histories unavailable in other written archives. Although the contents of these letters are topped and tailed by standard phrases from British and American epistolary reference books and are sandwiched between large chunks of wholly 'foreign' material excised from nineteenth-century letter-writing manuals, they seem to carry local voices in a richly textured *comédie humaine* of Nigerian urban experiences outside and beyond elite representations. Nearly 100 pages into Ralph O. Ability's pamphlet, for example, the following scene is described in a template letter demonstrating how to report a motor accident to one's insurance company:

> 44 Ihuegbe Lane, Owerri
>
> Dear Sir,
>
> I regret to have to inform you that I have had the misfortune at 5 o'clock this afternoon to be concerned in an accident with my motor-cycle in Ogide Road. I was passing stationary motor O Jesu bus when a woman who had been hidden from my by the bus crossed the road immediately in front of me. In my unsuccessful effort to avoid her, I skidded and knocked her down. She was cared by the police constable who took her to a hospital. I hope she has not suffered serious hurt. My own braises cuts and dislocated shoulder have been attended to by my own doctor … Should the woman claim compensation because she was walking on a Besha crossing. I wish to disclaim responsibility because she was completely hidden from me by the O Jesu bus which I believed to have been setting down passengers, and she neglected to exercise due care in making herself visible before emerging into the traffic stream. (1964: 99)

This letter conveys a powerful sense of the bustling infrastructure of Owerri, filled with cars, crowds, 'O Jesu' buses, absent-minded pedestrians, belisha beacons, policemen and hospitals.[4]

In other pamphlets, model letters contain vivid stories of conflicts between landlords and tenants, requests to senior family members for funds, complaints to headmasters from pupils about the poor-quality food in school canteens, polite requests to loud neighbours to reduce the noise pollution from their gramophones

---

[4] An 'O Jesu' bus is a decorated private minibus or 'mammy wagon' used for public transport. Remembering eastern Nigerian transportation in the 1950s and 1960s, Akachi Adimora Ezeigbo and Chris Uchechukwu Ezeigbo explain that 'O Jesu' could be an expression of adoration on the part of the owner, or a cry to God for help or even a prayer. Other citations one saw on the body of vehicles at the time included: 'No Condition is Permanent', 'Fear God' and 'Power Pass Power'. Most times, especially on mammy wagons, the captions were accompanied with an illustration of the inscription (personal communication, 2 July 2020).

and many other scenarios in which courteous, formal English correspondence replaces the impertinence, or hostility, that might be perceived by the presence of the signatories, who often occupy socially inferior positions to their addressees (Olisah 1962: 23–6, 27). In a section copied verbatim from a manual published in 1816, Njoku emphasised this point, insisting that letter-writers must respect the rules of politeness in which the writer's tone reflects hierarchies of age and status:

> To superiors, it should be respectful; to inferiors, courteous; to friends [and companions], familiar; to relation[s], affectionate; to children, simple and playful; in important subjects, it should be forcible and impressive; on lighter subjects, easy and sprightly; in condolence, tender and sympathetic; in congratulations, lively and joyous. (Njoku c.1964: 15; square brackets inserted to reproduce citation from Frank 1816 [American Edn]: xii)

Nigerian template letters carefully respect these social strata and reproduce their etiquette. The numerous local letters simultaneously respect and seek to move across socially stratified relationships in crowded urban settings: in them, epistolarity creates a positive effect in advance of, or instead of, face-to-face communications with the recipient.

Many of the localised scenarios described above are, however, borrowed and adapted from external sources. Indeed, they furnish evidence of (post)colonial networks of exchange that challenge colonialist models of English literary transmission in which literature is seen to flow in a single direction from London to the colonies and around the world. Large portions of Nigerian epistolary pamphlets are culled from popular letter-writing manuals published in India in the 1940s and brought into Nigeria after the Second World War for consumption alongside movies, magazines and other commodities from the subcontinent for trade in local markets (Osondu-Oti 2015).[5] These Indian pamphlets contain the same urban scenarios, template letters and extracts from nineteenth-century English manuals as Nigerian pamphlets. Some Nigerian pamphleteers adapted place names and terminology to suit the local environment, as in the model insurance claim letter from Owerri, but others simply cut and pasted sample letters without changing the Ahmedabad, Bangalore, Bombay, Delhi, Mahabaleshwar and Poona addresses. These appeared alongside model letters to the editor of the *Times of India*, references to temples and Hindu festivals and compositions on topics such as the need for the Boy Scout Movement in India to cure the 'physically weak' condition of Indian schoolboys, with their 'mind[s]

---

5 The history of the circulation of these Indian 'how-to' pamphlets in West Africa merits further examination. Critics have suggested that they were brought back to Nigeria by soldiers returning from Southeast Asia after the Second World War, but they don't begin to make an appearance in local literatures until the early 1960s (Obiechina 1973, Dodson 1973, Solanke 2014).

only stuffed with ill-digested matter' (see, for example, Njoku 1964: 37–9, 42).[6] Reflecting this Indian context, one such letter reads:

> Will you kindly accept the small gift for the New Year which accompanies this letter, namely a copy of 'How to Make Love' ... A year is the period during which the earth completes one revolution round the sun; and we of this globe, also perform this journey round the sun-God. On New Year's day, we must imagine ourselves standing before the gate of the temple to congratulate each other. (Njoku 1962b: 11–12)

An accusation of plagiarism involves the accuser in re-tethering quotations to sources, re-establishing intellectual ownership and asserting the authenticity of original texts. Plagiarism produces a territory in which poachers are caught red-handed by gamekeepers. Yet the concept of plagiarism does little to capture or explain local authors' relationships with multiple international sources, the epistolary manual's capacity for localisation – or re-routing – across anglophone (post)colonial times and spaces and the optimistic relationship between the genre and its readers, for whom access to models of English bourgeois discourse contributed to their self-representations and ambitions for self-empowerment as emerging classes in new postcolonial contexts.

While one could continue to try to disentangle 'foreign' from 'local', 'copies' from 'originals', and 'Indian' from 'British' or 'American' sources, or attempt to identify an authentic local corpus of letters in each national context unpublished elsewhere, such an approach would miss the point of the epistolary manual as a transnational genre. From the outset of the genre, model letters were offered for less well-educated readers to duplicate, adjust or adapt 'as copies for inditing letters on the various occurrences in life' (Cooke 1798: t.pag.). As Speedy Eric put it, 'The letters inside this book are designed in such a way that they could serve as ready replies to the letters written to you. You can copy out any one of them that suits your reply' (1964: n.pag.).

The same fountain pen and disembodied male arm feature on the covers of numerous letter-writing guides. The pen-holding hand is a metonym for all the opportunities made possible to Nigerian men by English literacy. With the suggestion of a jacket and shirtsleeve (or a wristwatch), and increasing attention to the detail of pen, the masculine 'modernity' and white-collar status of the hand are increasingly asserted until the fountain pen *is* a man's access to the prestige and power reserved for elites in colonial society (Figs 5.2 to 5.4). Far from referring to the unique signs made by authors as their singular thoughts flow onto paper, the fountain pen marks the potential for readers to successfully copy out the product

---

[6] This appears to be a reference to F. G. Pearce's (1918) pamphlet, *The Indian Boy Scouts, and How They Can Help Motherland and Empire* (Madras: Commonweal Office).

Figure 5.2 Cover of Okenwa Olisah's (1962) *How to Write Good Letters and Applications* (Onitsha: Highbred Maxwell, Students Own Bookshop).

Figure 5.3 Cover of N. O. Njoku's (1962b) *How to Write Better Business Letters, Good English, Applications, Telegrams and Important Invitations* (Onitsha: Njoku and Sons).

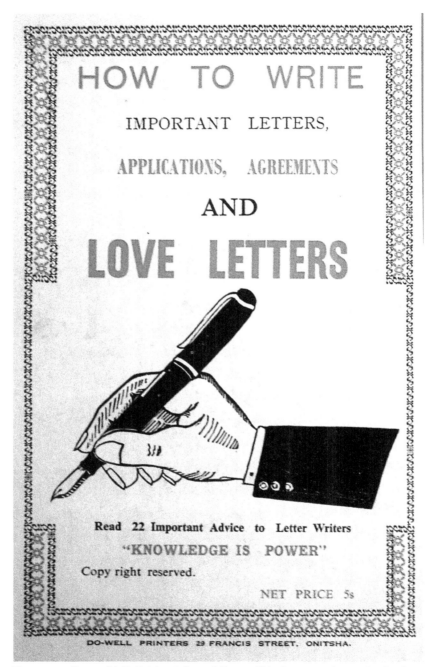

Figure 5.4 Cover of J. C. Abiakam's (c.1972) *How to Write Important Letters, Applications, Agreements and Love Letters* (Onitsha: J. C. Brothers Bookshop).

of this hand, to re-inscribe the printed text with their own pens and progress in the world of white-collar work. Letter-writers are constantly reminded to copy templates neatly and accurately and not to smudge their lines, for employers will judge their literacy from the quality of their hand (see, for example, Njoku 1964 duplicating Brumder 1888: 3–4). In this way, letters are presented as a genre, a discourse and a system of knowledge to be mastered by readers.

Such was the extent of verbatim copying across the century and a half of the English epistolary manual's global circulation that the genre itself – rather than the agents of its (re)production – can be described as inherently plagiaristic. More accurately, this is a genre characterised by generosity rather than theft. Nigerian pamphlets include their own local material, of course, but in general, as a genre, they comprise 'copies of copies' of global English-language publications. Ralph O. Ability and his Nigerian peers participated in a long international tradition of copying as self-help dating back to early nineteenth-century epistolary manuals designed to help people with little experience of letter-writing as they tackled the great variety of English language registers required for different types of correspondence. Rather than jeopardising a country's hard-won freedom from colonial rule, the duplication of English models in America, India and Nigeria was regarded by authors as contributing to national empowerment in each of the newly independent cultures in which the genre was taken up. Hogan's template letters for American readers were, for example, positioned within a national tradition, described as 'carefully adapted to the circumstances of our own country, and a considerable number are taken from approved American writers, and were never before published in any work of this kind' ([1818] 1839: vi). His book, like those before and after it, was a composite text that rejected its own historicity and insisted on its continuous currency in the reader's time and national context. If the British coloniser's culturally superior tone persisted in some of these publications, it was repositioned as a different kind of superiority as newly educated classes asserted their status through epistolary ventriloquism of the English bourgeoisie. For these emergent social groups, English print culture provided a global resource for self-betterment, available to all who could read.

The solution to the paradox of these pamphlets' popularity in decolonising contexts does not lie in macro-level diagnoses of 'mental colonisation' at the national level, or micro-level accusations of 'plagiarism' against individual authors. Whether published in York, Philadelphia, Delhi or Onitsha, epistolary manuals are international halls of mirrors in which the search for originals will yield layers of further epistolary sources and quotations stretching back to the Ancients and forward to the family next door in the reader's home town. Beyond the pursuit of originals and attributions are important questions about form and genre, about the prestige (or otherwise) attaching to citation in different literary traditions, about pan-colonial circuits of textual distribution and consumption and about the literary value of copies and copying in different cultures and historical periods.

The art of copying is a neglected area in contemporary literary studies, even though literary criticism recognises repetition and doubling (in the form of traditions and genres) as necessarily coexisting with and giving rise to the prestige of the 'new'. Numerous influential theories of modernist intertextuality, postmodern pastiche, the 'anxiety of influence' and the subversive potential of (post)colonial mimicry have interrupted simplistic liberal notions of individual creative 'genius' and 'originality' in twentieth-century anglophone literatures. In his influential theory of originality and repetition, *The Anxiety of Influence: A Theory of Poetry*, Harold Bloom (1973) emphasised that the recognition of creative genius in the European literary tradition revolves around an author's difference from – and tense, difficult encounter with – established genres that are historically saturated with the works of other great writers. Even so, the discipline still has a tendency to prioritise originality as the defining value of published writing, whether fictional or non-fictional, creative or scholarly. A dichotomy persists in literary studies insofar as genres of writing that are regarded as formulaic or generic are excluded from, or set against, what is recognised in the discipline as properly 'literary' material worthy of study. If literary copying is not considered by critics to be playfully self-conscious or parodic, it risks being castigated as plagiarism.[7] Authors are caught in the double-bind(ing) of a print tradition in which copying and emulation are recognised as a part of the writer's inheritance, but the repetition of identifiable external templates within a piece of writing will expose them to accusations of fraudulence and theft. By contrast, great works of literature should sparkle with singularity and difference from their predecessors and peers, shaping critical assessments of the success or weakness of national literary traditions (see Gikandi 2001).

Be it published in England, America, India, or Nigeria, the epistolary guidebook could not be further from these ideals of original creativity. Here is a genre with ambiguous, anonymous or composite authors in which the competence of copiers rather than creators is rewarded at every level of production and consumption. If Nigerian letter-writing pamphlets in the 1960s compiled and adapted material from earlier publications, these earlier publications were themselves compilations and adaptations of material from earlier books that were themselves composite assemblages of earlier sources. Even the English 'originals' were printed in multiple undated editions that duplicated earlier materials: the *Classical English Letter-Writer*, for instance, contains a compilation of 'A judicious selection from the letters of eminent writers' and includes references to the letters of Pliny, Cicero, Saint Paul and distinguished commentators on letter-writing such as Locke, Gray, Dr Johnson, Dr Knox and Bishop Atterbury (Frank 1821: iii). American author David Hogan's *The New Universal Letter-Writer; or Complete Art of Polite Correspondence*

---

[7] Amos Tutuola was accused by some scholars of plagiarising Yoruba folktales in his novel of 1952, *The Palm-Wine Drinkard* (see Lindfors 1970).

(first edition 1818) is a reprint of an earlier British publication, Cooke's *The Universal Letter-Writer: or New Art of Polite Correspondence* (1788), which itself drew from earlier models and passed through numerous revised editions, expanding with new material and with reprints of models from other bestselling publications, including Dr Johnson's 'Criticism on Epistolary Writings' (1751) and a popular moral essay, 'A Minister's Advice to a Young Lady' (n.dat.).

As the discussion of Stuart-Young's response to Anyiam's 'theft' of a poem indicated, a preoccupation with originality as the cornerstone of literary value can cause influential genres and aesthetics to be overlooked, leading to the erasure of significant cultural movements in which creative innovation does not depend on singularity and difference, or on principles of unrepeatability. Copying was a prestigious form of cultural production for many centuries in Europe, from medieval manuscripts in which spiritual enlightenment was achieved through the illumination of religious texts to the aesthetic of emulation in European poetry and music and drama in the sixteenth and seventeenth centuries (Herissone 2013: 5, Gazda 2002). In numerous global literary contexts, repetition is regarded as homage, quotation as learning and emulation as a highly rated and respectable artistic endeavour. The rise of the anglophone novel as a genre that followed colonial routes of expansion in the late nineteenth and twentieth centuries occurred alongside, and without displacing, these older, established narrative traditions in local cultures, including oral recitation, storytelling, divination and proverbial quotation (see Orsini 2015, Barber 1999, Barber *forthcoming*).

Anglophone West African print cultures are saturated with citational practices that involved cutting and pasting from English-language publications. From the earliest days of mass-produced independent newspapers in the 1880s until at least the 1930s, editors regularly reprinted articles from regional and international newspapers that they considered would be of interest to readers. This gave the West African press a composite quality that encouraged readers to participate in literary culture by sending in contributions of their own (see Newell 2013). Diverse foreign materials were localised in this way in West African newspapers, duplicated and juxtaposed, assembled into composite, contradictory texts that often lacked the ideological coherence identified by Benedict Anderson (1983) as shaping newspapers' identities. Whether they were transforming an English Romantic poem into politically meaningful prose, critiquing an article in the British press by reprinting it, or cutting and pasting from nineteenth-century epistolary manuals, locally situated 'anglophone' writers often depended on the mobilisation of external printed sources for the presentation of their own ideas and arguments. To see this exclusively as a performance of English competence in order to seek recognition by the authorities in a context of British colonial hegemony would be to miss the local configurations of class, power, culture and prestige signified by West African approaches to English textuality. It would also miss how, within their quotations, writers often made use of local oral traditions of obfuscation and

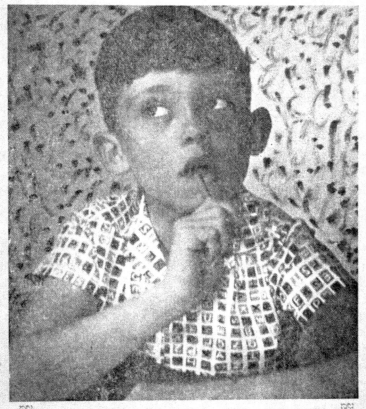

Figure 5.5 Cover of Chidi M. Ohaejesi's (n.dat.) *Quotations for all Occasions: Wise Sayings, Idioms, Proverbs, Good English and Compositions* (Onitsha: Minaco Bookshops).

satire that readers would have recognised and found both incendiary and highly entertaining, especially when quotations or distinctive literary registers were used to convey criticisms of authority figures (see Chapter 1).

The epistolary traffic described in previous chapters suggests a strongly scribal culture surrounding local literary consumption in West Africa, with readers' letters contributing not only to the public sphere of newsprint but also to the emergence, quite literally, of the class of 'men of letters' we encounter in Nigerian market literature, whose status was reinforced by the process of having their correspondence reproduced in print. By the 1950s and 1960s, when popular local pamphleteers emerged en masse in Nigeria, writers for newsprint had developed elevated ideals of the figure of the writer and the status of print. For mid-century pamphleteers, print was superior to oral records: 'illitracy is a disease,' writers declared, and without printed 'history book[s] for the generations yet to come ... a country can never be remembered or recorded in the world history' (Okeke 1964: 25, Olisah 1962: 14, Abiakam c.1973: n.pag.).

Unlike the pamphlet authors of the 1950s and 1960s, early twentieth-century West African newspaper editors always carefully attributed the items they culled, often in order to engage readers in correspondence and debate about controversial or disagreeable items published elsewhere (see Chapter 3). The 'imagined community' of readers was thus formed in the critical distance separating readers from the sources laid out for discussion in the press. Nonetheless, the pamphlets of the 1960s were similar to earlier newspapers in the way their quoted material stood out as extraordinary discourse, drawing attention to itself as uncommon and, in the process, inviting readers to pay critical attention to the text (see Fig. 5.5). In the case of Ralph O. Ability and his peers, the 'extraordinary' material attracted attention to the pamphleteer as a master of discourse, a well-read, wise and experienced 'man of letters', an author(ity) whose pamphlet was worth purchasing and whose texts were worth emulating. While sometimes gently parodic in the manner of 'Mr Ralphsco's' guest appearance, literary satire seems to have been far from epistolary pamphleteers' minds. Rather, through cutting and pasting, they demonstrated their ability to harness foreign genres and discourses and showcased their command of bestselling international forms.

It would be easy to argue that in a literary marketplace competing for readers with promises of newspaper-like currency and local relevance, authors stayed silent about the international sources of their compilations in order to heighten sales. In fact, pamphleteers displayed their 'foreign' discourse in such an overt, relaxed manner that they trumpeted, rather than muted, the transnational flow of imported texts into their reading spaces. In the 1950s and 1960s, whether they were producing epistolary self-help manuals, marriage guidance pamphlets or popular romances, Nigerian pamphleteers across the board cited freely from diverse sources, including Victorian and Edwardian popular novels and contemporary popular magazines such as *African Challenge*, *Psychology* and *Drum*. Foreign clippings were regularly pasted onto pamphlet covers to attract readers' attention and suggest the novelty and contemporaneity of publications: these images were culled from numerous sources including film posters, popular magazines, advertisements, knitting patterns and clothes patterns. From covers to contents, pamphleteers extracted and juxtaposed foreign materials, generating 'new' material while adhering to the rules of bestselling local genres (see Figs 5.6 to 5.8).

In this manner, pamphleteers produced 'original' texts that created impact and interest by their obvious difference from the covers of competing publications. What becomes clear from all of this cutting, pasting, collaging, assembling, quoting and collating is that 'new' indicated 'surprising' and 'fresh to the eyes of readers' rather than conforming to the definitions of 'original' and 'recent' in eurocentric literary value systems.

Pamphleteers' creative originality lay in their ability to identify material that would attract local readers. While some pamphleteers adapted their textual sources in order to expose and critique the ideologies behind popular forms, particularly romance, others projected themselves directly into their rough collages, not only identifying with but claiming foreign discourses as their own by etching slogans into pictures or, in the most engaging examples of this practice, cutting out photographs of themselves for insertion into the borrowed material (Fig. 5.9).

This reconceptualisation of literary originality helps to explain the recurrence of otherwise perplexing warnings against unauthorised reprints of pamphlets containing material lifted verbatim from external sources. 'You are permitted to copy any of my framed letters contained in this book which suits a reply to the letter you may receive', wrote Njoku in the introduction to *How to Write Love Letters and Romance with Your Girl Friends* (1965), but 'note that you are not permitted to reproduce it in any other book without a written permission' (n.pag.). In the same vein, Njoku's co-compiler and collaborator, Olisah, wrote a 'Serious Warning to Copists!' in *Man Has No Rest in His Life* (1965), a pamphlet containing several lengthy unattributed quotations. 'I have investigated and found out that some publishers and self-styled Authors grossly infringed the work of others', Olisah stated angrily: 'I hereby take this opportunity to issue a stern warning to the publishers and self-styled authors to give up such habit or damn the consequences' (1965: 24). Speedy Eric, another prolific borrower, also warned readers that while they may freely copy individual letters, 'don't attempt to compile a book with it' (1964: n.pag.).

Copying and originality were complementary rather than contradictory concepts in this literature, encompassing the generative production of new narratives from old templates. The mark of authorial distinction – or authority – was the pamphleteer's ability to master different literary discourses rather than to invent wholly new content. To see this literature as sometimes blatantly exhibiting its sources and sometimes carefully evading identification is one way of accounting for its creativity, but pamphleteers like Ralph O. Ability,

Figure 5.6   Back cover of Benjamin O. Chiazor's (n.dat.) *Back to Happiness* (Onitsha: Highbred Maxwell).

Figure 5.7 Front cover of Speedy Eric's (1964) *How to Write Successful Letters and Applications* (Onitsha: A. Onwudiwe and Sons).

Figure 5.8 Back cover of Nathan O. Njoku's (n.dat.) *How to Read and Write Correct English, Better Compositions, Sentences, Proverbs, Office Routine, How to Pass Examinations and General Knowledge (For Schools and Colleges)* (Onitsha: Njoku and Sons Bookshop).

Figure 5.9 Back cover of Wilfred Onwuka's (1965) *How to Study,* showing an educated local man pasted into a scene with fashionable East Asian women (Onitsha: Gebo Brothers Bookshop).

Speedy Eric and their peers worked in creative contexts where sources were neither explicitly acknowledged nor intentionally hidden. Epistolary 'how-to' pamphlets may contain considerably more verbatim foreign material than other local printed genres, with less parody and no obvious critique of the models, but they exhibit a similarly pleasurable relationship with their sources to that displayed in other popular local literatures, and need to be situated within the same local print cultures and aesthetic traditions to be understood.

A huge effort in translation was required on the part of Nigerian pamphleteers in order to select and extract material from early nineteenth-century manuals and render it comprehensible for local consumption. Few readers would have wished to copy out 'The lady's prudent answer' to a marriage elopement proposal from 'a young gentleman', with its careful, digressive grammar expressing shocked but polite refusal, shown in Figure 5.10. In re-presenting model letters from century old handbooks such as this, local pamphleteers tried to model how to use these letters by reducing, editing and simplifying the borrowed material. Even so, and importantly, at all times they preserved a formality of tone and, in so-doing, demonstrated their own authority as men of letters who were capable of duplicating epistolary English modes of address.

With multicultural English-language materials circulating around Nigerian markets in the 1950s and 1960s, local authors had every reason to believe their English writings were universal, capable of helping humanity at large and joining the swell of world literatures in English. 'Men are one and the same, all over the world,' wrote Stephen in *Be Careful! Salutation is not Love*: 'Thus, it can be clearly seen, that this book, is not restricted, to a particular race. This booklet, contains some lessons, which are very much indispensable to mankind' (n.dat.[a]: n.pag.). Such an idea of a universal reading public – or at least, the potential of a text to circulate globally – is one of the defining characteristics of the anglophone print cultures studied in this book.

Nigerian pamphlets contain a cornucopia of letters, including love letters, business letters, letters to officials, letters to landlords, letters to tenants, job application letters, letters seeking advice, letters of congratulation, marriage proposal letters and many other types of correspondence, each with its own distinctive language register for the reader to study. In order to appreciate Nigerian pamphleteers' relationship with the time of English letters, it is necessary to step back from plagiarism with its linear temporality and replace it with the 're-' of repetition. The prefix 're-' allows for an appreciation of the transformation of cultural forms through duplication and doubling; it allows for traditions of invention where the old and the new, and the old in the new, circulate in literary contexts where comedy, pleasure, rebellion and dissent, as well as assertions of individual authority, can occur through the words and texts of others.

Figure 5.10 Pages from Rev. Thomas Cooke's (1788) *The Universal Letter-Writer; or New Art of Polite Correspondence* (London: Osborne and Griffin), 58–9.

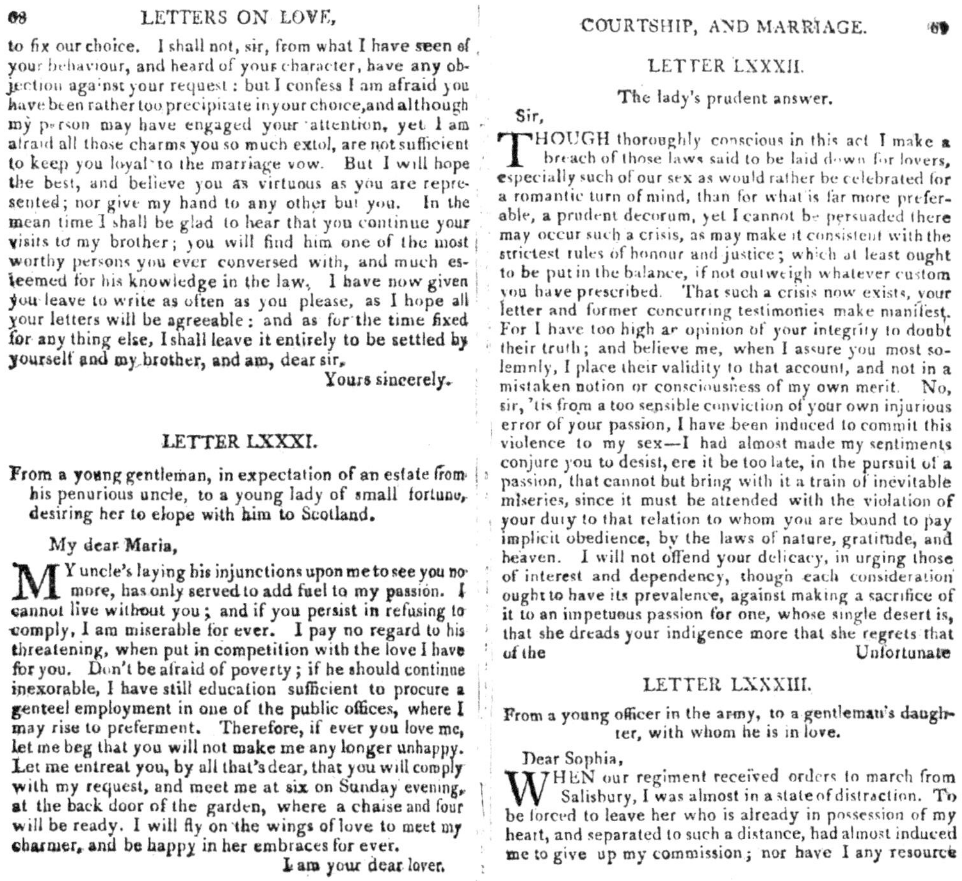

LETTERS ON LOVE.

to fix our choice. I shall not, sir, from what I have seen of your behaviour, and heard of your character, have any objection against your request: but I confess I am afraid you have been rather too precipitate in your choice, and although my person may have engaged your attention, yet I am afraid all those charms you so much extol, are not sufficient to keep you loyal to the marriage vow. But I will hope the best, and believe you as virtuous as you are represented; nor give my hand to any other but you. In the mean time I shall be glad to hear that you continue your visits to my brother; you will find him one of the most worthy persons you ever conversed with, and much esteemed for his knowledge in the law. I have now given you leave to write as often as you please, as I hope all your letters will be agreeable: and as for the time fixed for any thing else, I shall leave it entirely to be settled by yourself and my brother, and am, dear sir,

Yours sincerely.

LETTER LXXXI.

From a young gentleman, in expectation of an estate from his penurious uncle, to a young lady of small fortune, desiring her to elope with him to Scotland.

My dear Maria,

MY uncle's laying his injunctions upon me to see you no more, has only served to add fuel to my passion. I cannot live without you; and if you persist in refusing to comply, I am miserable for ever. I pay no regard to his threatening, when put in competition with the love I have for you. Don't be afraid of poverty; if he should continue inexorable, I have still education sufficient to procure a genteel employment in one of the public offices, where I may rise to preferment. Therefore, if ever you love me, let me beg that you will not make me any longer unhappy. Let me entreat you, by all that's dear, that you will comply with my request, and meet me at six on Sunday evening, at the back door of the garden, where a chaise and four will be ready. I will fly on the wings of love to meet my charmer, and be happy in her embraces for ever.

I am your dear lover.

COURTSHIP, AND MARRIAGE.

LETTER LXXXII.

The lady's prudent answer.

Sir,

THOUGH thoroughly conscious in this act I make a breach of those laws said to be laid down for lovers, especially such of our sex as would rather be celebrated for a romantic turn of mind, than for what is far more preferable, a prudent decorum, yet I cannot be persuaded there may occur such a crisis, as may make it consistent with the strictest rules of honour and justice; which at least ought to be put in the balance, if not outweigh whatever custom you have prescribed. That such a crisis now exists, your letter and former concurring testimonies make manifest. For I have too high an opinion of your integrity to doubt their truth; and believe me, when I assure you most solemnly, I place their validity to that account, and not in a mistaken notion or consciousness of my own merit. No, sir, 'tis from a too sensible conviction of your own injurious error of your passion, I have been induced to commit this violence to my sex—I had almost made my sentiments conjure you to desist, ere it be too late, in the pursuit of a passion, that cannot but bring with it a train of inevitable miseries, since it must be attended with the violation of your duty to that relation to whom you are bound to pay implicit obedience, by the laws of nature, gratitude, and heaven. I will not offend your delicacy, in urging those of interest and dependency, though each consideration ought to have its prevalence, against making a sacrifice of it to an impetuous passion for one, whose single desert is, that she dreads your indigence more than she regrets that of the Unfortunate

LETTER LXXXIII.

From a young officer in the army, to a gentleman's daughter, with whom he is in love.

Dear Sophia,

WHEN our regiment received orders to march from Salisbury, I was almost in a state of distraction. To be forced to leave her for who is already in possession of my heart, and separated to such a distance, had almost induced me to give up my commission; nor have I any resource

'Re' means 'again' (more accurately, 'again and again'), but it also means 'back' or 'backward' in the sense of a return. The pamphlets discussed in this chapter are 'again and again' *and* 'returning' texts from a decolonising country: they retype, retrace, reconstitute, remodel, repeat and, in some instances, revolt. They offer a positive model of repetition by offering empowerment through the mastery of English epistolary discourse. The further one delves into their reinscriptions and reroutings, the more international connections come to the fore, to the extent that, paradoxically, in these most 'English' of Nigerian pamphlets, the Global North is removed as the geographical source of anglophone knowledge-production and contemporary eurocentric ideas about authorship and times of composition are rendered obsolete in favour of different aesthetic criteria.

In Chinua Achebe's *Things Fall Apart,* the servile 'Yes Sah' of the colonised, christianised messenger at the end of the novel – an employee of the colonial regime – contrasts starkly with the eloquence and depth of Igbo understandings of life, which are, by the end of the novel, tragically silenced by empire (Achebe 1958: 147). Members of the newly educated class in Achebe's novel speak broken English, a sign that, no matter how intelligent, members of this class can only fail to achieve success and power in the colonial status quo.[8] Nigerian market literature was being composed at the same time Achebe wrote his tragic fable, but the linguistic markers of disempowerment are reversed. The ignorance of unschooled fathers and chiefs who cling to traditional power structures and oppose the romantic relationships of young, lettered Africans is continuously displayed through their shoddy English. Some chiefs are shown to be so illiterate they cannot even pronounce their own daughters' English names: 'Elibeth! Elibeth! Elibeth-ie!' are Chief Cookey's comic opening words in Olisah's classic, *Elizabeth My Lover* (1961a: 9).

Proud of their secondary school certificates and status as 'men of letters', pamphleteers took the side of Achebe's messengers. They attacked the power base of Africans with what they diagnosed as the 'disease' of illiteracy, further dismantling the authority of the chiefly class shown by Achebe to have been muted by colonialism. Pamphlets are packed with scenes of reading, printing and authorship. In just one novel, Ogali's *Okeke the Magician* ([1958] 1980b), for example, the protagonist visits libraries, consults esoteric books, reads and is written about in newspapers, has posters printed to advertise his shows,

---

[8] In tension with his pessimistic narrative of linguistic impoverishment and cultural disempowerment in the 1890s, however, Achebe's novel is written in English and contains a wealth of English literary references, showing the ingenuity of the author in using the colonial language and English literature to both commemorate and grieve lost Igbo cultures. Achebe describes villagers' songs, ceremonies, proverbs, conversations, desires and interior thought processes in English, offering explanations of some cultural practices while, at other times, leaving portions of untranslated Igbo to highlight the linguistic and cultural differences of his characters from anglophone readers in case the latter should be deceived by the ruse of cultural transparency.

purchases specialist tomes, writes letters and charms for global customers and studies 'various books by world-renowned authors, [which] made him develop very rapidly' (Ogali [1958] 1980b: 54, 68). Reading is the secret key that unlocks his access to power: literacy gives access to esoteric – if not occult – knowledge and enables its possessors to freely roam the world, gaining academic qualifications, fame and recognition.

Achebe's messenger, with his broken English, exemplifies precisely the reader to whom self-help pamphlets in English were directed. As the front cover of Olisah's *The World is Hard* (n.dat.) proclaims, 'Court Messenger lost promotion because of bad English'. Court messengers and their peers can improve their 'bad English', pamphlets promise, and rise up in the world.

Even when local authors copied English sources word for word, they manifested anything but a passive duplication of metropolitan texts. In studying the epistolary manual as a transnational genre with a long history, and in appreciating local authors' layering and juxtaposition of diverse source materials, this chapter has tried to complicate models of colonial mimicry and query the scholarly practice of judging literary quality according to principles of originality. The material under consideration here opens up a neglected strand of world literary history in which the literary merits of copies and copying attract prestige in different cultures and historical periods. As such, authors of Nigerian epistolary manuals can be regarded as contributing to world literature, even as they worked with genres and epistemologies that are not recognisable through contemporary institutional frameworks for literary studies in the Global North.

The 'again and again and returning' quality of the English quotations described in this chapter was not exclusive to letter-writing manuals. The genres discussed in the next chapter show how pamphleteers used English literary models to represent ordinary local men and women in critical situations with money, love, friendship and work. Like the letters in epistolary manuals, those published in local popular romances are highy derivative, showing authors' immersion in – and critical distance from – the works of globally circulating authors. However, as the next chapter also shows, romantic discourse is categorically *not* offered to readers for emulation. Material repeated from decades-old texts finds its way into the mouths of swooning local lovers, but the language of sincere, eternal love takes on the status of a repetition-turned-cliché that disrupts its own promises and serves as a warning rather than offering sentiments that 'spring from the heart' (Frank 1814: xii). Authors explicitly repudiate the emotionally extravagant language of romantic fiction in favour of a pragmatic tone that contrasts starkly with the 'high' language of popular novels. The textual repetitions that feature in the next chapter 'draw the attention of the general public to the every day occurrence in human life' as well as to the dangers of importing English romantic discourse wholesale into local life (Olisah 1960: n.pag.).

English Romantic Discourse: Women vs Men

6

> I regret to inform you that I treated [your letter] like a letter from a Jackass ... If I dear get your letter again, I will drag your name into mud and you will be left in the state of higgledy-piggledy ... So paddle your own canoe.
> (Okeke 1964: 36–7)

Besides letter-writing manuals, many other epistolary genres were produced in Nigeria in the 1950s and 1960s. Pamphleteers attracted their readership by promising to publish letters from members of their own communities, issuing invitations to readers to contribute to the contents of future pamphlets. 'Whenever you have any family problems or any other problem concerning life, write to us for solution', wrote J. O. Nnadozie: 'We shall give you the best advice free of charge. We have been helping so many Readers with advice' (c.1962: 21). Many how-to pamphlets were composed entirely of readers' letters, accompanied by commentaries and advice from authors, realising Stuart-Young's conjecture from the early 1930s that Nigerian newsprint could easily be dominated by epistolary material (*Comet* 30 December 1933: 9). Meanwhile, as the second part of this chapter will discuss, romantic novelists used letters as a plot device to develop love stories – or tales of seduction and betrayal – in fictional time.

Whatever their genre, and in a similar manner to Thomas's letters from Ṣẹgilọla, letters in Onitsha pamphlets were presented both as deeply personal and morally generalisable, as simultaneously real and a part of a fictional world conveying emotional interiority and communicating lessons to readers. Appearing to be from real people living at real addresses, readers' letters poured into the offices of Onitsha publishers from all over Nigeria and beyond, flowing back out into the public sphere in the form of printed texts in which they were repackaged as moral dilemmas or published in letter-writing manuals containing templates to be emulated. Most correspondents have Igbo or eastern Nigerian names. Even if only a fraction of these letters were from real people, they reveal the dispersal of pamphlets – and eastern Nigerians – throughout Nigeria and neighbouring countries.[1]

Unlike Sẹgilọla's correspondence in *Akede Eko*, which Thomas carefully calibrated with the temporality of his newspaper, this chapter will show how, both in self-help pamphlets and fictional romances, letters frequently occupy an impossible time zone. Whether in romantic novels or how-to pamphlets about love and marriage, pamphleteers' efforts to achieve newspaper-like currency through supposedly authentic letters often had the reverse effect, stymying time, inhibiting naturalism, raising questions about when and how these supposedly 'real' letters could have been produced and, in the process, revealing a great deal about the role played by English literacy in local writers' assertions of their status as an educated class.

Again and again in Nigerian pamphlets, letters obstruct rather than facilitate narrative flows. While newspaper correspondence was inextricable from the world it described, contributing to a public sphere where current opinion was shaped and serialised in daily or weekly instalments, the removal of letters into singular, one-off, bound pamphlets entailed a loss of currency. This had repercussions on temporality as well as literary form and meaning. In *I'll Rather Break My Sword and Die*, a racy thriller-cum-romance from 1964 by Alex Obiorah Okeke, a thug named Scorpion writes a warning letter to his love-rival, Jotsman, an equally murderous gangster who, in turn, composes a formal reply threatening 'to reduce you to a complete dependence of a walking stick' (1964: 43). The hoards of bloodthirsty crocodiles and armed robbers poised for attack at the start of this epistolary scene are placed in suspended animation while the two gangsters pen their violent missives to and fro, despatching them through minor thugs and waiting patiently for replies before penning the next batch of exchanges.

Similar scenes of writing a letter, posting a letter, anticipating the arrival of a letter, reading a letter and replying to a letter get in the way of the time-schemes and plots of numerous other local dramas and novels to the extent that letter-writing takes on more agency than narrative action and letter-writers themselves. Letters protrude out of plots, forcing characters apart solely in order for them to engage in epistolary exchanges. The representational relationship between reading and writing is reversed: thus in Onwudiegwu's romantic novel, *The Miracles of Love* (1965b), the first words of the Romeo character, Habero, take the form of an apology for being late to meet his beloved Princess Chandly

---

[1] The regional uptake of pamphlets is revealed in an 'Agents Wanted' notice posted by Port Harcourt publisher Vincent C. Okeanu on the final page of *The Surprise Packet*: 'Novel agents wanted throughout Ghana, Cameroon, Benin, Sapele, Warri, Ibadan, Lagos, Jos, Kano, Zaria, Kaduna, Sokoto. Eastern Region – Enugu, Onitsha, Aba, Owerri, Uyo, Oron, Calabar' (1960: vi).

because, as he explains, 'I was writing something at home' (3). With Chandly in his arms at last, his passion reaches a pitch of such intensity he is compelled to rush away from her again in order to compose another romantic letter. 'His letter reads thus', Onwudiegwu writes: '"My Chanda ... Love is mysterious. Love is wonderful. You are indeed, sweet and fair"' (1965b: 6). On receiving the letter, Chandly writes a reply, which she gives to her maid, who walks to the nearest Post Office to send on its way through the Nigerian postal system, and then patiently awaits her lover's reply (7–8).

Literary scholars influenced by the European realist tradition might regard these epistolary obstructions as signs of the failure of amateur writers to sustain verisimilitude at this particular moment in the evolution of books in Nigeria. Yet the repeated 'failure' of epistolary temporality across different genres of pamphlet literature can be studied through a more productive lens, read for signs of what letters reveal about local print cultures and reading practices as well as authors' searches for ways to represent time in their narratives. The invitation to such a reappraisal comes from the pamphlets themselves, as authors repeatedly halt the narrative clock to showcase letters and offer 'meta-commentaries' on epistolary genres (King 2018). The incompatibility of letters with the tempo of pamphlet production, the presence of these meta-commentaries, and the way English letters tend to inhibit, rather than facilitate, the progression of a story, all point to the presence of local debates about reading, writing, temporality and epistolarity that demand attention for what they reveal about the negotiation and crafting of local literary genres.

Letters published in how-to pamphlets communicate the urgency – and emergency – of a correspondent's predicament: 'I appeal to the son of Madam Nwugo Ekwerekwu to return home immediately', writes Speedy Eric in an 'Author's Note' inserted after a letter that was printed not as an appeal for personal advice but as a model for how to write to a family member in the epistolary guidebook, *How To Write Successful Letters and Applications* (1964: 29). Similarly, in an advice-giving pamphlet, *The Game of Love*, Abiakam publishes a desperate letter from a correspondent named Emmanuel Ucheaghuba begging for advice about his pregnant ex-girlfriend: 'I am quite sure that I am not responsible for her motherly state,' Emmanuel writes, but during the relationship he signed a '"foolish" document ... promising to marry her with £100, if she became pregnant' (1960: 15). Emmanuel requires immediate help from the author in an escalating crisis with a pressing deadline. The relationship has ended, but a summons from the girl's father has arrived ordering him to pay the bride price as promised in the document.

Clearly, the pregnant girlfriend and her litigious father in *The Game of Love* could not be suspended for the duration of the production schedule of Abiakam's pamphlet. Yet Emmanuel's letter is followed by other letters from readers presenting other scenarios requiring authorial assistance. The author's advice to Emmanuel, when it comes, is not at all helpful: 'you realise that you have acted in a foolish way by signing such document for your so called girl friend', Abiakam writes. 'It was a serious mistake for you and I am sure it has become a lesson for you', he continues (1960: 16). In this way, as with Ṣẹgilọla's letters in *Akede Eko*, the individual correspondent is rendered parabolic, as the specificity and urgency of the letter – Emmanuel's personal information, location, dilemma and appeal – are transformed by the author into the transcendent temporality of a general moral lesson to warn readers at large.

British and American letter-writing manuals in the eighteenth and early nineteenth centuries repeatedly warn that a handwritten letter is more binding than speech because of its status as a unique, signed document. It holds the status of a contract, signed by an identifiable person and dated in real time. Likewise, Nigerian readers are continuously warned to 'remember that what is written is written … you covered a full page of a writing-pad sheet … and sent it to your sweet-heart to read' (Obioha c.1962: 18–19). Whether irate or adoring, cowardly or bold, aspiring letter writers are reminded that what is handwritten may be used as evidence against the signatory, whereas verbal promises made without witnesses can always be denied. 'You should know that written words are not like spoken words', Abiakam warns: 'The written words remain indelible in the paper. The person you write the letter to may put you to court if you write bad words against him' (Abiakam n.dat.: 7).

Letter writing has a unique temporal quality, according to these pamphlets: no matter how long ago it was written, a letter leaves a trail of marks in the wake of its author in the form of promises and signatures that track the writer down and call him back into its own present moment. Letters have the potential to be eternal in their hold, to suck time out of letter writers' lives and fix their past in an eternal present. While love letters are the ideal medium to express 'personal feelings', extreme care should be taken not to articulate any visions of the future (Obioha c.1962: 20). Handwritten passion poured out on a page will commit its author to a contract far more permanent than the verbal expression of love: 'Don't make promise in writing', warns Olisah to young lovers in *How to Write Good Letters and Applications* (1962: 8). Lurking behind these male pamphleteers' warnings are visions of queues of pregnant girlfriends, and pregnant girlfriends' family members, waving documentary evidence of literate young men's textual passions.

The status of pamphlets as one-off publications, and their comparatively slow pace of production in relation to newspapers, meant that pamphleteers' efforts – and claims – to capture readers' everyday experiences through the exchange of letters are continuously absorbed into this other timescale in which readers' crises, emergencies and pleas for assistance are removed from clock-time and placed into a universal moral zone. Indeed, on close inspection, even the desperate letter from Emmanuel in Abiakam's pamphlet, if it was ever genuine, appears to have been modified in a similar manner to Ṣẹgilọla's self-conscious displays of herself as a lesson and warning to readers in *Akede Eko*. 'My Readers', Emmanuel writes, adopting the 'dear reader' mode of address, 'my main aim of relating to you this strange incident is to tell my fellow men to be careful for their girl friends, because they are in great majority dangerous' (Abiakam 1962: 16).

Other pamphleteers simply ignored the lack of synchronicity between readers and books. In J. O. Nnadozie's *Beware of Harlots and Many Friends*, 'harlots' are invited to send letters to the author 'to defend themselves in respect of the serious charges made against them' (Nnadozie c.1962: 9). Their letters should be addressed to 'the Critic Writer, J. O. Nnadozie, 30 Okweunu Street, Fegge-Onitsha' (Ibid.). Upon receipt:

> Mr J. O. Nnadozie shall undertake to publish your letter for the public to read. After six months of the publication of your letter, the Critic Writer shall invite some members of the public including five women to a meeting to consider your letter. After the conference of the members of the public, the Critic Writer who chairmans the meeting shall write you a letter. In the letter you shall be informed whether you defeated or knocked out our charges or whether the charges are still warning and holding the harlots tightly. The decision of the meeting is final. (10)

Nnadozie's scene of public justice presupposes that letters will be brought into live local contexts for circulation and discussion. By the time this pamphlet was published in the edition quoted here, however, Nnadozie had ceased trading and sold his copyright to J. C. Anorue, who had 'revised and enlarged' the pamphlet for a post-Civil War readership and inserted a 'public notice' informing readers of the copyright transfer. In printing the postal address of the original author in this call for correspondence, Anorue, like Tutuola in *The Palm-Wine Drinkard*, adopts an impossible temporality for the pamphlet, giving the printed word eternal currency while promoting the illusion that readers are letter-writers whose responses are coterminous with the contents of texts.

As with Ṣẹgilọla, Nigerian pamphleteers promoted the idea that life experience could be gained by proxy through the activity of reading and learning from other people's letters. The timescale of this proxy experience was superior to that of lived experience because the printed text contained the full trajectory of a story, showing the origins and consequences of particular behaviours over and against the slow, extended chronologies of people's lives, which could not be so easily condensed. In short, letters provided a second 'self' to readers. As Stephen wrote, 'life is based on experience. When anything good or bad happens, it serves as an example, worthy of emulation. But at the same time, it tends to give orthers, a warning' (Stephen n.dat.: 3). An experience read was an experience gained, as Stephen emphasised in the preface to another pamphlet, *How to Write Letters about Marriage* (1961): 'This booklet, is compiled for the purposes of amusing the reader and at the same time, letting him have some experiences, that might serve, as guiding factors to him, in love dealings' (n.pag.). Readers, in this model, should not need to undergo the same ordeals as characters in order to learn lessons about life.

The immediacy of personal letters attracted authors of another popular local genre in Onitsha: the romantic novel. British and American popular romances are filled with heroes and heroines who use servants – or pigeons, knotholes, or other means – for the exchange of letters swearing eternal love. The letter is indispensable to British and American romantic novelists as a plot device. Constrained by social conventions, young couples whose love is forbidden are dependent on third parties for the future of their relationships, and third parties are vital to romantic plots as catalysts for romantic elopements or, when the delivery of a missive fails, catastrophes in couples' carefully laid plans. Passionate bourgeois ladies trapped in heavily chaperoned spaces, unable to physically embrace their lovers, pour emotions into letters that depend on the availability of servants and other types of messenger for delivery across time and space to the expectant lover; or, in the anti-romance, they receive 'impertinent' declarations of love from inferior strangers, which etiquette obliges them to treat with 'silent contempt' (Bagot 1905).

Nigerian romances differ in numerous respects from the British and American tradition from which they draw inspiration. Rarely does the crooning, sighing, letter-writing 'I' in Nigerian romantic novels signify a morally exemplary protagonist; nor, authors emphasise, should readers 'lose' themselves in the emotional intensity of the story or empathise with romantic protagonists in the manner described by Janice Radway ([1984] 1991) in her influential study of women romance readers in North America. Packed with apologies, proposals, conflicts, jealousies, and more, these pamphlets open windows onto ordinary people's emotional preoccupations in the 1950s and 1960s and showcase the wisdom and erudition of authors as advice-givers, while insisting that the printed, literary nature of English romantic expression renders it useless, even dangerous, if mimicked in real life.

In Nigerian pamphlets, declarations of romantic love signal the presence of moral hazards. In the opening scene of Stephen's *How to Play Love*, for example, the romantic hero, Uba, writes a letter to a girl he has spotted at school in which he promises timeless love in return for her affection. 'I would dedicate my whole life to you should "Yes" be returned', he writes, 'and I assure you that I shall be yours for ever and ever' (Stephen c.1962b: 5). His sentiments appear to be both eternal and sincere. 'Please, do not address me again either in public or by any other means', Comfort responds sternly: 'You are mistaken if you consider me to tolerate such nonsense' (6). Uba's romantic discourse is regarded as 'nonsense' in the eyes of this anti-romantic local girl.

Rather than pursuing his one love and proving that he merits her affection in the manner of a courtly lover, Uba recovers immediately and 'writes to another girl'. In depicting this rapid recovery, the author overtly undermines both the timelessness and sincerity of the hero's love, and the language in which he expresses it, by rendering it serial and transferrable. 'Dear Pauly', the next letter opens, 'I do not know how to begin this letter as I have only met you last night' (6). Uba quickly gets into his stride, however, declaiming:

> Oh! Pauly! Will you drow me nearer and let me tough your smooth body and glance at your hairy hands? In fact, a look at your brown eyes and your pointed nose will remove all the devils of my foolishness and make me the happiest man ever lived.... Please, what I want from you is your sincere love, kindly love me as I love you. (6–7)

Uba waits for a reply, but his missive is met with silence.

Stephen's pamphlet satirises the English romantic epistolarity it quotes, revealing modern Nigerian women to be wiser and more cynical about men's sincerity than the heroines of popular British and American romances who, from one romantic novel to the next, repeatedly fall for men's seductive letters without learning from other literary heroines' mistakes. In Stephen's pamphlet, Uba mistakenly thinks romantic epistolarity is the problem, deciding that, 'it will be better for me to speak to any girl orally or personally rather than wasting my time in writing' (7). Having switched to oral delivery, he intercepts the first woman he lays eyes on and makes the following speech:

> I must be sincere. Your beauty is one of the charming that I ever came across … Love is something which is inevitable. It is indeed like death. Some people take it as a type of game. But I regard it as something very helpful in the day to day life of minkind … In short, I would like to have your love. (8)

If readers have picked up any clues at all from the previous two encounters, they will recognise that the problem lies with Uba's English romantic discourse rather than his mode of delivery. Indeed, rendering his declaration orally and personally makes his sentiments appear even more outrageous than they were in epistolary form. Like the modern girls before her, this girl answers scornfully, showing that she has learnt lessons from previous models and comically debunking the genre of the popular romance in the process:

> In those [old] days we had not known and so, took men serious in all that they spoke to us. But now, just as the day breaks and an-

other date comes, we are gradually coming to the realisation of the facts and figures. The days of flattery, seem to be going away ... You said that I am beautiful. Naturally, any woman with such make-ups as I have now, will surely look attractive ... It is not an easy thing to secure my love. There are certain terms that I go by. If you are really serious, then, I can tell them to you. (9)

The girl exposes and derides the boy's outdated methods, critiquing and historicising the English popular romance as a literary genre, exemplifying the critical consciousness of readers of popular pamphlets and issuing a warning in the process against the pseudo-sincerity of romantic discourse. Modern Nigerian women have outgrown romantic love, she demonstrates: they are wise to the English romance's potential for distortion and deception.

This is a 'how-not-to' pamphlet that critiques the entire field of English romantic textuality. Driving his message home in the face of Uba's unwillingness to learn his lesson and discontinue his romantic nonsense, Stephen twists the genre in a new direction packed with warnings about the outcome of such foolishness.[2] Uba's attempt to outwit Nigerian women with the false eternals of romantic love opens up the doorway into a punishment far worse than feminine ridicule and rejection. When he persists with the final girl, Helen, she accepts, and lays out her 'terms', including the ritual sacrifice and vampiric consumption of Uba's loved ones in return for wealth.[3] The 'for ever and ever' of Uba's fake sincerity is rewarded with eternal damnation.[4] No more thoroughgoing disavowal of romantic discourse can be found in Nigerian popular literature.

Nigerian pamphlets contain numerous examples in which men's love letters are critiqued by local women in a similar way, suggesting a deliberate and sustained critical intervention by male authors in the popular romances circulating around Nigeria at the time. 'I don't like to read letters full up with immoral words. Don't address me "My dear Sweet Heart." Just write "Dear Beatrice" or "My Dear Beatrice" is okay', the female recipients of love letters tell romantic young men, reminding them of the moral hygiene of letter-writing and critiquing men's overblown sentimentality (Abiakam 1960: 14). If 'letters

---

[2] In a similar reversal of convention, after a romance that nearly ruins him in *Miss Rosy in the Romance of True Love,* the hero, Joseph, 'married an illiterate – a big village illiterate, and he is still moving on financially strong' (Madu n.dat.: 30).

[3] This is a typical satanic wealth narrative in which economic commentary is mapped onto female sexuality (see Meyer 2003).

[4] The second half of this pamphlet departs from the Faustian Christian tradition by showing that the afterlife is run by a committee of War, Peace, Trouble, Hunger, Accident, Birth and Suicide, chaired by Death and administered by a clerk in the manner of a government committee. This part of the pamphlet fragments into a comic drama about a miserly, Scrooge-like millionaire who is visited by death.

play an important part in the game of love', as numerous authors insist, *romantic* letters play no role in building loving local relationships: 'My love solely bases upon the hint that you are a "quiet girl" with manners', one sensible boy tells his prospective wife in a letter modelling how to propose marriage to a girl (Ibid.: 13). The girl's reply is in a similarly 'low' language, using the formal register of a business letter adapted from an epistolary manual: 'I am acknowledging the receipt of your letter dated the 4th April 1959 the contents of which were clearly understood' (14). She goes on to explain her ambivalence about the boy's request: 'I wish to be in possession of a sound educational background after which I shall impart my knowledge to the uneducated elements, thereby contribute my quota to mass education in our independent country' (Ibid.).

In place of purple prose, authors inject young love with pragmatism and patriotic ideals. Even the most romantic-minded authors offer strategies to recover from failed relationships, refusing the eternities promised by globally circulating popular romances in favour of advice to 'forget such charming words like: ever yours darling; with love darling' (Obioha c.1962: 42). Practical advice abounds in reaction to failed romances. When choosing to end a relationship, readers are advised to do it 'in a tender way' without causing heartbreak (43), and on receiving a letter rejecting their romantic advances, they 'should realise that [… they are] not wanted and drop the friendship' (23). At the end of a romance, they should critically analyse what attracted them to a flawed lover, recognise the type, and change orientation: 'you should make up your mind that a boy or a girl should not win your love again with his or her sweet voice, or his or her dazzling smiles' (42).

In all of the examples given above, local young women forcibly collapse romantic discourse into the grounded complexity of everyday relationships. Indeed, the more promiscuous the male pamphlet 'baddie', the more epistolary his life is shown to be and the higher his romantic language register becomes, to the extent that the excessive number of love letters required to maintain Eddy's libertine lifestyle in Ogali's *Eddy the Coal-City Boy* contributes directly to his downfall: 'Because of daily letter-writing and reading in the office during the official hours, I messed up in my job', Eddy admits, as he is fired from the very post office that carries his duplicitious missives to their numerous unsuspecting targets ([1958] 1980c: 94). It is therefore surprising that, for all the dangers attaching to English romantic discourse, especially in contexts where pamphlets frequently provided models for readers to copy, many Nigerian authors use prose borrowed from bestselling English romances. Local male authors seemed to relish the luxurious English prose of the popular romance.

Given all the risks described above, why did Nigerian pamphleteers produce so many novels that duplicated the vocabulary and style of globally circulating romances? A section on the topic of 'Love Letters' in the epistolary guidebook, *English: The Language of the Modern World* begins to answer this question:

> When one writes to one's lover, and says only about 'I love you – you love me – I like you, you are my life. I will die without you. You are beautiful. More beautiful than day. Your kisses are unsurpassable. Oh! darling, I am dreaming of you. I want you. I want your body – I want you kiss…,' then the letter is completely ussless and nonsense. When you want this kind of letter try to buy my first novel, 'THE MIRACLES OF LOVE.' The novel is an interesting one full of fantasies. The outbursts of its contents keeps you gasping. (Onwudiegwu 1965a: 16)

Nigerian authors' relationships with transnational literary genres are illuminated in this moment of aesthetic clarification. As Onwudiegwu makes clear, if impressive displays of literary dexterity are unsuitable for the development of ordinary relationships on the ground, the popular romance retains a position of high literary distinction in authors' eyes. In splicing an advert promoting his own romantic novel into a paragraph dismissing the epistolary romance as 'ussless and nonsense', Onwudiegwu erects distinct generic boundaries between romantic novels and local self-help books about love and relationships. While he derides romantic language, readers are expected to be filled with astonishment and admiration for an author capable of writing the inflated English prose demanded by the genre of the popular romance.[5]

Popular romances provided platforms for local authors to display their virtuosity in English. Seen as literary displays rather than models for emulation, romantic expression is thus a sign of authorial distinction as much as its is a vehicle for descriptions of emotional interiority. Onitsha's romantic novelists quarantine romantic discourse in splendid isolation, from where readers are expected to appreciate their mastery of the English language and admire their abilities as men of letters capable of producing rich fantasies in dense English prose while also, crucially, adopting the critical consciousness nurtured in readers by decades of literary training in West African newspapers.

Locally published romances break away from the newsprint genres described so far in their refusal to offer models for emulation. Readers are firmly positioned on the outside looking in, invited to lionise authors for imaginative outbursts that they, as readers, will never be able to emulate. In composing romantic prose and brandishing their skills with this most complex – and flowery – English, local novelists claim their place in the highest echelons of literary expression,

---

[5] Onwudiegwu continuously advertises his publications in this way. In one romantic tragedy, *The Bitterness of Love*, he interrupts the crucial funeral scene with a parenthetical cross-reference to another of his publications: 'Refer to my interesting novel full of fantacies, "THE MIRACLES OF LOVE." Bridget is buried. May she rest in peace' (Onwudiegwu 1965c: 57).

setting themselves apart from readers and making the same kind of claims to prestige as the newspaper elites of previous decades who warned correspondents to study good literary models before daring to write for publication (Chapter 3).

Authors' mastery of different language registers was showcased through the playful havoc they wreaked with English romantic sources as much as through their reproductions of bestselling English templates. Time and again, creative writers subverted romantic language registers or juxtaposed 'model' printed genres with other models to render one or the other dysfunctional if applied to real life. In *Jonny, The Most Worried Husband* by H. O. Ogu, for example, Jonny's friend Big Tom asks, 'What is it that has reduced you to a size of a skeleton? Are you in love?', to which Jonny replies: 'Yesterday evening, ... I met a lady whose ... every movement was a piece of music. Her hair was an orb of heavenly frame where nature moulds the dew of light. Her paps were everywhere fed, resembling heaven by every wink' (c.1960: 1–2). This verbatim quotation from Thomas Lodge's 1590 poem 'Rosalyndes Description', popularised in the Victorian period in Francis Turner Palgrave's *The Golden Treasury* (1861), facilitates a movement out of everyday discourse, and Ogu's pamphlet dissolves into an action-packed adventure involving a quest to slay a giant and steal a golden spoon, a narrow escape from human sacrifice at the hands of shrine priests and numerous other adventures placing his romantic hero into an eclectic global archive of stories. As with Stephen's Uba, romantic discourse has unleashed forces and powers beyond his control.

The unromantically named Bob, hero of an earlier romance by Ogu, *The Love That Asks No Questions,* is thrust into exactly the same depths of Elizabethan poetic reverie at the sight of Stella's beauty:

> The girl's face was like a blushing cloud, that beautifies angel's face. Her lips which were like two budded roses that are apt to entice a deity. Her neck which looked more or less like a stately tower, where love itself imprisoned lilies. Her paps were centres of delight. The breasts were orbs of heavily frame, where nature moulds the dew of light. A selfsame colour was her hair, where all imperial glory shines, where in twines or be folded. (1958: 8)

The fact that Jonny's beloved and Bob's Stella have stepped straight out of 'Rosalyndes Description' does not change the status of the author's prose as inimitable. On both occasions, Ogu separates romantic discourse from everyday speech as a distinctive *printed* mode of enunciation, displaying his command of literary English through dense, archaic language designed to evoke admiration and pleasure among readers. And crucially, in the case of Ogu's Stella and countless other pamphlet heroines, high romantic language signals women's status as sirens and harlots rather than their moral worthiness – according to the English literary tradition from which they are drawn – as virginal objects of chivalric love.

This type of romantic language was referred to as 'Shakespeare's stylish way of writing' (Aririguzo 1960b: n.pag.). Chief among its admirers was Cyril N. Aririguzo, who repeatedly lifted material from English popular romances and spliced it into quasi-localised settings: 'My pleasure grounds were fringed with fragrant groves of orange and myrtle, where hundreds of full voiced nightingales warbled their love-melodies to the golden moon', gushes the first-person narrator of *Miss Appolo's Pride Leads Her to be Unmarried* (1960a), ventriloquising verbatim and at length from Bertha M. Clay's (pseud. Charlotte Mary Brame) international bestseller, *Love Works Wonders,* which had been published in 1878 (Aririguzo: 10). Marie Corelli's *The Sorrows of Satan* (1895) is cited next, as the narrator laments the circumstances of his father's death: 'every penny of the fortune I imagined he possessed was due to swarming creditors, and … nothing of all our house and estate was left to me except a jewelled miniature of my mother who had lost her own life in giving me birth' (Aririguzo 1960a: 15). These dense, verbatim quotations throughout the pamphlet give the story the status of an assemblage of fragments, each one funnelled more or less successfully towards the moral of the tale, revealed in the title, that Miss Appolo, like Stella and countless other 'romantic' pamphlet beauties, 'refused to marry at the proper time, that caused her failure in life' (Aririguzo 1960a: 10).

In 1960, Port Harcourt pamphleteer Sigis Kamalu used the preface to his novel, *The Surprise Packet*, to criticise his fellow authors for their plagiaristic dependence on works of English literature, castigating them for using material 'stolen from textbooks', offering 'mere imitation or adaptation of old stories and ideas' rather than original local material (1960: n.pag.). The opening page of Kamalu's own novel, however, will be familiar to any reader of Corelli and Clay:

> The late evening sun cast shimmering rays through the western windows into the large sitting rooms. The dancing speeks of light spread manifold hues over the luxurious room as glistering as the colours in a rainbow. Amidst this beauty in a heavy cushioned arm-chair sat the massive figure of a well-groomed middle aged man – the lord of all he surveys. His is the wealthy merchant of the Oil River, Claudius Opuene. (9)

Claudius's first vision of his love-object, Eremgbo, is conveyed through a similar register: 'as fresh as the lilies in a spring side and as beautiful as the flowers in blossom' (11), the young beauty appears at his door and the socially inferior girl, whose language is thoroughly unromantic (as befits morally upright women in pamphlet literature), submissively begs the older man for employment.

Rather than simply repeating its romantic templates, however, this novel comments continuously on the consumption of anglophone world literature in international settings. The wealthy older man possesses a 'rich library' in his mansion, from which he extracts gifts in his attempted seduction of the heroine:

> He led her past rows and rows of books in Politics, Travels, Trade and Commerce, Science, Religion and Literature until they came to the section of novels and story books. There were volumes of [Bertha] M. Clay like 'Married for Her Beauty,' 'A Woman's Temptation,' 'Love Works Wonders,' 'A Good Housewife,' there were the Maria Corneli 'The Sorrows of Satan,' 'Vendetta,' 'Thelma,' 'Romance of Two Worlds,' 'Barrabas' and 'Boy.' And on another shelf were several volumes of the Agatha Christie Series: 'The Big Four,' 'Death in the Air,' 'The Secret Adversary,' 'After the Funeral,' 'Case of the Moving Finger,' 'The Murder is Announced,' 'Holiday for Murder,' 'Man in the Brown Suit,' and other story books like Lamb's 'Tales from Shakespeare' and 'Arabian Nights Tale.' She became fascinated. 'What a precious collection'. (Kamalu 1960: 20–1)

This list reads like a library catalogue of the most popular British novels among Nigerians in the 1960s, suggesting the contents of a school library. In a gesture that speaks volumes about literate Nigerians' eclectic reading preferences and the absence of British gatekeeping over local intellectuals' literary tastes, Claudius gives Eremgbo three novels: Christopher von Schmid's moral tale, *The Basket of Flowers* ([1859] 1870), Clay's popular romance, *Beyond Pardon* (1890) and Jane Austen's classic, *Pride and Prejudice* (1813). All three books are positioned on an equal plane as great works of English literature.

The Surprise Packet is anything but 'mere imitation or adaptation': the giver of the literary gifts is also their target. Any reader familiar with *A Basket of Flowers, Beyond Pardon* and *Pride and Prejudice* will know that the high moral principles of the heroines of all three novels carry them through emotional challenges in patriarchal, bourgeois settings.[6] If Claudius intends these stories to transform his reluctant bride into a contented wife, the texts themselves obstruct her conversion.

---

[6] The ongoing popularity of *Beyond Pardon* with African readers is evidenced by this feedback on Amazon from a reader named Mabel Segeh-Yankuba in 2016: 'The book "Beyond Pardon" is one of the best of the best love stories I have ever read, the expectation, betrayal, disappointment and the full knowledge of what happened is mind blowing. I will recommend it to all love story readers. It can be scripted for movie' (https://www.amazon.co.uk/Beyond-Pardon-novel-Bertha-Clay/dp/B001G091K8, accessed 3 July 2022).

Through its layers of intertextual references, *The Surprise Packet* simultaneously critiques the British popular romance and endorses a pragmatic local narrative about conjugal relationships in which girls must be allowed to marry for love.[7] As in Stephen's story of Uga, Kamalu limits popular romantic discourse to the world-view of the 'baddie' and in so-doing renders the language of romantic love inextricable from a wealthy middle-aged businessman who believes, 'I am the king of money. The master of my own fortune. I can purchase the richest treasure on earth. This girl must be mine' (1960: 12). Kamalu trusts local readers to recognise what happens to romantic intertexts in the hands of the 'wrong' kind of reader. Without needing overt moral commentary, he offers a critical appraisal of the language of love in popular romances and invites readers to be sceptical of imported English reading matter.

The Surprise Packet is composed of numerous local as well as international intertexts. Characters' feelings and motives are established with reference to locally circulating pamphlets. There are no textually unmediated descriptions of characters' inner thoughts. On first meeting the heroine's father, for example, the reader is presented with a scene of reading in which the senior man's financial difficulties are disclosed covertly through his choice of text. Owupene 'is not gifted with reading, but as a sort of relaxation he picked up a pamphlet he had recently bought from a vendor and contemplated the title, "What Money Can Do." He opened a page and began reading aloud' (10). The author's critical commentary on local literary practices becomes active and reflexive at this moment. Any reader attuned to Nigerian how-to pamphlets will find what follows shockingly entertaining. The quotation Owupene reads aloud is a parody of local how-to pamphlets, cynically encouraging the worst kind of 'self-help' – a help-yourself mentality – and diverging from pamphleteers' messages about marriage for love. '"With money both old and young will call you master"', Owupene reads. '"With money irrelevant talk of yours is counted for wisdom … Every woman likes your company. With money parents court your friendship for their daughters to play their caps upon you"' (10–11).[8]

---

[7] Like so many of its peers dating back to *Veronica My Daughter* (Ogali 1956), the novel is underwritten by the storyline of *Romeo and Juliet*, which resonated with Nigerian creative writers because the tragedy is precipitated by Juliet's parents arranging a marriage of convenience to a political ally of her father's, an old man who is the polar opposite of the passionate young man of her choice. The most sustained, creative localisation of *Romeo and Juliet* is Iguh's *Alice in the Romance of Love,* in which the local love story is thickened with direct references to Shakespeare's play. For a discussion of *Hamlet, Julius Caesar* and *Macbeth* in Onitsha pamphlets, see Obiechina (1973).

[8] This quotation is a précis of the work of Olisah, the most cynical of Onitsha pamphleteers, whose misogynistic statements form part of a despairing misanthropy in works ranging in content from domestic to political relationships.

Without any outside interference from an omniscient narrator, this quotation positions Owupene as a duplicate of the stock figure of the obstructionist father who fails to appreciate that love is more important than bride-price in the modern world, asserting the new generation's legal rights under colonial legislation to marry the person of their choice and not to end up with 'the richest man' in the village 'four times [their…] age and an ugly piece of nature's work' (Nwosu 1960: 8). Crucially, however, Kamalu revises the 'illiterate chief' from classic pamphlets like *Veronica My Daughter* and *Miss Cordelia in the Romance of Destiny*, reincarnating him as a literate man reading the same pamphlet literature as readers of this narrative. Owupene's pamphlet repeats almost verbatim the misplaced logic of the protagonist, Claudius, who also believes that money can buy love. Luckily for Eremgbo and her beloved boyfriend Dikigbo, in the action-packed conclusion to *The Surprise Packet* they are saved from the shame of elopement that awaits other lovers in Nigerian pamphlets, and from the tragic fate of Shakespeare's Romeo and Juliet, by the convenient death of Claudius in a car crash while chasing his bride, who has escaped her forced wedding to the wealthy old man. Notably, Dikigbo, the sensible clerk who Eremgbo finally marries, does not produce or consume writing of any type in the pamphlet.

Claudius and Owupene duplicate the illiterate chief and unlettered father of *Veronica My Daughter* and its numerous successors but reverses the Onitsha classics' promotion of English literacy. Whereas educated characters in the bestselling pamphlets explain that the obstructive father's 'worst disease is his illiteracy. Being that he is not educated as to be able to read some novels to know about the work of love [so…] he foolishly opposes our friendship' (Olisah 1961a: 14), Kamalu shows the dangers of the wrong kind of literary consumption. Here is an author whose elitism toward semi-educated readers results in a pamphlet that preaches against an uncritical reading of its contents.

In a similar manner to the anglo-scribes and anglo-literates of the early twentieth century, the romantic novelists described in this chapter display an acute critical engagement with their sources, ventriloquising the style of British romantic fiction only in order to critique it. Over and over, pamphlets juxtapose extreme violence against women with scenes of male romance-reading. In Benjamin O. Chiazor's *Back to Happiness*, for example, the first-person narrator, Agatha, falls in love with a man whose addiction to English popular romances and aspirations to be a popular novelist obstruct, rather than facilitate, their relationship. The romantic hero, Lucky, spends all of his time reclining in the shade of a mango tree reading Clay's novels, oblivious to the goings-on around him and completely passive while Agatha, his beloved, who lives next-door, fetches and carries water from her house and is whipped by her father until she bleeds for putting Lucky above her parents' choice of marriage partner. 'Let's go to the C.M.S. Bookshop', Lucky suggests for the perfect romantic trip in the thick of this violence (Chiazor n.dat.: 24). Similarly, Onwudiegwu's *The Bitterness of Love* (1965c) depicts the hero 'sitting in his room reading a novel, *The Miracles of Love* – an earthly novel which keeps all hearts gasping written by J. Kenddys Onwudiegwu' (35). The romance reader in this embedded advertisement is presented both as eccentrically removed from reality and as a literary gentleman, a novelist and local intellectual for whom the scene of reading suggests social status and refinement, a transcendence of the ordinary rather than an escape from it. Nevertheless, as in Chiazor's romance, the heroine in Onwudiegwu's story breaks into the hero's scene of reading by delivering some alternative reading matter containing a story of violent abuse: the love letter she has written to him uses the highest romantic language to explain that his best friend has raped her.

While not explicitly criticising the storylines of western romantic novels, these pamphlets, often with overtly 'romantic' titles, problematise the lovestory's dreams while revering male literacy and authorship. In the process, the rules for educated couples in Nigerian love stories are shown to be more or less the same as for their unlettered peers. While 'there will be no happy marriage without love', readers are warned not to 'plan elopement and get married with your lover at your own will. What you will do is get the consent of your parents and face the situation squarely' (Obioha c.1962: 5).

In the end, as this chapter has argued, authors' impressive displays of English romantic literary dexterity were shown to be unsuited to the development of ordinary relationships on the ground. 'I must put it to the reader that I am not in the list of people who say that parents have no part to play in in choosing who will marry their daughters', wrote Abiakam in *The Game of Love* (1960), a polygeneric pamphlet containing a plethora of love letters and a dramatised 'secret conversation' between two girls, Agnes and Mary, describing how they exploit the language of true love to get money from their boyfriends. The best kind of love letter was one, in Onwudiegwu's words, where 'it is very hard to judge that [it] is a love-letter' at all (1965a: 17).[9] 'Real love is not like those ones that you see on the screens or those you read from novels,' readers are reminded: rather, 'real love develops slowly with its pangs and pains' (Obioha

---

[9] Only one example could be found of a local how-to pamphlet promoting high romantic expression in readers' communications with one another. In Speedy Eric's *How to Write Love Letters* (1964), a schoolboy's first letter to a girl reads, in homage to *Romeo and Juliet*, 'Oh! Sweet darling you are my queen and my joy … Indeed, Eliza, the Morning Gold, the evening Star, kindly may I have your love' (10). The boy meets his match in Eliza, for she replies in similar vein (11). Even so, Speedy Eric ends his pamphlet with section entitled 'Advice by the Writer to the Gentlemen and Ladies of Nowadays' in which he warns that 'it is very dangerous to trust anyone whether she or he loves you … Love sparkles and intoxicates like wine' and 'there are many people who do not know really what love is' (40–1).

1971: 6). Exciting, entertaining printed literature about romantic love could never double for 'the marriage type of love' (8). However, as this chapter has suggested, male authors wanted to have their (wedding) cake and eat it: high romantic English was simply too attractive as a literary discourse for authors to discard it altogether in favour of the grounded realism represented by 'quiet girl[s] with manners,' with their level-headed rejections of boys' charming words (Abiakam 1960: 13).

Female Critical Communities in Nigerian Pamphlet Literature: 'Beware of Women'

In her study of Black intellectual life in Paris in the 1950s and 1960s, Merve Fejzula (2022) argues that while women often participated on a par with men in the exchange of ideas, their presence is frequently overlooked by scholars for whom supposedly 'menial' forms of intellectual labour – editorial, secretarial and logistical – do not achieve the same recognition as the printed materials produced by men. To restore the visibility of women, Fejzula argues, historians require an expanded conception of the archives to include non-traditional materials and spaces, alongside a broader understanding of what constitutes intellectual labour to include 'chores' like fundraising and cooking, as well as other tasks undertaken by women (424). Using similarly expansive methods, feminist historians of Nigeria and West Africa have produced maps of women's intellectual labour and political power dating back to precolonial times, re-inserting women into traditional structures of political authority, and using the written archives of the mid- to late-colonial period to highlight women's robust presence in newsprint cultures as printers, editors, journalists and writers (Achebe 2011, Denzer 1994, Mba 1982, Gadzekpo 2001).

Given that only one Onitsha pamphlet, sadly no longer extant, was found under the name of a woman, Fejzula's injunction to expand our archives and methods to include the full infrastructure of intellectual production is all the more necessary if we wish to find signs of women's intellectual presence in Nigerian newsprint cultures of the 1950s and 1960s. The pamphlet – Cecilia D. Akosa's *Stirring of a Heart* – was purchased for £12 by the publisher George O. G. Ume-Ezeoke (aka 'Gogue') in 1950, making it one of the earliest Onitsha romances, predating Ogali's *Veronica My Daughter* by six years (Dodson 1974: 118). The existence of *Stirring of a Heart* implies the presence of an irrecoverable archive of locally published women's writing in a period when increasing numbers of Nigerian women occupied public positions as journalists and political activists, and when authors such as Flora Nwapa started to achieve international recognition, transforming African literature published in the Global North by giving sustained attention to female interiority.[1]

Women are occasionally named in the prefaces and introductions in Onitsha pamphlets, where they are thanked by male authors for their input as typists, proof-readers, storytellers and informants. In the preface to *Long Long Ago: A Novel* ([1957] 1980a), Ogali gratefully acknowledges the advice of 'Miss M. O. Emerih of Port Harcourt', who contributed to the shape of *Veronica My Daughter,* his runaway bestseller from the previous year (14). While the nature of her interventions is not described, Miss Emerih clearly assisted in both the improvement and the public circulation of the manuscript, for according to Ogali she 'not only made it possible for others to see the drama, but also made some fair and constructive criticisms on the characters' (14). Other pamphlets originated in women's oral tales: in *Adventures of Wonderful Buja,* the young author, Tesilimy Adekunle Senusi, acknowledges 'Mrs Fatumotu Sanusi and Mrs Titilayo Sanusi (both wives of Chief D. Sanusi) who submitted the original narration of this heart-suspending, enticing and original story' (Sanusi c.1962: n.pag.). Women were also employed at local printing presses: Don Dodson mentions 'three girls who set type and folded paper' in the early 1970s at the Trinity Printing Press in Aba, owned by Onwudiwe (1974: 154). Other pamphleteers credit women as teachers or typists who edited their manuscripts before publication, continuing the tradition of collective authorship discussed in Chapter 3.

Nigerian pamphlet literature at this time of national liberation is, however, loaded with young male authors' desires. In this space, a class of men identifying as intellectuals attempted to insert themselves into history, often against women and other residual authority figures, by producing their own versions of public opinion for posterity. As this chapter will suggest, in representing women's vibrant, submissive, subversive, repentant, bold, desiring, meek, or abusive presences on the printed page, male authors sought to consolidate their positions as English-speaking intellectuals producing moral discourses in print cultures that had, from the outset, been controlled by men.

As is evident in previous chapters, women are heavily mediated figures in newsprint literatures, determined by plot lines that favour authors' gender ideologies even as writers claim to present 'the photograph of what was actually happening' (Emedolu 1971, interviewed by Dodson 1974: 162). In male authors'

---

[1] Given that the details of Akosa's pamphlet were obtained directly from her publisher, it is unlikely that the pamphlet was written by a male author under a female pseudonym, as was common practice in newsprint cultures when male authors wished to represent feminine interiority (see Newell 2013). Flora Nwapa's *Efuru* was published in the African Writers Series in 1966, and she was one of the first women to establish her own publishing house, Tana Press, in the early 1970s.

representations, women's rebellions against patriarchal values take the form of 'harlots' who choose promiscuity and financial independence over marriage, or, on the opposite side of the moral spectrum, educated heroines who insist on marrying their boyfriends. Both kinds of independent woman serve authors' heteronormative conjugal goals: carried over from Ṣẹgilọla's infamous 'life-story' and the many Victorian moral tales that preceded and inspired it, the 'harlot's' life ends in misery and death (or, more rarely, repentance and marriage), while the 'Veronica' plot line cunningly inscribes the interests of male authors into stories promoting the girl's choice of a literate and poor young man above uneducated but wealthy middle-aged suitors.

A methodological problem arises for feminist scholars of Nigerian pamphlet literature who wish to attempt a project of retrieval similar to Fejzula's reclamations of a woman-centred negritude. In the absence of publishers' records from the period, it is tempting – especially for literary scholars trained in close reading – to turn to the pamphlets themselves as an archive and read for women's subjectivities, supplemented of course by oral history work and secondary materials.[2] However, given the plot lines described above, one cannot simply 'retrieve' and render visible females from the margins of archives that exclude them. As this chapter will argue, male pamphleteers recognised how female oral critical genres could undermine their status as literate young intellectuals and, in reaction, appropriated women's genres into their own written texts. Such a strategy was a great deal more deliberate and aggressive than allowed for by conventional understandings of printed texts as emerging organically from oral sources and developing out of oral traditions.

Fejzula emphasises the importance of the marginalised group's 'ambiguous relationships to the category of the intellectual' (2022: 425). Constituencies that are excluded from the knowledge-production of intellectual movements may be all too aware that public materials produced by the dominant group are embedded in ideologies that perpetuate processes of exclusion. If some of the men who dominated West African literary production in the first half of the twentieth century used their privileged access to print to endorse gendered hierarchies of power and knowledge, the educated, independent-minded women in their orbit would have been all too aware of how print contributed in public ways to women's exclusion from printed discourse, or

---

[2] A unique resource for historians of Nigerian pamphlet literature is Don Dodson's unpublished PhD dissertation, which contains an abundance of interviews with Onitsha printers, booksellers, authors and readers – all collected in the immediate aftermath of the Nigerian Civil War – and exemplifies the type of research that should be undertaken for literature regarded as ephemeral.

at least confined their public writings to 'feminine' genres such as cookery, fashion and other domestic topics.[3]

Additionally, and less subtly, male writers used print to publicly harass and humiliate women. In an interview with Dod Dodson in the early 1970s, Marius U. E. Nkwoh, the author of a pamphlet called *Cocktail Ladies* (1961) for the 'Facing the Facts Around Us' series, said the heroine was a real person, 'a telephone operator' at the Eastern Nigerian Broadcasting Service, whose boyfriend arrived unexpectedly one day when she was with another man: the boyfriend beat her up and 'dragged her out to disgrace her before the public … This is the beginning of the pamphleteering of my life' (Interviewed by Dodson 1974: 266–7). 'Miss Cocktail's' public disgrace in real life is doubled by Nkwoh's publication of her story as a pamphlet that condemns female promiscuity and endorses violence against women. Using print in a similarly punitive manner, Thomas Iguh, another prolific Onitsha author, became an active member of a University of Lagos club as an undergraduate in the early 1970s: the Nemesis Club, as it was called, 'published broadsides or cartoons every week "to fight moral laxity in the university" such as "girls who go off with the boys and then come back late at night". Although the targets were real, their names were disguised' (Interviewed by Dodson 1974: 248). This correctional campus tradition continues well into the present in popular blogs, newspapers, novels and Nollywood movies condemning female students' sexuality, especially at the University of Lagos.

Any reinsertion of women into histories of publishing dominated by men must therefore include not only the retrieval, wherever possible, of hitherto neglected female intellectual labourers, but also a consideration of how printed archives contain and structure women's ambiguous relationship with power, as identified by Fejzula. This is especially relevant in contexts with robust oral cultures in which women could take advantage of expressive modes outside the print genres and technologies controlled by male intellectuals. With these complexities in view, this chapter asks to what extent male-authored pamphlets can be used to gauge women's participation in Nigerian intellectual culture beyond the parameters of the repetitious plot lines and stereotypes about independent women to be found in local bestsellers. Can women's spaces of articulation be traced in the pamphlet literature of the 1950s and 1960s, and how does newsprint circumscribe their retrieval?

In societies where literate members of a household or community read printed matter aloud to unschooled members, where scribes read and write

---

[3] The 'Marjorie Mensah' column in colonial Ghana in the early 1930s combined recipes, fashion and domestic advice with brilliant feminist satires that mocked women's domestic positionality in local print cultures with fiction featuring assertive, intellectual, adventuresome girls (see Gadzekpo 2001).

letters on behalf of unlettered clients, and where non-readers are counted in the circulation figures of newspapers – constituting the majority of a newspaper's readership in some cases, as in the *Comet* (Chapter 3) – the concept of 'literacy' must be expanded to include more than a person's ability to read and write. As Isabel Hofmeyr (2004) shows in her study of the uptake of John Bunyan's *Pilgrim's Progress* in Africa, in the era of missionary expansion in Africa the contents of texts continuously moved off printed pages, or travelled ahead of the text into local communities to be reshaped into local genres and discussed and interpreted as part of the daily exchange of knowledge and opinion. In this way, texts were removed from the hands of the educated elites who controlled printing presses. Publications were absorbed into popular discourse, where literary characters and plot lines took on their own life as moral commentaries and maxims. Stories circulated through lettered and unlettered spaces alike with no respect for the supposed superiority of lettered men.

These circuits of transmission also allowed oral aesthetic values, genres and interpretive practices to travel onto the pages of printed literatures. Behind the slabs of high romantic discourse discussed in the previous chapter, the residual authority of the 'unlettered' masses persists in pamphlets, often in tension with writers' emphasis on young men's masterful penmanship. Nigerian pamphlet literature is packed with senior authority figures: parents, landlords, uncles, neighbours and community mediators continuously appear on the scene of conflicts, offering advice and collective understandings of morality and behaviour. Over and against the promotion of educated young people's freedom of choice, especially in selecting a marriage partner, neighbours and family members are called on repeatedly within texts to mediate in fights between fathers and daughters, or to intervene in romances that have turned into venomous marriages (see, for example, Olisah 1963a, Highbred Maxwell 1960, Abiakam 1960). The rejected father figures who star as disempowered, blustering 'illiterate old chiefs' in bestselling romantic dramas like *Veronica My Daughter* are recuperated in numerous pamphlets with a role in hearing both sides of a story and resolving disputes. Even in *Veronica My Daughter,* the consent of the obstructionist father, Chief Jombo, must be obtained before the young couple can proceed toward marriage. Romantic heroines are punished with misery, heartbreak, ill-health and death if they run away to get married or if, once married, they run away from their husbands in the manner of Segilola. In one or two cases, the 'illiterate' father is shown to be the only character to see through a duplicitous hero's fake romantic discourse and English literary wiles (see Iguh, n.dat.).

Non-scribal networks surround pamphlet protagonists on all sides, infusing stories, holding characters to account and, on occasion, challenging the promises and proposals contained in protagonists' letters and literary discourses. Over and against the model of self-empowerment through literacy offered by Nigeria's young male pamphleteers in the 1950s and 1960s, these artful non-literate characters are omnipresent in texts, often in the form of authority figures who have lost none of their cultural power. This is where women and girls come to the fore in Nigerian pamphlet literatures, for the patriarchal ideology of some of the most overtly misogynistic pamphlets is undermined by the presence of one particular constituency of female authority figures: oral performers who function within texts as moral choruses, noisily commenting on and critiquing characters from the margins of the plot. In a challenge to male authors' assertion of educated youths' superiority over 'illiterate' people, these oral commentators obstruct the operation of literacy itself, heckling letter-writers, preventing acts of reading and writing, inhibiting the exchange of missives and, crucially, producing competing, parallel accounts of the printed story for posterity. The presence and authority of these fictional women and girls within pamphlets helps to contextualise printed materials that stand out as starkly misogynistic in newsprint cultures produced by educated male elites. At other times, as in the example of *Mabel the Sweet Honey that Poured Away*, discussed in the second half of this chapter, female characters' erotic desires subvert authors' enforcement of heteronormative rules for female sexuality.

Many of the oral sources in Nigerian pamphlet literature take the form of quotations from British and American popular songs and Ghanaian and Igbo highlife music: these are sung and danced to by protagonists, transcribed and quoted to illustrate the vibrant modernity of the urban youths who feature in texts. On a single page of Okeke's fast-paced adventure-cum-romance, *I'll Rather Break my Sword and Die* (1964), for example, 'Aunty Christy' ('Auntie Christie' by The Ramblers, Ghana) is quoted beside 'Ben Beller' (Ichie Benbella Azuka and his Concert Band, aka 'Chief Benbella'), 'Bachelor Boy' (Cliff Richard), 'Iworiwo' (Cardinal Rex Jim Lawson), 'Worried Over You' (Keith Steward and Enid Comberland) and other hits as the ultra-cool gang members move between bars in Onitsha (Okeke 1964: 18).[4] Writing under a different name, the same author's *Adventures of the Four Stars* (Anyiche c.1962), a rollicking cowboy story set in Lagos, includes a 'signature tune' sung by the gang that readers would have recognised as a rendition of the last verse of Hoagy Carmichael's catchy hit, 'Somebody Stole My Horse and Wagon':

> Oh! somebody stole my horse and gone away.
> Oh! somebody stole my horse and wagon.
> Left my heart in an empty cabin,
> now I'm going to the trial I used to ride. (Anyiche: 23)

---

[4] Nate Plageman (2013: 132–3) includes a translation of the lyrics of 'Auntie Christie.'

Other pamphlets contain musical interludes in the style of popular American movies. Within four pages of the opening of Onwudiegwu's *The Miracles of Love* (1965b: 4–5), Chandly sings a long love-song to her beloved Habero:

> Love is a strange thing…
> Oh! love is a strong thing
> My heart throabs with excitement.
> My love for him, expands exceedingly.
> Love is throne to the rose of youth.

He replies in a Scottish register, crooning his own song with lines hand-picked and reworked from Robert Burns's song, 'I Love My Jean' (1788):

> Ah! the troubles and anxieties are bidden bye
> Yea! amidst all bias and odds, plenty …
> Oh, my Chanda I behold in the dewy flowers
> I see her sweet pleasant and fair.
> There's not a bonny flower that springs
> There's not a bonny birds that springs
> But reminds me of Chanda.[5]

Alongside these well-known popular songs and poems, pamphlet fiction is packed with local oral commentators who use songs according to Igbo oral genre conventions, especially to mock and memorialise the foolish life-choices of characters in the books (see Igwebuike 2020). In some pamphlets, writers use songs to change people's erroneous behaviour through lyrics that publically shame the errant individual; others include scenes of public singing designed to escort foolish protagonists into posterity, condemning their actions and fixing their reputations in time. 'If you doubt yourself that love can be bitter, well you have got to ask your way to the pleasant land of Awka and see for yourself', opens Nwosu's *Miss Cordelia in the Romance of Destiny: The Most Sensational Love Intricacy that has Ever Happened in West Africa* (1960), introducing a heroine whose first-person voice and direct mode of address echo Ṣẹgilọla's so closely as to suggest the influential presence of Thomas's heroine at the heart of this pamphlet, flushed out of her epistolary hiding place: 'it is as easy as anything to find me out for even the beggars know me and the dumbs have heard my story. Old women going to the market talk about nothing but Cordelia and her love intricacy. Market girls in their red cloaks sing nothing but my name' (Nwosu 1960: 8). Highbred Maxwell's self-help pamphlet, *Guides for Engagement,* also

---

[5] In addition to Burns as the obvious source for Onwudiegwu, his sentimental, Scottified lyrical style can be traced to the influence of Stuart-Young, discussed in chapter 3, whose mock-Scottish ballads and sentimental pastoral lyrics were widely published in the Nigerian press and influenced a generation of local poets.

describes how, after an expensive divorce case, the wife, who loses in court, wanders the roads singing 'a pitious song' to anybody who enquires about her circumstances (c.1962: n.pag.).

In a scene in Penn C. I. Oti's *£75,000 and 7 Years Imprisonment* (n.dat.) the husband's pilfering of his wife's immense trading wealth in order to fund his gambling addiction, and his subsequent destitution and imprisonment, are met with 'a popular song' composed and performed by local 'hotel ladies':

> Mr Poolsman is down, down, down
> Never to rise again,
> The boastful man is down and out,
> To rise no more,
> No more bread, no more butter
> No more fine dresses and no more laughter …
> No more money, no more ladies, but shame,
> Every hope is gone, gone never to rise again. (Oti n.dat.: 12)

Aririguzo's *Miss Appolo's Pride Leads Her to be Unmarried* (1960a) also includes a song of abuse performed by local girls who 'sing with Appolo's name'. Their song describes the downfall of the once-beautiful heroine who, like Ṣẹgilọla, chooses the 'foul game' of prostitution:

> What a shame! Appolo yea! Appolo yea! …
> An aged lady with the help of pan cake powder.
> Appolo runs from the window at any time,
> and all types of dance she has tasted them, what a shame!' (20–1).

Literacy might signify men's competence in copying registers and innovating with literary discourses, but even inside the papery world of male-authored pamphlets, posterity is produced through women's song: 'From my lonely sick bed', sighs Cordelia, who has been reduced to a skeleton by the dreadful disclosure that her beloved fiancé is her first cousin, 'I heard the pagan girls singing: Oh! what a shame/ She would die because she would not marry her cousin./ Oh! what a shame and how abominable./ May the gods help you to bear your shame' (Nwosu 1960: 40).

In a scene in Shakespeare C. N. Nwachukwu's Nigerian Civil War novel, *The Tragedy of Civilian Major* (1972), the promiscuity of the powerful soldier and the shame of his pregnant schoolgirl lover are memorialised as 'young girls sang with their names' while sitting around the Iroko tree. 'One of the songs ran thus', readers are informed. The young girls' lyrics are given in Igbo, summarised in English, and followed by a description of their emasculating effect on Civilian Major: 'this sort of song removed hairs from Major's body' (Nwachukwu 1972: 34). Major's response is to threaten the singers with his gun, but 'the girls refused to listen to him. The music became louder … the song went on' (34). Even after Major has fired into the group of girls to disperse them, 'the songs about Major and Caro continued in secret gatherings. New ones were formed' (Ibid.). Meanwhile, in the background, 'Major's mother sang in sorrowful sentimental tunes whenever Major returned home', using the traditionally sanctioned performance genre of women's song to present criticisms and historical reminders that could not be made to a powerful man such as this using common speech: 'Her enemies, she claimed in her songs were laughing at her. She called her son heroic names reminding Major that was her dead father come back-to-life' (Nwachukwu 1972: 33; see Vail and White 1991, Apter 1998).

Nearly all of the examples of oral creativity to be found in Nigerian pamphlets are similarly performed by women, as male-authored pamphlets expand to include low-ranking individuals like 'pagan girls' (Nwosu 1960: 40) and village girls (Nwachukwu 1972), socially castigated individuals such as 'hotel ladies' (Oti n.dat.: 12), 'beggars,' 'dumbs' and independent market traders who do not represent the Christian conjugal ideology that underpins pamphlet literature (Nwosu 1960: 8). The bustling social and cultural worlds surrounding and permeating pamphlets are reflected in the presence of these independent women and girls exercising their collective power to interpret stories and generate public opinion. Through these genres, women's knowledge-production emerges in numerous male-authored pamphlets, wrapped up within the printed text, asserting women's entitlement to critique men through song (see Matera, Bastian and Kent 2013). Women produce public memory with their critical interventions and interpretations of stories, simultaneously entertaining readers and imposing oral history onto the printed page.

Clearly, the different types of local song contained in these male-authored pamphlets illustrate the importance of women's oral performances as genres of censorious entertainment, producing people's reputations through cultural forms that audiences will recognise and remember. The fact that young male authors include so many scenes of memorialisation through female song demonstrates the undeniable cultural power of these performance genres. Women's choric function in pamphlets illustrates the way in which considerable control over public opinion resided with people positioned on the outskirts of literacy and pamphlet morality, outside writers' immediate realm of control. If writing for print was one of the few ways for young male authors to assert authority, their representations of the superiority of literacy seem to be undercut, even in their own pamphlets, by the presence of these representatives of other residual and more ubiquitous modes of cultural production.

While pamphleteers recognise women's central role in producing the historical record, however, the appearance of these scenes also indicates an appropriation of women's oral genres by male authors. Through the songs, pamphleteers claim status for their own printed narratives that was previously conferred on oral performance genres. Notably, the contents of fictional women's songs reinforce the gender ideology of pamphlets. Like the pamphlets in which they appear, songs carry warnings to audiences not to repeat the actions of their targets, nor run the risk of public ridicule for immoral behaviour. In Oti's £75,000 and 7 Years Imprisonment, for example, the 'popular song' circulated by the 'hotel ladies' reiterates sentiments expressed by the narrator in the preceding paragraph, where he chants a vindictive ditty at his fallen protagonist:

> No more cake and no more break,
> no more butter and no more milk.
> No more ladies and no more dance.
> No more fine dresses and no more laughter.
> No more money and no more pools. (Oti n.dat.: 12)

The very women whose lifestyles most threaten the conjugal morality of popular pamphlets are thus recruited as composers of popular songs that endorse – and in this case directly reiterate – the moral lessons of pamphlets against philandering and female promiscuity.

One of the moral lessons of pamphlets, in short, is that pamphlet morality should be preserved for posterity. The pamphlets display the work of young male pamphleteers as an emerging class of local intellectuals who simultaneously recognise and attempt to surpass women's cultural production. Male authors' versions of stories, as confirmed by their fictional female oral historians, should be absorbed into public opinion as authoritative accounts. The printed archive, in the end, circumscribes and inscribes women's performance genres while acknowledging their independence from the newsprint world.

Lesbian but not Queer? A Singular Romance in a Repetitive Genre

Only one pamphlet includes material that deviates from the heteronormative, conjugal morality of pamphlet literature as a whole. Featuring a young girl whose beauty fires the lust of everybody around her and who, in league with a close female friend, conspires to extract cash and gifts from men, *Mabel the Sweet Honey that Poured Away* (Speedy Eric, c.1964) adopts a storyline used by Thomas in the late 1920s and by numerous Onitsha authors in the 1950s and 1960s (see Fig. 7.1). Unlike these precursors, however, Speedy Eric makes the friendship explosively subversive in the form of a sustained lesbian romance. His pamphlet merits discussion in this chapter because, as with the female performance genres described above, the author attempts to harness an exclusively female space of expression to a heteronormative plot line but, in the process, produces anomalies that cannot be resolved by the logic he promotes.

The heroine has her first erotic encounter in the opening pages of this 'thrilling' story. Mabel works in a restaurant owned by her widowed mother:

Figure 7.1 Cover of Speedy Eric's (c.1964) *Mabel The Sweet Honey That Poured Away* (Onitsha: Onwudiwe).

there is no father to assert authority in the all-female household. In a similar manner to Thomas's depiction of Ṣẹgilọla and countless Victorian fictional prostitutes before her, Mabel's sexuality is presented both as cultural, being the product of her freedom to roam around the city, and as natural, being innate and excessive from birth. By the age of eleven she has 'the terrible desire to taste a young man', and by twelve she is 'plumpy and round. Her breasts were conical and had needle points' (Speedy Eric c.1964: 4). Whereas she might have been portrayed as a vulnerable girl exposed to abuse from adults, the continuous sexual assaults Mabel is subjected to from male customers in the restaurant are represented by the author as a form of self-empowerment and female agency brought on by the girl's excessive libido. Realising that 'she had something the men could like' (20), Mabel's moral compass is set away from marriage and towards damnation.

The heroine's encounter with her mother's employee, Margie, with whom she shares a bedroom, is unexpected. It is also unprecedented in Nigerian literature. 'Do you know what followed?' the reader is asked after Mabel has experienced arousal at the sight of Margie and a man having sex (10). 'Margie caught the virgin-girl by her waist and lay her on the bed and jumped on top of poor Mabel' (Ibid.). Mabel's request, 'I beg, Margie, no go do me like this again' is ignored (Ibid.). Designed to excite and scandalise readers, the lesbian scenes that follow oscillate between consent and assault, demanding a reaction. In the second encounter, when Mabel is asleep and dreaming of sex with a man, Margie mimics a male voice as she mounts her in the dark, and Mabel violently pushes her off. In the third encounter, 'Mabel stirred uneasily but responded to romantic touch' (34). By the fourth encounter she consents entirely (Ibid.). And by the fifth, it is she who initiates intimacy (65).

In each of these scenes, readers are addressed in the second-person, drawn as closely as possible through the narrative peephole by an omniscient narrator who relishes and exploits the 'dear reader' convention. From the outset of the pamphlet, the reader is positioned as a voyeur, implicitly male and heterosexual: 'Have you ever looked at a girl's skin and felt that if you pinched her she would shed blood?' readers are asked in the opening paragraph (3). Mabel's ravishing beauty is described in this section from the perspective of a lusty man gazing at a sexy girl: 'Can your imagination travel and gather all these qualities and then combine them at one place? Then you have a picture of Mabel' (Ibid.). 'WE SHALL SEE WHAT MABEL DID IN HER OWN CASE, READ ON, DEAR', the narrator interjects loudly, interrupting sexually explicit scenes (20; emphasis retained); 'You know what Margie did? Cool down and hear', he jokes confidently (24). Once the Pandora's Box of her voracious sexuality has been opened by Margie, Mabel is launched on her inevitable – according to pamphlet conventions – journey toward promiscuity and death: 'Dear reader you watch for yourself how the only daughter of Mrs Helen … is drifting slowly to her ruin', the narrator comments (23). Through these devices, Speedy Eric continuously subsumes the queer narrative into a heterosexual storyline that positions the heroine as the object of men's sexual consumption and the reader as the narrator's moral accomplice.

Allowing for the possibility that the second-person addressee might be a female reader, however, and bearing in mind the gendered division of interpretation that frequently occurs among readers of local literatures in West Africa, where there is a long tradition of audience interjection and debate, this pamphlet leaves scope for women readers to read against its heterosexual ideology.[6] Indeed, given the behind-the-scenes role of women in the production of pamphlets, described above, women may have been among its first readers.[7] The opening lines have a different inflection if imagined through a female gaze (Primorac 2021). This potential for revision from a queer reader's perspective becomes especially relevant when Mabel's first heterosexual encounter is described, for it is wholly non-consensual and occurs mid-way through the pamphlet, long after her transformation into a lesbian.

The 'corrective rape' of Mabel by the man who goes on to marry her is portrayed by the narrator as a necessary punishment and recuperation of the heroine's sexuality into the heterosexual economy (48). Mabel's subsequent abandonment of her marriage and entry into prostitution – commodified heterosexuality – enables a realignment of the story to the narrative template, prevalent in popular literature, where female sexual independence is punished by death. In the fast-paced final section of the story, Mabel becomes bored with her marriage and runs away to live a free life as a prostitute in Port Harcourt, where she dies alone and in agony, aged only seventeen, from a botched abortion in the lavatory of a brothel.

This narrative contains so many instances of male sexual violence against women that the relationship between Mabel and Margie – as young lovers and colleagues who protect one another from clients in the restaurant – becomes tender in comparison to the predatory behaviour of the men. Mabel's formative heterosexual encounter is a rape, which curtails her erotic relationship with Margie; her marriage is shown to be tedious and stultifying; and heterosexual intercourse, which leaves her pregnant, leads directly to her death. Framed by a heteronormative gaze in a narrative addressed to an implied male reader, and constrained by the unhappy ending of the 'Sẹgilọla' genre, the queer scenes in this pamphlet at least make visible alternative possibilities that readers would know about – or have heard of – in their own social worlds.

---

[6] For dicussion of the gendered division of interpretation in West African literary cultures, see Newell (2000).
[7] I am grateful to Merve Fejzula for this observation.

At the very least, this pamphlet invites a reassessment of the numerous close female friendships depicted in pamphlet literature by authors keen to eavesdrop on women's conversatons and decode their intentions. Whether in female first-person confessions such as *Miss Cordelia in the Romance of Destiny*, or in self-help pamphlets for confused male readers, such as *What Women are Thinking About Men: No. 1 Bombshell to Women* (Nnadozie c.1963) and *Our Modern Ladies Characters Towards Boys* ('Highbred Maxwell' 1960), pamphlet authors sought to fathom women's inner workings, separate the wheat from the chaff, and warn fellow men about 'the evil effects of having hundred percent trust on women' (Ogu c.1960: 1). 'Women have been and will always remain man's greatest source of failure', it seems (Nwosu 1960: 26): 'Beware of Women' (Njoku and Olisah c.1961). *Mabel* depicts a world in which misogynistic sexual abuse is legitimised by marriage, and where women's erotic desires occur outside the logic of pamphlets' masculinity. Even so, the fact that the heroine's downward trajectory occurs through prostitution and pregnancy, and not through female-to-female love, preserves a queer possibility in an otherwise punishing narrative where men's desire for the female body continuously morphs into violent misogyny.[8]

The case studies presented in this chapter show how pamphleteers carefully managed newsprint, presenting it as a public space characterised by debate while carefully appropriating women's voices as authentic speaking subjects.[9] 'Now, dear reader, I wish you to draw a moral for yourself from the stories of my life before you close this book', states Cordelia, Nwosu's first-person narrator, near the end of a punishing life-story in which she is transformed by the heartbreak of an incestuous romance from a 'beauty queen' into 'a little bag of bones with a shrunken head': 'what is your opinion about me and what do you think will be my end?' she asks, inviting interpretation of her story in the manner of the long-established local interpretive conventions discussed in earlier chapters (Nwosu 1960: 38).[10] As in *Mabel the Sweet Honey that Poured Away* and the other

---

[8] Another pamphlet that punishes women in a similar way is Miller O. Albert's *Saturday Night Disappointment* (c.1962).

[9] Fejzula notes that a large number of women who published essays or poems in the earliest West African anthologies moved into radio as their preferred medium. She speculates that radio may have 'presented a more attractive medium for female-gendered intellectual authority than male-dominated print technology' (Personal communication, 31 January 2023).

[10] For further examples of the 'dear reader' convention, see H. O. Ogu, *Rose Only Loved my Money* (1950) and *Jonny, The Most Worried Husband* (c.1960); C. G. Nwosu, *Miss Cordelia in the Romance of Destiny* (1960); N. O. Madu, *Miss Rosy in the Romance of True Love* (n.dat.); R. I. M. Obioha, *How to Write Better Business Letters* (c.1962), Cyril N. Aririguzo, *Miss Comfort's Heart Cries for Tonny's Love* (c.1960b); and Benjamin Chiazor,

pamphlets discussed above, the 'dear reader' convention, perfected by Thomas in the story of Sẹgilọla, is used here to stake a claim to the voice of the female speaking subject: 'My dear reader, do you believe me when I tell you that this story is no fiction', F. C. Nanni interjects in *Never Lose Hope* (c.1961), among the countless examples of this device.

Nevertheless, as this chapter has suggested, outside these carefully circumscribed female 'voices,' women's oral performances and intimate relationships flowed in and out of pamphlets. West African women may be scarce as authors of local newsprint literature in the first half of the twentieth century, but they are omnipresent on the printed page, not only as the blighted heroines of male authors' imaginations and educated heroines who are determined to marry the young men of their choice, but also, as this chapter has indicated, as oral historians who produce songs of criticism and remembrance and as lovers with desires of their own.

Given editors' and pamphleteers' repeated assertions of the superiority of print over oral forms of knowledge throughout the decades covered by this book, it might seem perverse to have looked to male-authored texts for evidence of the presence of women's voices in local literary cultures. Yet while 'harlots' and 'hotel ladies' occupy the wrong end of the moral spectrum promoted within texts, and are unanimously condemned by authors in pamphlets with titles such as *Beware of Harlots and Many Friends* (Nnadozie c.1962), in the context of the pamphlets described in this chapter, they shape protagonists' futures with catchy lyrics in which the reputations of characters are judged. Their words may be male-authored and inflected with masculinist bias, and their genres appropriated into printed texts, but the *presence* of these women powerfully suggests weaknesses in pamphleteers' assertions of patriarchal authority in local contexts where public opinion was produced by women far beyond the pages of pamphlet literature.

How to be the Friends of Girls (c.1965) which duplicates his pamphlet, *Back to Happiness* (n.dat.), under a different title.

Writing Time: African Cold War Aesthetics and Nigerian Political Dramas of the 1960s

8

This chapter asks what changes in our understanding of the cultural politics of the Cold War if we prioritise the publications of creative writers who did not travel to international conferences or place their manuscripts with publishers in Paris and London, but who avidly consumed international news stories and produced texts about them for local circulation. Focusing on Onitsha dramas produced in the thick of the Congo Crisis of 1960–61, it asks about the ways in which locally published literature contributed to debates about Cold War politics and aesthetics, especially when the 'global Cold War' entered creative writers' own backyards in the form of political crises in new nation-states (Westad 2005). To neglect this archive is to ignore cultural artefacts that were produced and consumed during Cold War emergencies by the very populations the superpowers attempted to tether to their poles. As the chapter will argue, attention to creative writing by local intellectuals furnishes additional perspectives that complement and triangulate the work of Cold War literary scholars of Africa, who generally focus on the work of transnational elites.

The dramatists at the centre of this chapter – Ogali A. Ogali, Thomas O. Iguh and Felix N. Stephen – made bold and original interventions in a crisis that is widely recognised to be the first Cold War proxy conflict in postcolonial Africa.[1] Calling on the English literary canon for inspiration, they responded instantly to

---

[1] The youngest of the three dramatists, Iguh was born in 1942 in Okigwi. His father was a well-educated civil servant and all of his siblings went to university. One of his brothers was a lawyer and his sisters included two doctors, an engineer and an architect (Iguh interviewed by Dodson 1973: 244). Like Iguh, Ogali was better-educated than his peers in Onitsha: born in 1931 in Item (Bende), Umuahia Province, he worked for the United Africa Company (UAC) between 1950 and 1954, then took a job at the Nigerian Railway Corporation in Enugu. In 1957, Ogali briefly worked as a teacher in a Methodist school before pursuing his dream to train as a journalist (Back cover, *Patrice Lumumba: A Drama*, 1961). Though prolific, much less is known about Stephen: he was 'reportedly a journalist' who did not always wish to be named on his pamphlets. He asked the publisher Nathan Njoku to take credit for *How to Behave and Get a Lady in Love*, but as Njoku recalled, 'the grammar there! In fact it's above my own' (Interviewed by Dodson 1974: 322, 259).

political developments and used the genre of drama to interpret the unfolding news story of Patrice Lumumba's assassination, adding imagination and artistic weight to the news. Their genre was not unique: bestselling romances like *Veronica My Daughter* and its successors were also presented as dramas, and how-to pamphlets about love and marriage were frequently spliced with dramatic scenes. Yet the Lumumba plays were extraordinary for the way they featured real, named – and often still living – political personalities.[2]

The authors of these dramas were intimately caught up in the timelines of colonialism, the Cold War and nationalism in the mid-twentieth century. Ogali, Iguh and Stephen responded to recent events while remaining 'quite unlike the familiar postcolonial canon', as Francesca Orsini (2023: 76) describes similar local literatures in India. As with Orsini's local archive, the materials considered in this chapter typify vibrant print cultures that fall outside the parameters of debates about Cold War aesthetics in which the literature of commitment is widely associated with an allegiance to communism, while experimental art forms are associated with the ideology of democratic freedom in the West (Popescu 2020).

Events in Congo offered a ready made plot to Onitsha pamphleteers. From the late 1950s, Congo had been under scrutiny by Western intelligence agencies as a site for Soviet infiltration on the continent (Williams: 135–42). The instability that followed Independence on 30 June 1960, when the Congolese army mutinied against the Belgian military commanders who remained in the country, increased consternation in the West. Exploiting the instability, Moïse Tshombe, premier of the mineral-rich state of Katanga in which Belgium had mining interests, seceded from the federal republic with the backing of Belgian forces.

In July 1960, the Congolese prime minister, Patrice Lumumba, was summoned to the US to discuss a solution to the crisis with the Eisenhower administration, but the president was so alarmed by Lumumba's confrontational anticolonialism and Marxist rhetoric that the meeting resulted in covert American support for Lumumba's assassination (Williams 2011, 2021, Nzongola-Ntalaja 2002). Meanwhile, the Secretary General of the United Nations, Dag Hammarskjöld, dispatched UN forces to Congo at Lumumba's request, but their instructions were to avoid miliatary conflict on the ground. The situation deteriorated with the secession of South Kasai under Albert Kalonji's leadership on 9 August 1960: at this point, desperate at the ineffectiveness of UN forces, Lumumba asked the USSR for military assistance (Williams 2011: 35–6).

---

[2] The Lumumba pamphlets inspired later dramatisations of key political events by Onitsha pamphleteers, including plays about the trial and imprisonment of Obafemi Awolowo 1963, and plays about the deposition of Nkrumah and other African leaders in the 1960s. The tradition of printed political drama inaugurated by the Lumumba plays merits considerable further study, not least for what it reveals about African nationalism among local intellectuals in eastern Nigeria before the outbreak of the Civil War.

Violence escalated when, on 5 September 1960, with CIA and MI6 approval, the president of Congo, Joseph Kasavubu, dismissed Lumumba as prime minister and Colonel Mobutu Sese Seko staged a coup d'état, remaining in power with Western backing until 1997. Lumumba was placed under house arrest in October 1960, from which he escaped. Recaptured in January 1961, he and his allies, Maurice Mpolo and Joseph Okito, were secretly flown to Katanga, where they were murdered by Belgian mercenaries alongside Katangese forces, their remains disposed of before Lumumba's death was officially announced (Williams 2011).

Lumumba's death triggered protests around the world, including demonstrations in Lagos, where crowds brandished an empty coffin and called for the executions of Tshombe, Kasavubu and Mobutu (Olisah 1961b: 19).[3] Furious newspaper editorials condemned Congolese leaders for allowing the Western powers to exacerbate the crisis. A poem by the journalist, creative writer and president of the Nigerian senate, Dennis Osadebay, conveyed Nigerians' widespread dismay at the betrayal of anticolonial nationalist ideals at this time, using archaic English to mark the gravity of the moment. In a warning to the rest of Africa, Osadebay wrote:

> Ye independent states of Africa, rise;
> Ye are not free, no, not free;
> Ye have changed one kind of chains
> For a more degrading kind of chains;
> Rise and fight for freedom, ye slave;
> Weep for Lumumba, weep for murdered
> Youth;
> It is done. (Osadebay, cited in Olisah 1961b: 17)[4]

Nigerians had every reason to be nervous in the volatile climate of a postcolonial Cold War that permeated the national politics of every African

---

[3] This powerful visual symbol of the disappearance of Lumumba's corpse and people's desire for the perpetrators to be brought to justice reappears in several Nigerian plays, often carried by striking workers or by revolutionary anticolonial crowds waving banners and palm fronds in declarations of war (see Iguh 1961). In Iguh's *Dr. Nkrumah in the Struggle for Freedom* (1971), the Nkrumah character has a large coffin conveyed through a crowd of protestors in Accra, which he sets on fire immediately before the riot during which he is arrested and imprisoned (37).

[4] In Nigeria there were also popular gramophone records narrating the details of Lumumba's life and death (Post 1964: 405). Ghanaian novelist Ayi Kwei Armah was so deeply affected as a young man by the murder of Lumumba that he changed his degree programme at Harvard University from literary studies to the social sciences, before leaving Harvard without completing his degree. After hospitalisations for mental and physical collapses in which he felt 'my entire being, body and soul ... had broken down,' he returned to Ghana and turned to creative writing, full of ambivalence about its usefulness as a tool for social and political transformation (1985: 1752–3).

state. Directly and indirectly, the Cold War created political instabilities throughout the continent. For the Western powers, a failed state was preferable to a communist government in postcolonial Africa. Lumumba himself argued that the Congo crisis was continental in scope because conditions in his country were duplicated in other newly independent nations (Wenzel 2002: 243). Even without access to the full story, which was shrouded with cover-ups and denials for many decades, Nigerian intellectuals noted the ease and immediacy with which Congolese Independence had been overrun by Cold War interests, making a mockery of the credo of non-alignment endorsed by African leaders at the Bandung Conference of 1955 and jeopardising the principle of self-government that Africans fought so hard for in preceding decades.[5]

Published in Onitsha in the months immediately after Lumumba's assassination, and only weeks after Nigerian Independence, the Lumumba plays offered parabolic warnings to Nigerians to beware of duplicating, in their own nascent federation, the conditions that caused the crisis in Congo. These dramas were 'specially designed to bring home in, to the reader the manner in which Patrice Lumumba was killed', fleshing out a political plot that was already circulating in the public domain and filling it with new temporalities that would resonate with Nigerian readers (Iguh 1961: n.pag.). In them, Onitsha authors re-shaped the Congolese nationalist leader's forward-looking ideals into a life destined for a premature end: African nationalism is shunted into the conditional tense just as it appeared to have been realised across the continent.

Onitsha pamphleteers recognised that the assassination of Lumumba and his allies was not a one-off national tragedy caused by unique conditions in the ex-Belgian Congo. 'All nationalists should mourn for Mr Lumumba. Weep for him', Okenwa Olisah laments in *The Life Story and Death of Mr. Lumumba*, a non-fictional pamphlet which reads like a eulogy for the continent's lost future (1961b: 28).[6] Secessionist pressures in Nigeria had been carefully contained in the negotiations preceding decolonisation, but local intellectuals were clearly nervous that Nigeria might suffer the same fate as Congo: 'You can agree with me', Ogali tried to reassure readers in his second Lumumba play, *The Ghost of Patrice Lumumba* ([1961] 1980e), 'that if African States had handled the matter, Congo today would have become a united country with a strong central

---

5   Decades before the facts emerged, it was clear to political commentators around the world that the murder had been carried out with US backing. Newspaper editors speculated about the extent of international vested interests in the Congo, and Nigerians keenly read about Andrew Tully's book *C.I.A. – The Inside Story* (published in New York by Morrow in 1962), a review of which was culled from the international press and published in the *West African Pilot* in March 1962. In the review, the CIA and 'U.S. Imperialism' were described as the '"main culprit" in Lumumba's death' (Post 1964: 407).
6   The temporality of these plays reverses the future-oriented temporality of the self-help pamphlets discussed in Chapter 4.

Figure 8.1 Cover of Thomas Iguh's (1961) *The Last Days of Lumumba (The Late Lion of the Congo): A Drama* (Onitsha: Onwudiwe).

government as the Federation of Nigeria' (248).[7] The political vision Lumumba espoused is shown to fail in the plays: they depict the tragic fall of a nationalist hero and no restoration of sovereignty in Congo. The treacherous usurpers retain power at the end of the plays.

This nervousness among Nigeria's local intellectuals may explain the keenness with which Onitsha pamphleteers listed the differences separating Nigerians from Congolese. 'The Belgians, unlike the English, did not like to give us some academic training which will eventually make the country produce graduates and well read men and women who would not fail in culture', says the Lumumba character in a clunky pro-British aside for the benefit of Nigerian readers in Stephen's *How Tshombe and Mobutu Regretted after the Death of Lumumba* (n.dat.[b]: 10).[8] Olisah also notes that during his research for *The Life Story and Death of Mr. Lumumba*:

> I was informed that Congolese boys are in a great majority rough. They extravagantly spend, and are womanisers. They get money but lavish all in bar. They cannot save. All they think is to dance, drink wine and chase women. The betterment of their futures do not come into their minds … In Nigeria, Indian hemp, is seriously unlawful, but these Congolese boys smoke it and that is why they do not hear. (1961b: 21)

Congolese women do not fare any better under Olisah's notoriously gender-conservative pen:

> I was also told that Congolese girls are in the same majority, lovers of bar lives. They have no shame and do immoral things in public places. They are easily got by boys, but do not keep long with one man, run up and down. They regard life as nothing and so play it to the last. (Ibid.)

Echoing colonialist racial stereotypes about hedonistic natives, these authors turn an anthropological gaze onto the Congolese, using the opportunity for critical comparison to promote an image of the new Nigerian citizen as an educated person and book lover. In this way, pamphleteers cleverly flatter

---

[7] By 1963, conflict over the federal distribution of resources based on census results for the regions, and violence against Igbos in the North, had caused newspaper editors to warn of Balkanisation in Nigeria and appeal for peace (Daly 2020).

[8] K. W. J. Post (1964) notes that Congolese people come off as politically inferior in another of Stephen's plays, *The Trials of Lumumba, Jomo Kenyatta and St. Paul* (n.dat.), where the anticolonial consciousness of Kenyans is contrasted with the drinking and dancing culture of the Congolese: 'These two, you would appreciate, cannot go a long way to bring about the progress of any nation', Stephen interjects (cited in Post: 409).

readers at the moment of literary consumption, positioning them as cultivated citizens whose abstemious lifestyles will prevent similar political tragedies from occurring in their homeland. Critical, reflective and intelligent, local readers exercise rational political agency and 'bring about progress' and 'peace and harmony' in the view of pamphleteers, over and against the more fractured (because frivolous) Congolese (Stephen cited in Post 1964: 409, Olisah cited in Post 1964: 409).

Past, present and future are woven together in unique ways in these plays. Pamphleteers used their imaginations for historical interpretation, rearranging events and opening up recent history to the insertion of alternative timelines. Prominent among these is Ogali's second Congo play, *The Ghost of Patrice Lumumba,* which appeared in print only weeks after the plane crash that killed Dag Hammarskjöld in September 1961. This play features the mournful ghost of the murdered nationalist quoting his own lines from Ogali's first Lumumba play, *Patrice Lumumba: A Drama,* published in June 1961. The ghost warns a still-living fictional Hammarskjöld of his impending demise: 'Your sun is set and your stage is closed … You are now dead' ([1961] 1980e: 253–4). Next, the ghost visits each of the remaining leaders in Congo in a manner reminiscent of the spirits of Christmas past, present and yet to come in Charles Dickens's *A Christmas Carol*, informing each of them that 'Congo's Union must be maintained' and terrifying Tshombe into agreeing to return Katanga to the federation (263).

Through the device of the ghost, Ogali resolves the suspended temporality of the Congolese federation by resurrecting the murdered nationalist and having him direct future policy decisions by the country's living leaders. In this way, Ogali plays with time, transforming the 'not to be' of Lumumba's life into an affirmative 'to be' of future national unity in which Lumumba takes up an official position as 'spiritual father of the Republic of Congo', allowing an atmosphere of hope to settle over the political tragedy (251). The ongoing crisis is treated with hindsight by the ghost, made into a totality through which the usurped timeline of African nationalism is reinstated. Through the literary figure of the ghost, then, Ogali resolves – or perhaps evades – the real political problem of how to achieve postcolonial nationhood in the time of the global Cold War.

In her forceful reconsideration of the capacity of leftist postcolonial leaders and intellectuals to realise their political goals under Cold War pressures, Bhakti Shringarpure identifies three incompatible but synchronous ways of thinking about and experiencing postcolonial time. The first 'bind of time' is the ideological legacy of colonialism, in which the Western world positions indigenous populations outside history, progress and modernity, peripheral to centres of knowledge and power in the Global North (2019: 15). The second, and contrasting, bind of time describes the ways revolutionary leaders placed newly liberated populations 'into the waiting room of history' at Independence, postponing popular demands for immediate qualitative improvements to their lives in order to pursue long-term goals for the nation like five-year plans and infrastructure development projects (Ibid.). The third bind of time describes Cold War interventions in new nations by the Western powers that supported assassinations and coups against leaders identified as Soviet sympathisers and sponsored national politicians who upheld the strategic interests of NATO (Ibid.).

Permeated with violence, the clashing temporalities Shringarpure describes produced realities on the ground and shaped domestic and international policy. Understood through her model, the Congo crisis was caused by the intrusion into a nation state of two global hegemonies: on the one hand, an intractable colonial state attacking Lumumba for obstructing its residual economic interests, built up during decades of colonialism; on the other hand, the United States and its mid-twentieth-century Cold War allies wishing to eliminate Lumumba as a threat to Western power and ideology. As for the nationalist bind of time, as Shringarpure shows, African countries at Independence included many highly educated Marxists and African socialists, some of whom had been members of the Communist Party in previous decades, while others had been suspected of communism in the colonial era and came to the continent via Russia: their ambitious five-year national plans deferred the promises made at Independence, rendering them vulnerable to destabilisation by Cold War interests.

As a consequence of these competing binds of time, Shringarpure argues that failed postcolonial revolutions under these leaders should not be dismissed as 'grand failures of a utopian Marxist left' (2019: 15). Rather, the country specific conditions produced by the three overlapping temporalities obstructed the smooth transition of many countries – most notably those with leftist governments – from colonial rule to peaceful postcolonial nationhood. An understanding of the different binds of time is therefore vital to discussions of failed nationhood in postcolonial states: only in this way, Shringarpure emphasises, can Cold War cultural studies be 'rescue[d] … from a tyrannically linear historicism' that serves the interests of the Global North's capitalist victory narrative (6).

Shringarpure's argument that postcolonial 'national trajectories' were usurped by the 'corporeal and temporal interventions' of the Cold War is clearly demonstrated in the Lumumba plays (15). In them the Congo crisis is staged as a juxtaposition of temporalities, from colonialist to nationalist and from nationalist to Cold War, with clear connections drawn between old colonial interests in Africa and the Western alliance in the new Cold War. Published in a world divided into two superpowers, with a United Nations unfairly skewed toward neocolonial interests, the plays cling to national time – stolen, aborted, compromised in Congo – as the only remaining form of non-alignment in a bifurcated world. Nationalism is shown by authors to be an egalitarian and humanist assertion of African equality with other self-governing nations in the early 1960s.

Onitsha pamphleteers dramatise and expose the competing temporalities of postcolonial Africa in the period of the Cold War. Lumumba's story becomes a complex parable for local readers: the unfolding plot creates shock and suspense, but readers turn the pages knowing that the protagonist's namesake is already dead. A parable is a finished story that sits beside the listener or reader, occupying an imaginative space adjacent to their lived reality, inviting comparisons with their experience and, in its state of completion, indicating directions and possibilities for their unrolling lives. Through the parable of Congo, Nigerian dramatists could comment on Lumumba's assassination and also project and rehearse their own nation's political arguments for economic independence from Britain and for federal unity. Their fictional Lumumba unfurls his egalitarian vision for Congo in the present time of the plays, occupying the stage as a nationalist leader with a vision of African freedom, innocently facing what authors highlight and readers know: the impending tragedy of his removal from history. Predetermined by history, the Lumumba of Onitsha market literature vibrates with tragic temporality and historical precedents: 'Was Gandhi not killed after securing the independence of India?' Ogali's Lumumba asks in a brave reply to his wife's prophetic vision of his death, adding another foundational precedent: 'Was Abraham Lincoln not killed after maintaining America's Union?' ([1961] 1980d: 233).

In considering these local plays as responses to the Cold War, two further temporalities may be introduced to Shringarpure's three binds of time. The imaginative works that accompanied Lumumba's assassination combine the temporality of crisis with the temporality of tragedy. In crisis time, chronological time is unravelled: plans come undone and interpretation flounders. Crisis brings speculation and a destabilisation of goals, removing the precedents that offer people tools for recognition and understanding. In tragic time, by contrast – at least in its literary manifestations – the moment on stage is continuously wrapped into its outcome, read through its future, endowed with moral permanence through the presence of destiny or fate. In tragedy, past, present and future are rolled up together in a way that accommodates ghosts, spoilers, prophesies, repetitions, foreknowledge, completion and moral certitude. Lumumba's murder, when it comes, is a tragedy thoroughly foretold. Moreover, in *radical* tragedy, which is how the Lumumba dramas can be positioned, the supposedly inevitable fate of the protagonist is continuously interrupted by the possibility of alternatives. Radical tragedy insists that things would have been different if only human agents had acted otherwise in history (see Dollimore 1989).

Onitsha's political dramatists pack the dramatic present with foreboding and forewarnings about Lumumba's end, as foretold by the news. Even so, they use their creative imaginations to invoke a future tense for Congo and other African nations, reclaiming deferred – or stolen – national time into the temporality of the self-help pamphlet and revitalising the crisis in Congo with tragic ghosts and futuristic visions, all presented as part of the present action of the play. In doing so, they reminded readers of the vital role of the imagination in producing truths and identities and in judging current affairs. In short, Iguh, Ogali and Stephen present a radically tragic vision of an African crisis, opening up linear time in order to depict Lumumba's fate as entirely avoidable. Through these literary devices for representing time, the playwrights give the nation a future made possible by the work of their own, and the reader's, imagination.

Every moment in which Lumumba's life is presented in the plays is thick with imaginative interventions showing how recent events should have been otherwise and must be otherwise for countries like Nigeria. While readers wait for the outcome of a political tragedy that is already known, the plays' progression towards Lumumba's violent end is halted, every step of the way, by attention to the human agents behind the plot. 'O God! Please pardon me', Mobuto cries remorsefully in the final pages of Stephen's *How Tshombe and Mobutu Regretted after the Death of Mr. Lumumba*, a play that shows how Congo's new leaders, having gloated about the torture and murder of Lumumba, are in the end capable of remorse (n.dat.[b]: 35). Similarly, as Tshombe is taken away to prison on Kasavubu's orders at the end of this play, he cries to God for forgiveness (38). Stephen's pamphlet has a picture of Tshombe on the cover, captioned 'Tshombe of Katanga (Oh! I Have Regretted)'. The text beneath a photograph of Mobuto on the flyleaf of the pamphlet reads:

> Mr Mobuto Congolese Army Officer
> 'Oh! I have regretted for the death of Patrice Lumumba.
> May heaven and earth forgive me my sins towards him'. (Ibid.)

If the Cold War, rather than nationalism, 'is the afterlife of colonialism', as Shringarpure argues, then the ghost of Lumumba and the other futuristic visions in these political plays represent an optimistic afterlife for anticolonial nationalism: it haunts the imagination where the nation is not allowed to die (2019: 85).

Onitsha's political dramatists broke with previous literary traditions in one crucial respect in their responses to the assassination of Lumumba. Judged by the colonial censorship and sedition laws of previous decades, they adopted high-risk strategies in their accounts of the crisis, defaming world leaders and scandalously accusing living Congolese politicians of murder.[9] In this, they followed the lead of Nigerian newspapers, which named culprits and suggested plots, often singling out Dag Hammarskjöld as a figure for blame. In the plays, world leaders such as the UK prime minister Harold Macmillan, Hammarskjöld and King Baudouin of Belgium are not only named but incarnated as cloak-and-dagger villains involved in murderous plots. 'If there is any way to get rid

---

[9] For information about censorship and sedition in British West Africa, see Newell (2013).

of this man who is called Lumumba, you too will be a big man. Do you not like to become a President?' a Belgian officer asks Tshombe at the opening of *How Tshombe and Mobutu Regretted after the Death of Lumumba* (Stephen n.dat.[b]: 7). 'If there is any way in which your people can help me, I can at once storm the whole nation' comes the wicked reply, eliciting a promise of military weapons and personnel from the West (Ibid.). Scenes such as these could not fail to have aroused readers' indignation at the hypocrisy of the Western world.

The long-established newsprint tradition of allusive naming was abandoned in the Congo crisis. Dramatists unhesitatingly decried 'the political ambitions of the Congo vampires, to wit Tshombe, Kasavubu, Mobutu, Joseph Ileo, Albert Kalonji, as well as Belgian and the Western imperialists' in print for all to see alongside their photographs (Ogali [first edn. 1961] 1980d: 221). The dramas depict what happened behind the scenes at secret meetings of world leaders in Brussels and New York, bringing international media speculation to life in the form of dialogues and disclosures by named political figures. These representations are uncharacteristically direct, blatantly discrediting public figures involved in the crisis and naming Tshombe, Kasavubu and Mobutu as murderous, power-hungry African thugs who lack political ideals and break up the federation on behalf of Western interests.

Nigerian readers would have laughed in shock at these scurrilous representations of world leaders. The only precedents in print were the courtroom farces published in Onitsha in the late 1950s and early 1960s, in which a trial of Adolf Hitler was imagined featuring dramatis personae that included Winston Churchill, Joseph Stalin and Franklin D. Roosevelt (Anorue n.dat.[b]: n.pag., Oleyede c.1959, Olisah 1963b). Published for laughs, these plays used distortion, historical error and exaggeration to turn European history into a spoof in which the Germans have 100,000,000 troops and 50,000,000 police officers, all of whom use toy weapons such as water-pistols and pea-shooters to further their wicked goals, and where Hitler shoots his way out of the International Court of Justice in New York as the judges run helter-skelter, so that 'Nobody could tell Hitler's whereabout up till today' (Anorue n.dat.[b]: 6, 36; see also Olisah 1963b).

Fast-paced, violent, entertaining and parabolic, the plays about the Congo crisis encapsulated the spirit of Onitsha market literature, disclosing characters' sinister intentions in advance of the action and using the present-time of dramatic action to expose 'what really happened' on the international stage. Yet even as their works include photographs of the main political actors, and while characters quote real political speeches and act out incidents attributed to their namesakes in the press, pamphleteers insisted that their dramas were not intended to represent actual people or events in Congo. In the prefaces and introductions to plays whose dramatis personae are listed as Tshombe, Mobutu, Hammarskjöld and Baudouin, authors stated that 'all the names used here are simply accidental and have no connections with any human being' (Iguh c.1961: n.pag.). Treading a fine line between fact and fiction, they claimed, 'this drama … is an imaginary story compiled to interest the reader for his leisure and amusement' (Iguh c1961: n.pag.). As Iguh insisted, 'the drama is fiction and does not in any way represent the true accounts of the Lumumba episode. It is all imaginary' (Ibid.). Stephen gave the fullest explaination of the imaginary status of these works in *How Tshombe and Mobutu Regretted After the Death of Mr. Lumumba*:

> This is just an imaginary play, based on the life and death of the first Prime Minister of the Congo, Patrice Lumumba. In the main, the play is quite fictitious and all the statements herein contained, do not in any form, go to reflect to the prestige of the personalities mentioned. It is only for the purposes of intertainment. (Stephen n.dat.[b]: n.pag)

These disclaimers are significant for the way in which they assert the special status of imaginative literary discourse over and against newspaper writing. Inspired by the news, pamphleteers pushed the conventional book disclaimer to its limits, marking a separation of truth from reality and literature from news. The moral permanence of truth – separated from reality by the insertion of authors' literary imaginations – replaces the quotidian world reported in the news. In this way, well-known political personalities could be percolated through genres in which they took on literary and parabolic rather than realist credentials, becoming eternal during a time of crisis and uncertainty in the news.

Lumumba stands in isolation in the plays as a selfless African nationalist whose egalitarian vision for the continent, natural leadership qualities, commitment to Cold War non-alignment and popular pan-Africanism remove him to a tragic space of his own in plays thick with literary and biblical quotations about betrayal and self-sacrifice.[10] Crucially, at no point in any of the plays is Lumumba positioned as a Soviet sympathiser. In so doing, the dramatists repudiate the Western powers' rationale for Lumumba's removal and show how the prime minister's enemies use 'Communist' to discredit him. 'Tell me the truth Patrice, are you a communist?' Ileo asks Lumumba in Stephen's *How Tshombe and Mobutu Regretted After the Death of Mr. Lumumba*: 'I can assure you that I am not' comes the curt reply (n.dat.[b]: 16). Instead, Lumumba's rise and fall is presented in purely nationalist terms, as stemming from neocolonial interventions by Western powers to prevent African political self-determination. Western leaders are accused of political meddling in Congo in the interests of

---

[10] Lumumba's two allies, Maurice Mpolo and Joseph Okito, who were murdered alongside him, feature in the plays, but for dramatic effect Lumumba is kept in the spotlight.

neocolonial capitalism: 'Britain and America killed me', laments the ghost in Ogali's *The Ghost of Patrice Lumumba*, adding: 'they blamed Tshombe openly, but supported his selfish policy of divide and rule privately' ([1961] 1980e: 259).

Debates about communism flourished in local West African print cultures in the 1960s. In newspapers and pamphlets, local intellectuals discussed the merits of socialism and communism as ideologies suitable to postcolonial Africa. Several Nigerian journalists who also wrote local pamphlets in the late 1960s and early 1970s had undertaken tours of the USSR sponsored by the Novosty Press Agency of the Soviet Union and other Soviet cultural organisations wishing to influence thinking on the continent (e.g., Ajiboye 1967, Umoh c.1971). One of the most prolific Onitsha pamphleteers of the 1960s and early 1970s, Thomas Iguh, was overtly pro-communist.[11] Another author from the early 1970s, Eddy N. Ekesiobi, was public relations officer for the Czech Socialist Embassy in Lagos (1964: n.pag.). Together these authors debated the compatibility of nationalism and communism for non-aligned countries in the postcolonial world.

Perhaps as a consequence of these discussions of communism, without exception, all of the Onitsha plays about the Congo crisis interpreted colonialism as an extractive form of capitalism and showed how neocolonial interests continued to pervade postcolonial states. Ogali quotes directly from King Baudouin's speech at Congolese indendence, in which the Belgian king outrageously suggested that Africans had secured Independence prematurely. 'It is with the greatest regret that we allow you to try your own hands on self-determination', Baudouin tells Congo's new leaders in *Patrice Lumumba: A Drama*, exhibiting colonialist nostalgia at the very moment of handing Congo to its future leaders (Ogali [1961] 1980d: 221). Displaying the leadership qualities that Baudouin implies are lacking in Africans, Lumumba repudiates the king and accuses Belgium of under-developing Congo during the colonial era. Quoting Lumumba's own Independence Day speech, Ogali has his hero say: 'We are not going to be puppets and I now say without mixing words that we are going to Congonise the civil service forthwith ... Belgians must work under Africans, and when their pride allows them not, they must pack and leave the country immediately!' (222). Ogali loads the historical moment of African Independence with the knowledge of what comes next for Congo. In

---

[11] Iguh attended St Francis School, Opubra, in 1948 and in 1958 entered the Church Missionary Society (CMS) School in Abakaliki. In an interview, Iguh described Thomas Paine's *Rights of Man* as 'the first real serious novel I ever read': as the interviewer, Don Dodson, comments, '[Iguh used] "novel" as many Nigerians do, to refer to any book that is not the Bible or a text. "I was so carried away by the forceful oratories that were used. It was surely writing! And I felt I could dvelop along that line"' (Dodson 1974: 244). In his many pamphlets about Nkrumah, Kenyatta and Lumumba, Iguh is considerably more pro-revolutionary than the other Onitsha pamphleteers: see *Dr. Nkrumah in the Struggle for Freedom*; *The Last Days of Lumumba (The Late Lion of the Congo)*.

an instant, the global Cold War usurps the nation as Belgian and Katangese soldiers murder Lumumba with backstage US, British and UN support. The entire Western political conspiracy is exposed.

Collectively these dramatists show that there is only one reason why European governments would oppose decolonisation in Africa: as one British character states rhetorically in Abiakam's drama about the life and death of Nkrumah, 'If we grant them Independence, where can we get gold and cocoa to sell to the World Market? Where can we get fat cows and goats to eat?' (Abiakam c.1971: 21). Similarly, in Iguh's play about Nkrumah, *Dr. Nkrumah in the Struggle for Freedom*, a pamphlet that debates the pros and cons of violent armed resistance to colonialism, one of the characters says: 'these Britons have been allowed to feed fat and exploit our natural resources to their own exclusive benefits for over fifty years now' (1970: 6).

There is considerable overlap between this material and the Soviet premier Nikita Khrushchev's speech at the United Nations during the Congo crisis, which was widely covered in the Nigerian press. 'The colonialists and their servile supporters say that Mr. Lumumba is a communist', Khrushchev stated. 'Mr. Lumumba is, of course, no communist; he is a patriot and is honestly serving his people in its struggle for freedom from the colonial yoke' (UN General Assembly 23 September 1960: 71). Carefully appealing to anticolonial nationalists, Khrushchev demanded the end of all forms of colonialism and accused neocolonial powers of conspiring against patriotic Africans:

> Raw materials for nuclear weapons ... that is what the monopolists are afraid of losing in the Congo. That is the true motive behind the plot against the Congo, the threads of which lead from Brussels to the capitals of the other major NATO powers ... It is deplorable that they have been doing their dirty work in the Congo through the Secretary-General of the United Nations, and his staff. (UN General Assembly 23 September 1960: 71)

Khrushchev's understanding of colonialism was widely supported in the Nigerian press, forming part of what K. W. J. Post describes as the 'almost talismanic use of the word "Socialism"' in Nigeria in the early years of Independence in reaction to low wages and the high cost of living (Post 1964: 410–11). As one Onitsha pamphleteer observed through a well-known quotation from Marx and Engels, 'During the period of our Colonial tutelage, contact between Nigerians and the Soviet people was frowned upon and actually discouraged ... But [now] the capitalist world is being haunted by the spectre of Communism' (Aniweta 1962: 1). In Nigeria at Independence, the lifting of colonial restrictions on communist publications allowed the emergence of new media outlets such as the socialist publishing house, Pacific Printers, in Yaba, and the weekly newspaper, *Advance*.

Several communist organisations – including trade union groups, branches of the Toilers Brigade and the Afro-Asian People's Solidarity Organisation and a Nigerian-Soviet Friendship Society – were also formed in the early years of independence. Many of these organisations were disbanded after the military coup of 1966, but large numbers of leftist local pamphlets remained in circulation, including work by Baba Oluwide, who continued to produce Maoist pamphlets fro the Young Toilers Brigade of West Africa well into the late 1960s.[12]

While only Iguh was an active supporter of communism, all of the dramatists discussed above repeated the Soviet interpretation of imperialism in their political dramas, condemning the UN secretary general for complicity with Belgian neocolonial interests while shielding the Congolese leader's reputation from the anti-communist bias that motivated his assassination. In representing Lumumba as a hero of anticolonial independence struggles and a non-aligned national leader, they removed him – and themselves – from Cold War polarities in order to emphasise his advocacy of non-alignment: 'We are not going to support any particular world power block – East or West', Ogali's Lumumba informs a crowd in *Patrice Lumumba: A Drama,* again quoting from Lumumba's Independence Day speech (Ogali [1961] 1980d: 222): 'keep the Cold War out of the Congo' (222, 231).

The Cold War and Transnational African Literature

Situated in the thick of overlapping and competing temporalities in an era when decolonisation coincided with the rapid escalation of the global Cold War, Africa's new electorates and media consumers were, in the view of the USA and ex-colonial powers, highly susceptible to Soviet propaganda. In response, during the 1950s and 1960s, the blunt instrument of the Western allies' colonial media censorship morphed into more subtle forms of cultural influence. Taking the form of public relations strategies so 'soft' as to evade detection, cultural organisations like the CIA's Congress for Cultural Freedom (CCF) monitored debates about the role of literature among postcolonial

---

[12] Other titles include *The British Political Shooting of the Nigerian Coalminers in November 18, 1949* (Ojiyi 1965) and *On the Current Divergencies* (Oluwide 1968). Oluwide merits further study as a Maoist revolutionary activist. He describes himself as 'author of innumerable essays and booklets of a sociological novel and other unpublished and unpublishable "works". To advance revolutionary career and to keep from starving has been kindergarten teacher, kitchen porter and paratrooper, grammar school headmaster, copy writer, milk salesman and oil executive (for precisely 30½ days), taxi driver, law clerk and economic consultant. Many hairs breath brush with the Law, having been arrested on countable occasions, threatened with jail on uncountable ones, and confined to the most despicable cells meeting the most colourful criminals on both sides of the Sahara' (1968: 37).

intellectuals, subtly seeking to shape the imaginations of people through their sponsorship of conferences and financing of literary magazines such as *Black Orpheus*, *Transition*, *Quest* and *Hiwar*, among others (Djagalov 2023, Davis 2021, Popescu 2020). The revelation that the famous African Writers Conference at Makerere in 1962 was underwritten by the CCF drew a bitter comment from Ngũgĩ wa Thiong'o in 1986: 'It shows how certain directions in our cultural, political, and economic choices can be masterminded from the metropolitan centres of imperialism' (30).

Urgently asserting principles of non-alignment at this time of seismic political shifts and conscious of cooptation by either side, many postcolonial African intellectuals endeavoured to connect with one another in non-aligned networks like the Afro-Asian Writers Association, where they could define their own aesthetic principles and consider postcolonial goals independently of the superpowers. Even so, the Cold War seeped into postcolonial intellectual production through literature and the arts, even as writers – as so many did – sought to decolonise their cultures, disengage from Cold War binaries, and occupy national political and cultural spaces that were not aligned with either side.

In her study of Cold War aesthetics in 1960s African literature, Monica Popescu focuses on the superpowers' strategic forms of cultural surveillance and writers' responses to the Cold War in order to challenge any suggestion that postcolonial African literature occupies a 'peripheral' space in world literary systems. Popescu shows how postcolonial creative writing in the era of the Cold War became a strategic source of intelligence to both sides, forming a particular kind of archive. New African states were part of a bifurcated world order where leaders were under pressure to nail their national flags to Western or Soviet poles: African intellectuals were, she shows, equally tied into the logic of the Cold War. The Cold War permeated continent-wide debates about the roles and values of postcolonial writers, sending 'shrapnel from politico-aesthetic artillery across the Iron Curtain' into the twenty-first century, influencing present-day 'understandings of the social function of the writer and modes of evaluation of literary worth' (Popescu 2020: 3). Only a myopically Eurocentric and historically uninformed model of world literature, she argues, would place capitalist countries at the 'centre' and postcolonial African literature at the 'periphery' of such a world system: 'it is only by restoring the Cold War as the background and shaping element of the decolonization struggles and the postindependence engagement with neocolonialism that we can grasp the full significance of the aesthetic and ideological choices made by African writers' (7).

Popescu examines the tensions generated by this worldliness in 1960s Africa, when politics and aesthetics collided in overtly ideological ways. Clearly, as she argues, we cannot ignore either the desire of the superpowers to monitor postcolonial intelligentsias through sponsorship and surveillance or the political engagement of postcolonial writers at a time of nationalist activism and global political realignment. She also highlights an ethical dilemma: if later scholars treat local artforms as always tethered to Cold War aesthetic criteria and timelines, they risk reinforcing colonialist and Cold War ideologies in which artistic movements are regarded as originating elsewhere, arriving late and loaded with ideological baggage in the decolonising world, already predetermined by extrinsic values.

In addressing this, Popescu briefly notes the existence of 'local aesthetic debates' in Africa that 'have nothing to do with the Cold War' (77). In acknowledging this third space, she carefully avoids replacing one Cold War hegemony with another by including all African cultural production in a Cold War framework determined by the superpowers. However, by neglecting a discussion of 'local aesthetic debates' in the Cold War era, Popescu risks overlooking archives packed with political and cultural ideas about the Cold War in the form of plots, characters, advice, suppositions and deductions, as well as literary genres that engaged with politics and aesthetics beyond the limits and intersections of modernism and realism. Such a gesture risks inadvertently excluding the authors and publics whose worlds the colonial powers and Cold War superpowers were wanting to shape. If writers deemed to be local – such as the Onitsha dramatists discussed above – are relegated to a zone outside the global Cold War, an impossible historical scenario is produced in which some local intellectuals appear to be untouched by the Cold War, even as it helped to constitute the world in which they lived.

Local print cultures were considerably more complex on the ground than allowed for by the framework of Cold War power relations. As Peter Kalliney writes in the afterword to a recent book on the Cold War and (post)colonial print cultures, 'intellectuals in the decolonizing world pursued their own agendas' (2022: 302). Even the most avowedly Marxist proponents of committed literature in the 1960s did not adopt the Soviet aesthetic wholesale in postcolonial contexts. As Chana Morgenstern observes in her study of the anticolonial Arabic cultural journal *Al-Jadid*, writers 'creat[ed] counter-hegemonic community-based narratives that blended news, history, political critique and radical imagination', achieving local traction through vernacular material that was published alongside translations of socialist realist writing (2023: 58). Local print media were always slippery and boundary crossing, filled with 'varied and competing internationalisms in the context of the Cold War' rather than exhibiting singular affiliations to one side or the other of the conflict (Orsini 2023: 74). Paying attention to local print cultures allows for these additional temporalities – national, non-aligned and decolonial – to be added to the historical timelines determined by the global superpowers in the twentieth century.

The authors discussed in this chapter crafted Cold War characters to carry debates about good leadership in the perilous period of decolonisation. They took up roles as home-grown political moralists, turning crisis into critique and using the genre of tragedy to expose the conditional tense of African nationalism. Their works were also nonaligned because they were written outside the parameters of the modernism versus socialist realism conflict that seemed to dominate the aesthetic debates of transnational postcolonial elites. Local Nigerian dramatists produced critical frameworks through which Cold War politics could be read locally with the question, 'What do *we outsiders* think about this [issue]?' at the forefront of interpretation (Anon., n.dat.: 22; emphasis added).

The first principle of African nationalism, as articulated by Lumumba and the other deposed political heroes of Onitsha political dramas, is the rejection of interference by the Global North. In this anti-metropolitan articulation of nationalism, these plays contribute in significant ways to the study of Cold War literature, containing Nigerian understandings of the relationship between colonialism, nationalism and the Cold War at a time of major international crisis in Africa. They exemplify the 'triple bind of time' identified by Shringarpure and produce further 'binds' through their status as literary works that re-assemble the crisis according to temporalities made possible by the creative imagination.

In their careful avoidance of Cold War alignment and insistent retrieval of nationalism in deferred, displaced and supernatural forms, Onitsha's political dramatists merit a place in studies of African literature in the era of the Cold War era. Even though they were insistent about the fabricated nature of their plays, their plots and characters offered truths, if not facts, about recent events as they ventriloquised the speeches of living political leaders, used their creative licence to interpret media reports and forcefully inserted their imaginations into the 'Cold War temporalities' identified by cultural historians of the Cold War.

'How now my man?': The Problem of Realism in Political Plays

In reflecting on whether he would rather live in comfort or die as a hero, Ogali's Lumumba gives a version of Perseus's reply to Pallas Athene from one of the many versions of Charles Kingsley's popular Victorian rendition of Greek mythology, *The Heroes* (1856), in circulation around colonial schools in the first half of the twentieth century. 'Is it not better to die in the flower of youth on a chance of winning a noble name as the founder of Independent and United Congo, than to live at ease like a sheep and die unloved and unrenowned?', Lumumba asks rhetorically ([1961] 1980d: 233, citing Kingsley 1906: 9). In Iguh's play, *The Last Days of Lumumba*, the hero's dignified speeches to 'citizens of Congo' combine quotations from Lumumba's speeches with Shakespearean stage directions: in the manner of a Shakespearean king before battle, Lumumba 'mounts on the back of his horse dressed in the uniform of a commander in chief armed with a sword and spear' (Iguh 1961: 9). Borrowing from *As You Like It*, Lumumba declares, 'Let's be on the move my men for every inch of delay is a South Sea of discovery' (Ibid.). All of the Lumumba plays use the same 'high', archaic style of dialogue: 'How now my man?' ask characters of one another (Ogali [1961] 1980b, 252); 'Stay, thou traitor, stay!' Lumumba cries to his assassins (Stephen n.dat.: 26); 'How now, my Lord, what is wrong?' Lumumba's devoted wife asks (Ogali [First edn 1961] 1980d: 223). At all times, these classical and Shakesperean quotations are spliced with distinctly Nigerian turns of phrase: in Iguh's *The Last Days of Lumumba (The Late Lion of the Congo) A Drama*, for example, Lumumba combines the local term 'pack away' with Mark Antony's famous speech in *Julius Caesar*: 'Comrades Mpolo, Okito and the rest, lend me your ears ... Belgium must pack away and that must be now or never' (1961: 8).

In a similar manner to the quotations discussed in Chapter 6, these literary references confer dignity and detachment on the figure of Lumumba while also displaying the credentials of pamphlet authors as intellectuals with English literary materials at their fingertips, extracting wisdom for the benefit of readers. Through Shakespearean soliloquies, battlefield orations, quotations from the speeches of world leaders, as well as references to Christian saints, maxims, popular proverbs and British and American literature, the Lumumba dramatists secured readers' admiration for an eloquent tragic hero who knows one thing for certain: that his days are numbered. Through multiple layers of literary cross-references, the dramatists added weight to the newspaper coverage of Lumumba's assassination and flaunted their own wisdom, producing laments for Lumumba, praising the great nationalist and abusing his enemies. Lumumba emerges as a nationalist martyr with a humanist consciousness and a place in the Christian line-up of saints: 'Patrice, your sacrifice was great. It is only fitting that you have been numbered among the Saints', wrote one correspondent in the *West African Pilot* at the start of this tradition of sanctification: 'Like the Christ of old, you came to your people but your people knew you not' (cited in Post 1964: 406). In this, the Lumumba dramas are the earliest examples of a tradition of sanctification of Lumumba that continues to the present day (see Miller 2020).

Jennifer Wenzel (2002) suggests that some of the Lumumba plays have an uncontrolled relationship with real time, partly as a consequence of this intrusion of quotations from anglophone literature into local dialogue (236). Bernth Lindfors jokes that the Shakespearean style makes the Congolese premier sound more like a bourgeois English gentleman than a francophone pan-African leader of a popular anticolonial movement (cited in Wenzel 2002). Moreover, these critics point out that unrealisable stage directions, in which dramatists require the presence of 'surging millions' and 'ten thousand soldiers' undermine the plays' realism (Iguh 1961: 9, Wenzel 229). For these commentators, the plays' grandiosity prevents the prospect of theatrical realisation. All these inflationary devices have a paradoxically 'deflating effect', according to Wenzel: they 'complicate communication' and frustrate the plays' aspirations to represent recent events (236).

Judged by the criteria of realism and naturalism, Lumumba's rousing anticolonial speeches are anything but loyal to the leader's national context. Onitsha dramatists appear to make no effort to 'Congonise' their subject, to use Lumumba's word for the nationalist principles that must replace colonisation. But what if realism and naturalism are not the yardsticks by which these dramas should be judged by their readers? What if other aesthetic conventions were prevalent at the time of their composition, shaping local authors' and readers' appreciation of their literary value?

Seen through the creative practices described in this book, the plays turn recent history into morality, transforming the temporality of current affairs by vividly presenting Lumumba's – and Congo's – story as a tragic totality. Onitsha's dramatists took the position of moral overseers, distilling public rage and shock at Lumumba's death into plot lines filled with repetitions where secrets are exposed, moral truths produced and critical distance assured, all sealed in the high literary language of a centuries-old Shakespearean tradition. Had the Lumumba playwrights adopted the principles of dramatic naturalism in form and style, their works would have stood out as anomalies in relation to the pamphlets surrounding them on all sides. In local West African creative writing, as previous chapters have shown, the 'literary' was characterised by moral prescriptions, overviews, lessons, warnings, advice and thick layers of quotations. The lives of fictional characters were portrayed as parables, not unfolding in time but continuously 'spoilt' by forward projections and summaries of their ends.

All these forms of interruption and repetition were designed to prevent readers from becoming immersed in the plot. The authors' primary goal was to reduce the risk that readers would empathetically over-identify with protagonists; they wished, instead, to ensure the critical distance required to extract moral lessons from the story. In Onitsha pamphlet literature the life stories of protagonists are framed in such a way that their temporalities cannot – and should not – synchronise with readers' lived realities. Life stories in local creative writing are presented reflexively, from a parabolic space outside and alongside readers' lives. With the outbreak of the Nigerian Civil War, however, the parabolic aesthetic and high literary language of Onitsha pamphlets gave way to new forms of realism necessitated by the representation of the conflict, drawing English-language Nigerian fiction into the aeshetic space of vernacular newsprint literature from earlier decades.

9 Romances from the Nigerian Civil War: Veronica's End

Onitsha pamphleteers were among the first to fictionalise the Nigerian Civil War. Unlike their plays about Lumumba, Awolowo, Nkrumah, Kenyatta, and other deposed African leaders in the 1960s, national heroes were largely absent from creative writing about the Civil War. If anticolonial nationalism provided a vantage point for pamphleteers seeking forms of Cold War non-alignment in political dramas about African crises in the early to mid-1960s, as described in the previous chapter, the war confused authors' loyalties and muddied the nationalist solution to postcolonial crises.

'Biafra's history is short', writes Samuel Fury Childs Daly, but 'it would shape Nigeria's politics long after 1970, both for what it taught the country's leaders and for how the public remembered it' (2020: 6–7). Creative writing is fundamental to this process of public remembering and interpretation. The pamphlets discussed in this chapter are among the earliest in a long tradition of Civil War literature by Nigerian creative writers that continues to the present day and includes Flora Nwapa's *Wives at War and Other Stories* (1980), Buchi Emecheta's *Destination Biafra* (1982), Ken Saro-Wiwa's *Sozaboy: A Novel in Rotten English* (1985), Chimamanda Ngozi Adichie's *Half of a Yellow Sun* (2006) and Akachi Adimora-Ezeigbo's *A Million Bullets and a Rose* ([2011] 2022), among many others (see Coundouriotis 2014). The women writers on this list – Nwapa, Emecheta, Adichie and Adimora-Ezeigbo – all focus on the experiences of women caught up in the conflict, while the anti-war writers, including Nwapa and Saro-Wiwa, use fiction to try to seek 'humanity in a world gone mad' (Nwapa 1975: b.pag.). Other authors have been more politically partisan. In his collection of poetry, *Nigerian Civil War Soliloquies* (1977), the anticolonial leader, first president of Nigeria, renowned nationalist newspaperman and Igbo 'son of the soil,' Nnamdi Azikiwe, described the leaders of the federal government as 'scapegoats of history' and attempted to use poetry to reinstate a Nigerian national identity (v). By contrast, in his 2013 memoir, *There Was A Country*, Achebe maintained a clear pro-Biafran perspective consistent with his wartime work for the Biafran Ministry of Information as a diplomat and fundraiser in Europe.[1]

Events unfolded as follows: on 30 May 1967, General Chukwuemeka Odumegwu Ojukwu declared the Republic of Biafra in the eastern region of Nigeria after a period of increasing political instability that included the assassination of the premier of Northern Nigeria, Ahmadu Bello and the Prime Minister of Nigeria, Abubakar Tafawa Balewa, among other political leaders in the military coup of January 1966. Led by two Igbo officers while President Nnamdi Azikiwe was out of the country, the January coup was widely interpreted in Nigeria through the lens of ethnicity as an Igbo push for power. What resulted from this interpretation of events was carnage. Tens of thousands of Igbos were massacred in the north of the country, and hundreds of thousands were displaced to the eastern region from their homes all around Nigeria.

In response to Ojukwu's severence of ties with the federal republic in May, Nigeria invaded Biafra on 6 July 1967 with the support of Britain and the United States. According to the Red Cross, an estimated 1.5 million people died over the next three years and Eastern Nigeria became 'hell on earth' (Nwapa 1975). Among the war dead was the avant garde poet Christoper Okigbo, who joined the Biafran army at the outbreak of the war and was killed in action only three months later. Many thousands of people died of starvation as the federal government blocked trade routes in their attempt to force easterners into submission. Theft, armed robbery and fraud proliferated in Biafra, with lasting repercussions in Nigerian society (Daly 2020).

Most pamphleteers fled Onitsha at the onset of war. Commentators in the early 1970s describe the popular publishing industry as decimated by the conflict as printing presses and libraries were destroyed by federal troops advancing through Biafra (Obiechina 1973, Dodson 1974). The few Onitsha publishers who continued to produce pamphlets during the conflict boldly declared their location as the Republic of Biafra and gave prices in the new Biafran pound. Even so, the scarcity of newsprint under federal blockades severely restricted the production of printed material. One of the few publications from the period, *The Biafra-Nigeria War – A Human Tragedy* by Godfrey C. Okeke (1968), printed in London, responded to the ongoing conflict with a critique of neocolonialism and a condemnation of corruption

---

[1] In response to the conflict, Achebe famously stopped writing novels altogether in favour of more concise literary forms such as short fiction and poetry; he did not return to book-length fiction for twenty years. Other university educated authors also paused before writing novels about the war, or approached it circuitously, with intense anguish, focusing on topics such as madness and corruption rather than direct accounts of the conflict (Emenyonu 1973: 50–1, Ezeigbo 1991).

in Nigeria, while a trickle of pro-federal pamphlets by non-Igbo easterners during the war swore allegiance to the nation:

> Convey my love to GOWON now
> Our peaceful Head of State,
> Reluctantly he fought a war
> To keep Nigeria One. (Efiom 1968: 9)[2]

As soon as printing presses started to function again in Onitsha after the conflict, pamphleteers returned to the genre of the romance (see Anafulu 1973). Pamphlets such as Iguh's *The Last Days of Biafra: A Drama* (third edn 1977) and *Love in a Bunker* by G. C. Osakwe and A. Odogwu (c.1972) transplanted the classic *Veronica My Daughter* template into a wartime setting, keeping the romantic plot but adding to its cast list and rejuvenating the classic story by splicing in current political figures and political commentaries. Ogali's Veronica (and her countless successors), her educated young fiancé, her greedy father, her loyal mother, and the old illiterate chief who wishes to marry the girl against her wishes, are situated in wartime scenarios: wartime crises and moral inversions reshape the decisions of their 1950s predecessors. And in at least one case, discussed below, the quintessential protagonists and storylines of prewar romances are inverted by the war, giving rise to a new local genre that made a break with the parables of past decades.

Written by authors who witnessed or were involved in the conflict, the new war romances boldly incorporated recent history into readers' favourite local romantic storyline, demonstrating the resilience of a local literary culture in which writers transposed current events into 'entertaining and educative' texts and attracted readers' attention with promises of relevance and innovation in true Onitsha style. In Iguh's loosely structured drama, *The Last Days of Biafra* (1977), the familiar 'illiterate chief' of *Veronica My Daughter* and the many other forced-marriage plays that were published in its wake reappears as the character 'Chief Nweke, Illiterate', alongside major political actors from recent history, plus journalists, a judge, a prosecutor and a juju priest. In other postwar romances, such as *Love in a Bunker,* discussed in more detail below, the war is foregrounded to the extent that the 'Veronica' blueprint is challenged and transformed.

The difficulty of eastern authors' reintegration into the federation is exemplified by Shakespeare C. N. Nwachukwu's *The Tragedy of Civilian Major* (1972), a novel that fictionalises the life and suicide of Uchenna Nweze, a demobbed Biafran soldier who became a gang leader and armed robber at

---

[2] In a poignant poem entitled 'Lamentation', Azikiwe mourned the loss of his beloved library, named after the anti-colonial nationalist and Nigerian intellectual Herbert Macaulay (1864–1946), that held 40,000 items. Referring to his books as 'My priceless jewels. Nutrition of my soul', Zik cries, 'Dreary life/ Now confronts me/ For my books are gone' (1977: 38–40).

the end of the war (Fig. 9.1). The novel is based on oral accounts of the real 'attack trade' gangster, including Igbo popular songs in which the celebrity criminal was memorialised.[3] Yet Nweze was no hero: the Civil War spawned no dramas featuring Nigerian leaders facing martyrdom at the hands of dastardly local conspirators in cahoots with neocolonial capitalists in the manner of the Lumumba plays. The Lumumba template was simply not available to authors in a region faced with the task of reconciliation in the aftermath of two murderously incompatible nationalisms within the same postcolonial state.[4] The difficulties are exemplified by Azikiwe, first president of Nigeria from 1963 to 1966, who turned from federalism at Independence to secessionism in 1967, and back to federalism in 1970, when he called on Biafrans to rejoin Nigeria, earning denunciations as a 'defector' on Radio Biafra and the wrath of committed Biafrans (Daly 2020).

M. N. Nwanekezi's foreword to Osakwe's and Odogwu's *Love in a Bunker*, published in Onitsha two years after the war, outlines the moral and epistemological crises faced by authors. 'This small novel', Nwanekezi writes:

> is one of the very many books, written and yet to be written, that will tell the story of that three year experience of hardship for many and enjoyment for a few, of extreme moral degeneration, of desecretion of sacred tradition, of cowards becoming brave overnight and lording it over the naturally brave. (1972: ii)

As Nwanekezi suggests, the war threw eastern Nigerians into the indefinite now of crisis time. Their futures became unmoored from the present. Prewar public opinion in the form of morality and 'sacred traditions' lost value as anchors for making sense of the world. Books that 'tell the story' of the war will, Nwanekezi suggests, need to fix the perverted morality of war time into the absolute past, a temporality that Nwapa (1975) described as the 'never again'.

In the aftermath of the war, some Onitsha publishers returned to the city to retrieve what remained of their presses and bookshops. Njoku, one of the prewar publishers to re-surface after the conflict, named his new business 'Survival Bookshop', marking his resilience (Dodson 1974: 176). He was joined by new pamphleteers who purchased the rights to classic titles from publishers whose businesses had been destroyed in the war and reproduced

---

[3] 'Attack trade' describes the commercial activity that continued across the borders between Nigeria and Biafra, often carried out by women traders, in violation of the federal blockade (see Daly 2020: 139–40).

[4] In *The People's Right to the Novel*, Eleni Coundouriotis (2014) studies war novels in which the Biafran leadership is put under the spotlight for malpractices such as hoarding, corruption and false propaganda, and where social and class inequalities are highlighted (151).

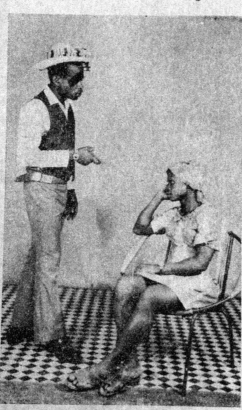

Figure 9.1 Cover of Shakespeare C. N. Nwachukwu's (1972) *The Tragedy of Civilian Major* (Onitsha: Nwachukwu Africana Books).

the old bestsellers alongside new pamphlets about current affairs. In this way, Onitsha's pamphleteers ensured intellectual and literary continuity, helping to build bridges between the past and the present, restoring a semblance of cultural continuity to a society traumatised by war. When Dodson travelled to Onitsha in 1972 to study the postwar pamphlet industry for his doctoral dissertation, he found a vibrant, resurgent literary scene in which new entrepreneurs sought to transcend the impact of war.

Postwar market literature drew from and expanded the bestselling genres of the previous two decades. As in the 1950s and 1960s, pamphleteers showed a great talent for reproducing the most popular local narrative templates. New editions of classics such as *Veronica My Daughter* and *How to Know When a Girl Loves You or Hates You* were published alongside compilations of wartime speeches extracted from the newspapers, including *Short History and Speeches of Azikiwe, Shagari, Aminu Kano, Waziri, Awolowo* (Anorue n.dat.[a]) and *Important Records on Nigeria Civil War from 1966–1970* (Abiakam 1972), which used newspaper reports to compile a chronology of the political events leading up to the outbreak of hostilities and carefully listed, without taking sides, the postwar line-up of Nigerian national leaders.[5] The tradition of eulogistic political plays continued with the publication of Iguh's *The Struggles and Trial of Jomo Kenyatta* (Iguh 1971) and *The Complete Life Story and Death of Dr. Nkrumah (History and Drama)* (1972), which mixed transcripts of speeches with imaginary scenes featuring global figureheads in the manner of the Lumumba plays. As of old, new pamphleteers put their own names to old works and augmented publications whose rights they had acquired, sprucing up the covers and adjusting the dates of letters to give new readers the impression of novelty and currency. 'New favourites' were produced on familiar topics, such as *Money is Good But Hard to Get: Old Money and New Money, Which is the Best?* by Emman Eleonu (c.1972), which is an abridged version of Okenwa Olisah's *Money Hard to Get But Easy to Spend* (c.1965). Similarly, *How to Know When a Girl Loves You or Hates You*, by S. Eze, was re-published in 1970, declaring itself an 'enlarged and corrected' version of the original under the editorial hand of J. C. Anorue.

A handful of Onitsha publishers dominated the book market after the war. In particular, Anorue, who also used the names J. Abiakam and Rufus Okonkwo, republished a large number of old titles in the 1970s, helping to revivify the shattered book industry (Dodson 1974: 158). These pamphleteers entered the postwar market with a combative style of publishing in which they aggressively asserted ownership of their lists with warnings to rivals against all forms of

5   Eleni Coundouriotis suggests that eastern Nigerian pamphleteers may have played a greater role in postwar reconciliation than elite novelists writing about the Civil War: the latter often continued to describe a 'Biafran' consciousness in their work (Personal communication, 12 February 2023).

borrowing: 'Mr. J. C. Anorue is the only person who has the right to print and sell the copies of this booklet', reads a 'Public Notice' at the start of the new edition of the classic, *Beware of Harlots and Many Friends*: 'J. O. Nnadozie the Former Publisher has entirely sold the Manuscript to Mr. J. C. Anorue on 14th May 1970' (n.pag.). Others like Njoku, the dynamic 1960s entrepreneur who purchased the rights to bestsellers from authors such as Okenwa Olisah in the early 1960s, stepped away from the industry and sold their lists to new publishers. 'Public notice: Mr N. O. Njoku the Former publisher of this booklet has entirely sold the copyright to Mr J. C. Anorue', ran the preface to the new edition of Olisah's *Life Turns Man Up and Down* in which the author's name is removed from the cover: 'Therefore Mr J. C. Anorue is the only person who has the right to print and sell the copies of this booklet. Any reproduction in part or whole without permission from him is entirely prohibited' (Anon c.1970: n.pag.).

Locally published dramas continued to use the 'Veronica' blueprint invented by Ogali in the mid-1950s, in which obstructionist fathers and chiefs speak pidgin English to signify their ignorance, while the progressive modernity of young lovers is conveyed through their ability to speak good English. As in the 1950s, 'high' language in these plays is confined to bombastic, over-educated youths who provide comic relief by spouting polysyllabic nonsense that neither side understands.

If postwar drama maintained continuities with the 1950s, however, the genre of the romantic novel underwent a significant transformation from the styles described in Chapter 6. In the new romances of the postwar period, the dense, quotation-rich English prose of the previous half-century – where citational discourse took priority over naturalistic modes of description – is gone. In the process, Nigerian romances lost much of their English literary coating.

As previous chapters have argued, 'high' English prose was always subject to deliberation, scrutiny and critique in local romances, often shown to obstruct rather than facilitate loving relationships and repeatedly debunked by wise local girls. However, in the new local fiction of the early 1970s, creative writers incorporated fresh styles of representation into familiar local genres and started to detach themselves from the citational practices of previous generations. For scholars who witnessed this transformation, such as Emmanuel Obiechina and Ernest Emenyonu, the explanation was simple: escapist genres and flowery forms of English writing failed to adequately reflect a society recovering from war (Obiechina 1973, Emenyonu 1973). Other critics seemed relieved at the transition of English-language fiction away from derivative prose, albeit laced with nostalgia for authors' lost innocence.

While it would be reductive to understand these changes exclusively in relation to the cultural impact of the Civil War on local intellectuals, one of the best examples of the stylistic shifts described above can be found in a war novel composed in the immediate postwar period. In Osakwe's and Odogwu's *Love in a Bunker* (c.1972), the trauma of the recent war is rendered as a love story whose setting is anything but timeless. Lovelorn African aristocrats in manorhouse libraries overlooking rose gardens and lawns are replaced, in this novel, by a setting where love between a local girl and a soldier occurs in the thick of food shortages, the destruction of towns and villages, and sexual violence and starvation as weapons of war. This is a novel produced 'out of an experience red-hot with the memories and physical wounds of a most excruciating civil war' (Obiechina 1971: vi). The preface to the novel states that the story will focus on 'the social conditions and feelings of some people in the war-torn area at the time' (Nwanekezi c.1972: n.pag.). Local experiences of the recent war interrupt the transnational, century hopping English style of the prewar romances, replacing it with references to inflated prices, smuggling across federal lines, starvation, the military presence and the necessity of sex work by women keen to secure money and goods.

The wartime setting has another equally striking narrative consequence: the progressive modernity represented by Onitsha heroines and their educated boyfriends – for whom arranged marriages to illiterate old men for the enrichment of the patrilineage are displaced by marriages for love with the consent and agency of both parties – is destabilised in favour of other moral norms made necessary by war conditions. *Love in a Bunker* reactivates the most popular local plot template: in it, a beautiful girl rejects the polygynous, illiterate old chief chosen by her father, who is greedy for brideprice and political connections, in favour of the handsome man of her choosing. 'What will money matter when I am to marry a man who loves me and whom I love' (20), the 'Veronica' character, Nkechi, tells her sympathetic mother, who embodies the progressive mothers to be found in local dramas and asserts what the 1950s plays insisted – in an adoption of phrasing from the Universal Declaration of Human Rights that was regularly quoted in 1950s newspapers – was girls' 'fundamental human right' to choose their own marriage partners against the wishes of their fathers (Olisah 1961a: 19). Duplicating Veronica's mother in Ogali's original play, and the countless mothers who followed in her shoes, Mrs Ike unconditionally supports her daughter and expresses repulsion toward the dirty 'heathen' chief (Osakwe and Odogwu c.1972: 20, 22).

Wartime conditions test the limits of the prewar popular romance, however, showing its inherent incapacity to describe the choices facing African women in conditions of political crisis. As the rebellious heroine states towards the end of *Love in a Bunker*, when she witnesses the wartime conditions at home, 'hunger [was] written all over her mother's face and had there been no Kenzo, she would have decided to marry Chief Ogbuefi Okonji so that she could feed both her mother and grandmother properly' (59). When the handsome soldier, Kenzo, is killed in battle shortly after, the heroine goes ahead and marries the illiterate old chief. Thus is Veronica – the feisty, resilient 'modern girl' of peacetime romances – broken by the crisis time of war.

The exigencies of war introduce other major obstacles to this 'Veronica's' happily ever after ending. In an internal monologue in the opening pages, readers find out that the soldier Nkechi has 'fallen in love with … at first sight' and wishes to marry happens to be already married to a woman in another town (8). As a handsome stranger, the soldier problematises the 'Veronica' template and opens it up to other local narrative threads. The soldier personifies the fickle boyfriend from 1960s epistolary romances who flitted from girl to girl promising marriage to each in suspiciously flowery English (see chapter 6). Sergeant Kenzo has no intention of marrying 'this small girl' (42). All his promises of wedlock are 'just a ruse to achieve what he had just achieved', he jokes to himself while rolling with the love-struck heroine in his bunker (Ibid.). Lurking behind this figure, of course, is the 'complete gentleman' of folktales and novels, the handsome outsider who exploits his status as a man whose background cannot be discovered in order to deceive local women into marriage.

Love in a Bunker critiques the characters in prewar romances in other ways. When placed in wartime conditions, the educated modernity of the girl and her mother – both of whom oppose established male authority figures such as husbands, fathers and chiefs in prewar literature – is shown to throw domestic patriarchy into crisis and disrupt men's social control of women. In an animated scene in the opening pages, Nkechi's mother eavesdrops on an all-male gathering convened to hand over the girl to the chief and then rushes away to urge her daughter to flee from home and take refuge in her maternal grandmother's house. In response, Nkechi's father offers a lengthy condemnation of local women for copying the ways of white women (25). The village chief imposes a public punishment on Mrs Ike for disobedience to her husband: in order to re-learn her place in the marriage, she must kneel and ask for her husband's forgiveness in front of all the men, cook food for them and serve drinks submissively (28, 30). The overarching lesson, as one character puts it in this extended scene of patriarchal reassertion, is 'if we don't handle these women this way we will become their toilet papers' (29).

Love in a Bunker is a dystopian masculinist novel, set one year into the war at a time when 'young men were scarce on the streets except those in Khaki. It was an era of female supremacy … They were the bread-winners, they were the farmers … Many women took advantage of this situation to boss their husbands' (8). Throughout the novel, Mrs Ike's domestic coup is enacted through her encouragement of Nkechi's love affair with the soldier against Mr Ike's wishes. In this way, the authors revise the progressive mother figures of prewar romances who facilitate the conjugal union of young lovers. The war exacerbates these domestic conflicts by removing men from the home and giving women free rein. When Nkechi's father leaves on a lengthy trading mission in an effort to bypass the federal government's blockades against Biafra, his wife takes total control of the household. The novel's central focus is this 'abomination' – as the jilted chief terms it – of women's power (28).

The political is the personal, not the other way around: women exploit wartime conditions to seize domestic power from their husbands. Federal forces do not feature in this fiction. The local romance is not deployed to symbolise national reunification or a rehumanisation of the Nigerian 'enemy'. The romantic entanglements in Onitsha war novels occur between Igbo girls and Biafran soldiers. The primary conflict is shown to be elsewhere, between men and women, represented in the war of Mr Ike and the jilted chief, on one side, over and against Nkechi and her mother on the other side. Put another way, conflict and violence at the national level open up power struggles at the domestic level. Osakwe and Odogwu make these parallels explicit by juxtaposing descriptions of the head injuries sustained by Kenzo in the battlefield, blow by blow, with an account of Mr Ike caning his wife for allowing Nkechi to abscond from her forced marriage to the chief. In this vivid scene of domestic abuse, parallelled by the enemies the battlefield, Mr Ike continues to beat her even after she appears to be dead (36). Set side by side, the national war and the domestic gender war reflect on the violent nature of shifts in power. In rendering the two wars comparable, the novel participates in the process of postwar reconciliation as Biafra is reabsorbed into the federation. As an illegitimate 'boss,' Mrs Ike is on the receiving end of extreme forms of discipline and correction from men asserting their authority. Likewise, 'a period of serious and heavy battle' results in head injuries and near death for the Sergeant Kenzo, who is killed (34–6, 38). The novel by no means offers a pro-federal reading of the war, but these parallels between women and Biafra restore patriarchy at the domestic and national level with the killing of the married soldier who seduced a girl away from her father's chosen marriage partner. The 'happily ever after' of this novel is Nkechi's marriage to the illiterate chief.

Love in a Bunker is riddled with ambiguities that mark it out from the prewar romance tradition where Christianised and educated – 'modern' and 'progressive' – youths win the battle of ideas against outmoded patriarchs. Yet in spite of its masculinist posturing and scenes of extreme violence against women, the novel has dialogical elements and is subject to the same complications to its gender ideology as the sexually violent material discussed in Chapter 7. Osakwe and Odogwu problematise both sides of the debate about women's rights before and during marriage. In spite of the collective male approval of Mrs Ike's public apology, for example, Mr Ike is accused of 'warmongering' by male elders in his family, and is abandoned by them for the ferocity of his response to his wife's disobedience (47). Meanwhile, wartime conditions complicate the morality of Sergeant Kenzo's extra-marital affair with Nkechi. In spite of the deceitful behaviour that marks him out as a rogue, Kenzo helps to support Nkechi and her mother after Mr Ike and the village chief have banished them from town, saving their lives with money and food supplies. The 'Veronica' love story is thus complicated by the war: past parables dissolve into uncertainty.

Love in a Bunker contains no authorial interruptions, no love letters and no explicit moral commentaries by an omniscient narrator. The novelist 'trusts the tale' to deliver its moral, showing confidence in postwar readers' ability to interpret local narratives after many decades of training in newsprint aesthetics. As with the Romantic poets and popular romances incorporated into English-language literatures in previous decades, however, the realist turn must be historicised and contextualised for its local specificity to be appreciated. Crucially, verisimilitude is not achieved through authors' attention to the unique personalities of characters using a European tradition of realist portraiture. Nigerian war fiction achieves its reality effect through the naturalistic portrayal of places rather than people. Four decades after Thomas's meticulous attention to urban cultural history and production of a new kind of moral realism – through references to what one correspondent described as 'names, neighbourhoods, times and all kinds of other things' such as popular songs, well-known nicknames and historical proverbs (Barber 2012: 60) – these war romances in English introduce their own innovative form of literary realism into Nigerian print culture.

For the first time in local anglophone literary production, fictional characters proceed through the narrative unaccompanied by moralising authorial chaperones. Formulaic, familiar character types and plots from the prewar era are inserted into realistically portrayed locales marked by war. Classic, iconic, popular and familiar literary character types like the 'harlot' and the 'illiterate chief' are pressed into well-known settings in this literature. The assertive Veronicas and the coquettish, sensational Stellas and Cordelias of prewar market literature are suspended by the war, replaced with local beauties caught up in the struggle to survive scarcity and starvation. The necessities of survival inject realism into the prewar romance. *Love in a Bunker* produces a new, local form of realist writing in which hitherto invisible backgrounds are thrust into the foreground. The novel opens with a stark description situated in calendrical time: 'the Guards strike Force of the 12th commando Division arrived Nnokwa on a sunny November afternoon in 1968' (3). In turning away from English romantic discourse and literary quotations in order to describe wartime conditions, Osakwe and Odogwu nudge local English-language creativity toward mimetic representation. This is not simply an adoption of a transnational genre with European origins, however: in their engagement with local prewar character types and the familiar 'Veronica' plot, the authors continue the parabolic literary tradition of previous decades and produce a local form of realism in which environments and social settings are intricately described but characters remain moralistic types, resounding with familiarity and packed with lessons for readers. In a similar manner to Thomas's epistolary narrative, where the iconic prostitute describes the songs and popular memories of Lagos so accurately as to appear to mingle with readers in the empirical world, Onitsha war novels are pervaded by realist specificity without an interfering narrator. Deploying realism for the settings and parabolism for characters, local novelists in the early 1970s honed literary forms and styles that remained influential well into the 1980s and 1990s. As Shakespeare C. N. Nwachukwu's adopted forename makes clear, however, they did not dispense altogether with English literary influences.

At the end of the conflict, Onitsha pamphleteers responded to the bloody landscape of Biafra in typically innovative ways, rethinking popular character types and plot lines from the past and using fiction to reflect on the region's recent history. The heroes and heroines of the prewar era, idealised and universalised through high romantic quotations, are not abandoned. They are, however, brought down to earth in this literature, immersed in realistic wartime settings and placed in conditions of starvation and crisis in a war that demanded new aesthetic priorities from authors and necessitated a depiction of the contexts in which characters' decisions, actions and relationships took place. Finally, perhaps one might say that male authors had caught up with their own female characters, discussed in Chapter 5, who warned young lovers to 'forget such charming words like: ever yours darling; with love darling' in favour of more pragmatic goals (Obioha c.1962: 42).

Conclusion: Local Aesthetics

> The general mode for the postcolonial is citation, reinscription, rerouting the historical.
> (Gayatri Chakravorty Spivak, cited in Gikandi 2012: 309)

> Black counter-historical projects ... have never been able to install themselves as history, but rather are insurgent, disruptive narratives that are marginalized and derailed before they ever gain a footing.
> (Saidiya Hartman, cited in McCorkle 2020: 132)

> For many people caught in the vortex of colonialism and what comes after, the main indexes of time are the contingent, the ephemeral, the fugitive, and the fortuitous.
> (Achille Mbembe, cited in Daly 2020: 6)

In an article published in *The New York Times* in 2014, the creative writer and journalist Adaobi Tricia Nwaubani highlighted the centripetal power of Western literary markets and their distorting effect on local literary cultures. 'Some of the greatest African writers of my generation may never be discovered', she wrote, 'either because they will not reach across the Atlantic Ocean to attract the attention of an agent or publisher, or because they have not yet mastered the art of deciphering Western tastes' (*NYT* 28 November 2014). As Nwaubani's ironic tone indicates, the celebration of African literary 'discoveries' in the West contributes to the naturalisation of uneven global economic and cultural power relations: the identification of greatness by Western literary agents and publishers propagates Eurocentric categories of discernment circulating around literary markets in the Global North. However, she also indicates that an abundance of great literary works circulates locally outside Western centres of taste and recognition.

This book has sought to show how anglophone literary tastes were negotiated in colonial West Africa within local print cultures that occupied distinctive times, political spaces, literary logics and relationships with international English-language genres. Literary tastes in West Africa were shaped by educated elites throughout the colonial period in the context of British colonial power. Led by educated local intellectuals for whom the printing press provided an ideal vehicle for the expression of individual and collective opinions, newsprint writing involved agreements and disagreements within and between diverse publics, the exercise of cultural power, persuasion and exclusion as well as public displays of rules about what readers ought or ought not to derive from print. As I hope to have shown, studying these past literary processes yields fascinating details about the negotiation of local aesthetic principles as part of new class formations in the colonial and immediate postcolonial periods.

The creative writing discussed in this book supports arguments for a reconceptualisation of the category of the local in literary histories of the Global South. Without careful attention to local aesthetic and political concerns, it would be easy to miss the ways in which West African intellectuals and creative writers in the early twentieth century positioned themselves and their readers, not as marginal to world affairs, nor as centrally involved in them, but as balanced external critics of happenings in Africa, Europe and America and producers of their own literary conventions. Theirs was a comparative, counter-historical consciousness: as Ali pointed out continuously in the Lagos *Comet* in the 1930s, '"civilization" is a purely relative term' (*Comet* 4 January 1936: 6). Promoting 'intelligent borrowing' from Europe and Asia, and echoing the literary cosmopolitanism of earlier pan-Africanist intellectuals, Ali and his contributors encouraged readers to think in broad terms about the political and cultural formations that might replace imperialism (*Comet* 7 September 1935: 18).[1] As interpreters of events in Europe, West African intellectuals used printed English to assert egalitarian principles of African self-determination and non-alignment in direct response to colonial and Cold War interventions on the continent. In so doing, they problematised Eurocentric views of the world, encouraged local readers to become critically involved in the printed materials circulating around their communities and connected readers with international discourses about anticolonial nationalism, antiracism, romantic love, humanism and human rights.

While local elites and literary tastes changed over time, one factor was constant in the first half of the twentieth century: with the exception of a handful of highly educated women, anglophone print cultures were dominated by men. Taking the form of grammatically correct literary gentlemen such as 'Dick Carnis' (Chapter 1), 'Mr. Ralphsco' (Chapter 5) and upper-class romantic bachelors like Claudius Opuene in the library of his mansion (Chapter 6), local newsprint writings were packed with men who quoted and borrowed from globally circulating English literatures. Some of these repetitions fit so badly

---

[1] For many local intellectuals, E. W. Blyden was the exemplar of comparative cross-cultural thinking. Blyden believed 'that the African should assimilate the European cultures … but all these acquisitions should, by a process of analysis and synthesis, be investigated and examined and their counterparts in the African race cultures should be strengthened in the race' (*Comet* 22 June 1935: 18). See also Nwangoro on Blyden (*Comet* 7 September 1935: 18).

into their West African settings that they appear to be tragic or comic failures rather than strategic engagements with colonial masculinity, highlighting the impossibility of West African authors' aspirations to emulate, or come after, the English literature that fills their pages. Seen in this way, many of the authors and fictional characters discussed in this book perform the imaginative failure of a future-oriented project of gendered self-definition and liberation in West Africa, revealing the flaws of choosing English literature as a vehicle of creative expression in colonial contexts. All of these 'anglo-' men – fictional and real – were inspired by English literature, but, if viewed chronologically in relation to their literary models, were doomed to fail in their 'counter-historical project [to…] install themselves as history' (Hartman cited in McCorkle 2020: 132).

Nevertheless, writers used the printed page to ventriloquise across race, gender, generation, and other core colonial subject-positions, often under pseudonyms, keeping open a diversity of possibilities for authorship and attribution (see Newell 2013). They imaginatively crossed in and out of the racial, class and gender identities under which they were marked as colonial subjects, expressing opinions from a mobile and transcendental – because printed – subjectivity. The uniform appearance of print on the page seemed to make possible an unbinding of subjectivities, giving writers platforms to deconstruct local and colonial hierarchies and to play with English literary forms. For local intellectuals, newsprint subversively enabled a pluralisation of identity in colonial contexts where writers often lacked social and political power and were fixed according to racial categories.

The colonial-era writers and reading publics analysed in this book did not simply exist, independent and ready made, awaiting the arrival of publishers and texts. Nor, as Chapter 6 explains, did they emerge organically out of local oral cultures, which were often their counterpoints in terms of gender and power. The literatures and readerships described in this book need to be visualised as uneven and plural rather than singular. Local readers who consumed printed mass media in the colonial period were anything but coherent entities with interpretive codes gleaned from shared cultural influences or common educational backgrounds in the colonial school system. The fact that so much editorial labour and commentary were involved in encouraging the activity of literary criticism among readers from the 1880s onward shows how readerships had to be actively produced and renewed on a continuous basis in newsprint cultures, attracted with promises of currency and relevance (see Barber 2007). When authors quoted freely from globally circulating English literature and debated the rules of reading and writing in newspapers and pamphlets, they absorbed English-language texts into their own print cultures and attempted to replace existing gatekeepers of culture and taste. Studying such works helps to make visible acts of resistance, political critiques, the articulation of literary tastes and the presence of readerships that have hitherto largely been omitted from the consideration of anglophone world literatures.

The poet Derek Walcott famously wrote, in response to the stultifying omnipresence of slave history in Caribbean consciousness, 'what has become necessary is imagination, imagination as necessity, as invention' (Walcott [1974] 1993: 53). Similarly, for the local intellectuals studied in this book, the creative imagination had the potential to provide a space of critical freedom for those entangled in colonial histories. For men who had passed through colonial and mission school systems, and who identified as readers and writers of English-language texts, the creative imagination could be harnessed to newsprint to reshape the ways recent history was understood and offer alternative interpretations of current affairs. As such, newsprint creativity and print ephemera merit our attention as forms of understanding and producing history.

Newsprint creativity was historically productive in numerous ways, shaping how readers imagined subjectivity and society, influencing their interpretations of political crises and helping them to imagine futures for themselves. In an understudied area of literary history touched on in this book and meriting further study, local authors recognised the capacity of print to represent time itself. As Chapter 4 suggested, the 'experience' offered on the pages of printed texts would, writers promised, pre-empt readers' futures, forewarn them of obstacles and, with careful study, give them the power to recognise and evaluate events that had not yet occurred in their lives. These locally formulated temporalities infused genres such as epistolary romances and political dramas, and contributed to the formation of genres that cannot be described using European categories. Defined as a mode of historical thinking, newsprint creativity helps us to appreciate the work of writers for whom print enabled the articulation of topics and temporalities that attracted the attention, to use Nwaubani's terms, of local rather than Western literary gatekeepers and only 'reach[ed] across the Atlantic Ocean' to borrow resources for local readerships. These English-language literatures were not cut off from the global cultural flows that helped to produce them, but, as this book has suggested, their conditions of production, circulation and consumption during the decades of colonialism were markedly different from those for transnational literatures published in the Global North and disseminated through international circuits.

A reorientation of linear conceptualisations of African literary history may be required to appreciate the histories contained in West Africa's newsprint archives. The literatures at the heart of this book refused to be left behind or superseded by other texts. All of the material considered herein was produced by dominant or aspiring elites for whom locally published literature in English was intimately connected to anglophone literary cultures elsewhere. Authors flattened cultural differences and insisted on the global transferability of printed modes of communication. Through quotation, juxtaposition, repetition and assemblage, as well as through their individual visions, writers shaped genres and plots that attracted large readerships.

The techniques of quotation and repetition to be found in newsprint literatures exemplify the erasure of historicity that occurs in the time of 'post'. Authors complicated temporal models of repetition as 'coming after' in colonial contexts. In local newsprint literatures, one finds synchronicities, juxtapositions, doublings, quotations and repetitions rather than before-and-after lineages as authors replaced British colonial mythologies about the cultural superiority of Europeans – including their supposedly advanced stage of civilisation and right to dictate African endpoints – with alternative temporalities. In these literatures, to adopt Gayatri Chakrovorty Spivak's terms from the epigraph to this chapter, 'citation' and 'reinscription' were used to re-route linear colonial timelines – the chrono-logics – through which before and after, source and copy, original and repetition and success and failure were fixed in colonial society.

When nineteenth-century British letters are cited in texts from the new republic of Nigeria via texts from the new republic of India, themselves reproduced from texts from the new republic of America, as discussed in Chapter 5, local expressive cultures come into visibility that bear little resemblance to Eurocentric notions of literary originality, (post)colonial models of 'writing back' to the centre, or world literary models of centre and periphery. Such techniques invite a questioning of chronological frameworks for understanding postcolonial print cultures in order to make space for the contributions of literary producers who localised global aesthetic movements and stripped them of linearity even while being inspired by earlier models of their forms. Emily Hyde puts the problem succinctly in her study of the Guyanese artist and intellectual, Denis Williams, who helped to shape international Modernist art and literature from Nigeria in the 1960s: linear understandings of Modernism were a source of anxiety to Williams, Hyde points out, precisely because they positioned him permanently behind the West, a problem he resolved intellectually by cultivating 'skepticism about academic disciplines because of their grounding in the colonial logic of historicism' (2023: 238).

In thinking beyond their locations within specific histories and places, and asserting intellectual connections with the entire English-speaking world, the West African writers studied in this book postulated what Said describes, in his reflections on travelling theory, as 'intellectual, and perhaps moral, community of a remarkable kind, *affiliation* in the deepest and most interesting sense of the word' (Said 2000: 450; emphasis added). The gestures of global affiliation and critique to be found through the practices of citation and repetition in West African newsprint cultures were properly post-colonial: writing in English modelled a cosmopolitan vision of a world where writers and readers moved transnationally through space in print while remaining inextricable from their colonial locations. Such notions of print, in which the empirical, the critical and the visionary combine side by side, where neither the global nor the local constitute the starting-point, offer fresh ways to think about (post)colonial and decolonial intellectual networks in the twentieth century.

At present, as scholars in the arts and humanities work to retrieve African epistemologies as part of the task of (re)writing Black history in what Hartman calls 'Black counter-historical projects', the vast, neglected archive of locally produced African literatures demands to be included alongside the outputs of transnational intellectuals in the twentieth century. If postcolonial experiences of time involve exclusion, postponement and interruption, as forcefully emphasised in the epigraphs to this chapter, then the local intellectuals examined in this book experienced writing and print as positive spaces of participation, emancipation and empowerment.

Whether in British West Africa or other (post)colonial locations, locally published literatures provide an archive in which aesthetic debates and epistemologies can be set against the frameworks that have come to dominate world literary studies in the twentieth century. The questions they raise about feelings, relationships, national identities, history, politics and the future overlap with, but do not duplicate, the problems posed by transnational postcolonial authors published in the Global North in the colonial and Cold War eras.

Ephemera is insufficiently complex as a category to describe literary cultures that, as their producers reiterate, contain material that was deemed to be 'above the ordinary' rather than simply a product of it (Okeanu 1960: ii). This reading matter was global in its influences but local in its production and circulation: to describe it as 'ephemeral' is to impose a temporality that did not necessarily apply at the time. By definition, 'ephemera' is so common as to be deemed unworthy of collection, and so unremarkable as to fail to earn a second glance, signifying matter that is intended to be disposable. However, in the print cultures studied here, there was no expectation that newsprint materials should be thrown away after use. As one contented letter-writer in the mid-1930s commented with anti-ephemeral conviction in a letter to Ali, 'The "Comet" is not a newspaper merely to be read, and thrown aside or passed for parcelling articles, but one to be read, bound and kept for the coming posterity to enjoy' (1 September 1934: 1; see also 8 February 1936 and 8 August, 1936).[2] This was a sentiment repeated across

---

[2] West African readers amassed substantial collections of back issues of newspapers, and often demanded that editors provide binding services for the storage of their unwieldy stacks in their personal libraries. A letter published in the *Comet* in February 1938 highlighted the difficulties faced by readers who struggled to find their own forms of cataloguing and preservation for their favourite items: 'Sir – In each number of your weekly paper as well as in the *Lagos Daily News*, I find one or two interesting articles and paragraphs which I cut out for future reference. I have these catalogued under different headings, but, alas! I have yet to find the perfect scrapbook. I would be grateful for

the West African newspaper archive in the first half of the twentieth century, demanding that later scholars query the labelling of newsprint as disposable.

Read on their own terms, the local literatures considered in this book were anti-ephemeral rather than ephemeral: the manner in which creative writers used newsprint to produce parables, archetypes, moral universals and lessons about human behaviour gave an air of immutability to their fictional characters and plots. Whether through warnings about the contractual implications of love letters or invocations of the ghost of Patrice Lumumba, local literatures contributed to posterity, promising readers up-to-the-minute material where moral truths – deeper realities – could be extracted from readers' life experiences and endowed with permanence. Authors promised that through the wisdom absorbed by reading printed material, a person could transcend their difficulties and gain understandings of other people's behaviour for all time.

In one crucial respect, however, the literatures described in this book can be regarded as ephemeral. Comprising matter that does not matter later on, ephemera is marked by forgetting and erasure, describing texts that do not appear on the horizons of later cultural and literary scholars as they sweep the past for significance. Local in their specificity and plural in their forms, the texts considered in this book capture the everyday temporalities of local cultures within and alongside the political crises and conflicts that shaped postcolonial states. Faced with their medley of styles and genres, later scholars tend to label these literatures as emergent, nascent, amateur and derivative, spaces of experimentation in which future genres were conceived rather than literary texts in their own right. An overemphasis on the experimental or emergent status of local literatures in relation to later writing, however, risks depleting their status as substantial textual commodities and missing (or dismissing) their aesthetic integrity, imposing a future on them rather than appreciating their experimental – and indeed emergent – relationships with present and past literatures.

Newsprint literatures in British West Africa adhered to aesthetic principles that were shaped over decades of local literary production and differ from what is recognised as originality in mainstream European literary culture. Ranging from the 'pleasure of influence' described in Chapter 1 to the careful delineation of rules for good copying in 1960s epistolary pamphlets, the art of quotation, as a locally recognised form of repetition, took the place of *mimesis* as a core aesthetic principle in much local creative writing. Western literary genealogies, such as the division of Modernism from realism, or the emergence of the romance from the epic, are inadequate to describe these distinctive modes of representation and the trajectories they enabled. At the very least, the local creative practices described in this book do not illustrate the inevitable 'global

---

suggestions from your readers as to how to house paper cuttings' (*Comet* 12 February 1938: 2).

triumph of neoliberal capitalism' that gives many contemporary world literature scholars the 'world' with which they work (Popescu 2020: 32; WReC 2015).

Rather than regarding this vast body of anglophone writing as making space for the mature African literature that came after it, we should study it for evidence of alternative literary and cultural trajectories, local ways of understanding art, time, genre and representation that are more subtle than the straight lines of capitalist globalisation and the cultural theories these spawn. To bring this literature in from the margins and make it visible within the parameters of African literary studies is to open the door to book history as it happened, allowing a consideration of moments in African literary history that did not become institutionalised in subsequent decades.

Beyond a celebration of obsolete micro literatures, however, why should we study these writings? Other than offering insights into moments of past creative practices, what is the significance of newsprint literatures by unknown and largely unremembered authors? How are these texts relevant to postcolonial anglophone literary cultures today, or to the study of contemporary African literatures?

This book has argued for an appreciation of literary texts in situ over and against the retrospective application of genealogies and genres. In thousands of critically unmarked (by later scholars) creative writings published in West African newspapers and pamphlets, one can find textual moments that might or might not form genres, and trajectories that might or might not form traditions. Outside current scholarly tastes and academic frameworks of recognition, these archives of literary experiments offer productive comparisons with later literary cultures as well as connections with local literatures elsewhere.

If contemporary literary historians can appreciate the specificity of past creativities and consider what local genres contributed to posterity according to the texts' own logics, then it may become possible to identify alternative – more aesthetically localised and accurate – genealogies for contemporary African literatures in English. An indicative example of these local genealogies can be found in the *Comet* in the mid-1930s. In his regular column, 'About It and About', the eastern Nigerian writer S. O. Nwangoro addressed general moral topics such as envy and good citizenship, often in the form of short stories in which readers were invited to critically intervene at the end.[3] One such story, published in the Christmas 1935 issue of the *Comet*, features a wrestler named Okereke, 'whose back had never been known to touch the ground', and whose masculinity (and marriage prospects) are tested in a championship during the New Yam Festival, where different villages come together for music, feasting and

---

[3] Nwangoro also contributed to the *Daily Service* in the early 1940s. He was trained as a teacher at the Hope-Waddell Training Institution, Calabar, from where he witnessed the outbreak of the First World War (*Comet* 27 August 1938: 8). He taught for 26 years at the Baptist Academy in Lagos (*Comet* 8 April 1939: 4).

competitive sports (*Comet* Christmas Number 1935: 67–8). With its parabolic style, descriptions of wrestling, details of Igbo ceremonial apparel and use of tragic irony and quasi-anthropological explanations of traditions, Nwangoro's story anticipates Chinua Achebe's *Things Fall Apart* by more than twenty years, giving the canonical transnational novel a local literary lineage in relation to the newspaper fiction in circulation during Achebe's childhood (see Ochiagha 2015).

Nwangoro's story lacks the cultural nationalism of Achebe's novel: in a plot-twist filled with dramatic irony, just as the hero claims victory in the wrestling match, his bride-to-be is struck down with sickness because false news has reached her of Okereke's defeat. Nwangoro's contributions to the *Comet* often ended with invitations to readers to 'weigh and consider' a problem (22 April 1939: 6). True to form, this story concludes with a question: 'Did She Survive?' (*Comet* Christmas Number 1935: 68). While this interactive aesthetic would be unsatisfactory at the end of a narrative published in the Global North, in the *Comet* it exemplifies what Achebe referred to, in 'The Novelist as Teacher', as the 'complex of relationships' connecting West African authors with readers, in which authors were expected to inspire debate and correspondence about the morals of their tales ([1965] 1975). Indeed, a Ghanaian teacher whom Achebe encountered reacted with consternation to the lack of clear authorial moral direction in *No Longer at Ease*, making the 'accusation … that I had squandered a rare opportunity for education on a whimsical and frivolous exercise' by not having the protagonist overcome the obstacles and 'marry the girl he is in love with' (42).

Resituated in local newsprint cultures, it becomes possible to appreciate that Achebe's complainant was not a naïve reader wishing for moral leadership from the author, but a participant in long-established reading practices who was disappointed by Achebe's turn away from the norm. As Achebe wryly admitted, while university educated African writers wrapped themselves in European Modernist notions of authorial alienation and art for art's sake, local African readers regarded authors as teachers and moralists and expected transnational publications by African authors to comply with their aesthetic expectations (40).

Rochona Majumdar comments that all the scattered textual materials outside official, institutional archives in the first half of the twentieth century contain 'traces, in print, of cultural histories of the formation of artistic value and aesthetic judgment in a new postcolonial nation' (2023: 301). Materials such as amateur film society journals and minutes of meetings, she argues, constitute alternative archives that force a rethinking of the colonial, national and postcolonial narratives contained in the official archives (Ibid.). West African newsprint literatures are similarly vast and para-institutional to the Indian archives Majumdar describes, although it must be emphasised that from the early 1900s newspaper proprietors were required by law to lodge a copy of each issue with the colonial governor, thereby creating the newspaper archive used by contemporary scholars. Nevertheless, attention to the circulation of newsprint literature outside the school curriculum, unabsorbed into Western literary canons, helps scholars to produce fresh genealogies for postcolonial literatures.

One obvious field of contemporary literary activity connects with this para-institutional historical archive. With heterogeneous, disorderly texts that defy quantitative study, contemporary social media creativity, like the old newsprint creativity, confounds orthodox methods for literary analysis and problematises metaphors of time and space while often performing gendered power relations among other forms of struggle. The internet archive, like the newsprint archive, is a form of mass media that thrives in undisciplined spaces and oscillates between singularity and repetitious layering, and is subject to similar problems of institutional recognition as the old newsprint literatures.

In a similar manner to the newsprint cultures described in this book, online creativity involves readers as core participants in responsive textual communities. As in Onitsha, where authors were publishers, publishers were printers and printers were booksellers, in many contemporary digital networks, members 'can be writers, readers, publishers, bloggers, editors and scholars. Writers also function as readers, and readers may function as publishers. There are also scholars who are creative writers, and who also function as publishers' (Adenekan 2021: 23). Social media creativity and colonial-era newsprint cultures thus offer productive parallels: twisting and looping through expansive, uneven, unregulated literary spaces where authors are frequently anonymous, the two literary fields raise similar formal and methodological questions about how to approach texts that are historically evasive and often too plural to suit conventional genre classifications (see Bode 2019, Bosch-Santana 2015, 2018, Langmia 2016, Willems 2019).

'Compared to the curated treasure troves of our literary archives', Ainehi Edoro-Glines writes of African online creativity, 'social media might appear to be a landfill of textual trash' (2022: 523). Social media and newsprint forms of literary creativity both demand an expansion of the parameters of literary studies to accommodate genres and aesthetic values in which clocks, worlds, timelines and subjectivities are uncoupled from global centres of power while also remaining embedded in global circuits of culture shaped by colonialism and capitalism (see Bode 2019). Ephemeral and plural like colonial-era newsprint genres, social media texts produce a 'new sense of the literary' with rules and genres that may, Edoro-Glines writes, be 'untranslatable in literary terms', particularly if the 'translation' requires Eurocentric genre categories for the recognition of literary forms (2022: 524).

Any comparisons or genealogies of this kind must, however, respect core differences between these media in terms of their technologies, accessibility and dissemination. With its reliance on paper and imported heavy machinery, colonial-era printed literature differs substantially from contemporary internet creativity and gives rise to different literary forms. In particular, digital participants are not tethered to markets and booksellers like the textual communities described in this book: rather, their reading matter is often shaped by algorithms that, in turn, influence the style and tone of their responses (see Yékú, 2021). Digital readers and writers gather and disperse according to the layered temporalities of the web, disrupting categories of analysis based on social identity and challenging scholarly quests to locate authors in particular places of production.

The two archives invite juxtaposition, however, not least because the erasures of place, gender, identity and class exploited by internet users have clear precedents in African newsprint cultures. Contemporary social media scholarship can provide frameworks and methods for understanding print ephemera from the past, just as newsprint scholarship can help scholars of African internet creativity to historicise sources that often appear to defy contextualisation. Linear temporalities such as pre- to post-, and binary spaces such as centre versus periphery, or author versus reader, are too basic to accommodate the fleeting historicity and simultaneity of these creative spaces. Online identities, like local literatures, do not require the thesis of colonialism and the antithesis of anticolonialism in order to make sense, nor do they fit easily into the model of a dominant metropolitan space set over and against peripheries of cultural production in the Global South.

Similar methodological, conceptual and disciplinary questions thus arise in both fields. In both cases, traditional approaches to literary history may be too narrow for the appreciation of literary forms where fragmentation, repetition, 'accumulation and miscellany' are core components of the aesthetic, and where influences are often plural, networked and global rather than linear or binary (Edoro-Glines 2022: 523, 534, 536). As James Yékú (2021) observes, in a comment that brilliantly encapsulates the practices of repetition and quotation at the heart of this book, social media consumption often involves 'the act of self-inscription into the performance of another' (211). African social media users, like newsprint communities a century earlier, are not therefore 'local' in opposition to the global texts and genres they invoke: they are local in ways that require more complex understandings of power, emplacement and identity (see Bosch-Santana 2018).

Inspired by the question of what literary historians can *do* with all of those texts that have no obvious place in the literary and cultural logic of our hindsight, this book has been part of the larger project within postcolonial print culture scholarship to retrieve neglected texts and reconstitute them into archives, inserting local perspectives, genres and practices into the study of world literatures. Colonial-era newsprint texts and the contemporary internet forms that inherit their unruliness may be where the greatest challenges to Eurocentrism lie, including challenges to the historicism of mainstream literary studies.

Albeit with limited circulation, the newspapers and pamphlets studied in this book provided platforms for all kinds of literary activities among colonial populations. A large portion of this writing seems to be so localised in its time and place as to jam the historical radar of scholars seeking trends, movements, epochs and genres. The English writing styles and plural literary influences of the material discussed in this book perhaps lead nowhere when judged through generic classifications of realism, Modernism, postmodernism, speculative fiction or the romance. Some of the writing described in this book is so singular in form and style as to be beyond recognition in relation to established literary genres. Other material is too 'trashy' – too repetitive or generic – to seem worthy of reading as an original contribution to literary culture. Released from the need for lineages and trajectories connected to dominant Western genres and tastes, however, West African newsprint creativity becomes alive with its own logics, containing local articulations of postcolonial identities, local understandings of reading and literary taste and complex local enquiries into the concepts of time, freedom and history.

Bibliography

Primary sources

Printed Primary Sources

'A Native'. ([1886–8] 2002). *Marita: Or the Folly of Love* (ed. and intro. S. Newell) (Leiden: Brill).

Abiakam, J. C. (n.dat.). *How to Write Business Letters, Correct Agreements, Telegrams, Good Letters and Applications* (Onitsha: J. C. Brothers Bookshop).

—— (1960). *The Game of Love: A Classical Drama from West Africa* (Onitsha: J. C. Brothers Bookshop).

—— (1965a). *How to Speak in Public and Make Good Introductions. A Hand Book on Public Speaking, Introductions, Don'ts, Greetings and General Instructions for Schools and Colleges, Teachers, Traders and Workers* (Onitsha: J. C. Brothers Bookshop).

—— (1965b). *How to Speak to Girls and Win Their Love* (Onitsha: J. C. Brothers Bookshop).

—— (1972). *Important Records on Nigeria Civil War from 1966–1970* (Onitsha: J. C. Brothers).

—— (c.1972). *The Complete Life Story and Death of Dr. Nkrumah (History and Drama)* (Onitsha: J. C. Brothers Bookshop).

—— (c.1973). *Complete Speeches of Ojukwu and Some Comments of General Gowon (History and Drama)* (Onitsha: J. C. Brothers Bookshop).

—— (c.1987). *How to Speak to a Girl about Marriage* (Onitsha: J. C. Brothers Bookshop).

Achebe, Chinua. (1958). *Things Fall Apart* (London: Heinemann).

Adichie, Chimamanda Ngozi. (2006). *Half of a Yellow Sun* (New York: Vintage).

Adimora-Ezeigbo, Akachi. (2022). *A Million Bullets and a Rose* (London: Abibiman Publishing).

Ajiboye, Adegoke. (1967). *Behind the 'Iron Curtain'* (Yaba: Pacific Printers).

Albert, Miller O. (c.1962). *Saturday Night Disappointment* (Onitsha: Chinyelu Printing Press).

Amadi, Elechi. (1973). *Sunset in Biafra: A Civil War Diary* (Oxford: Heinemann).

Aniweta, Obiekwe. (1962). *The Church and Communism* (Onitsha: City Printing Press).

Anon. (1864). *Bob, The Crossing Sweeper* (London: The Book Society).

Anon. (n.dat.). *Arab-Israeli War: Israeli Brave Soldiers in Action During One of their Successful Operation Against Arab* (Onitsha: J. C. Brothers Bookshop).

Anon. (c.1970). *Life Turns Man Up and Down* (Onitsha: J. C. Brothers Bookshop).

Anorue, J. C. (n.dat.[a]). *Short History and Speeches of Azikiwe, Shagari, Aminu Kano, Waziri, Awolowo* (Onitsha: Good-Way Printing Press).
—— (n.dat.[b]). *Complete Story and Trial of Adolf Hitler (Drama)* (Onitsha: J. C. Brothers).
—— (c.1973). *How to Read and Write Welcome Addresses, Correct English Applications, Compositions, Business Letters, Speeches, Toasts and Agreements Without Mistakes* (Onitsha: J. C. Brothers).
Anyichie, Okeke, J. A. (see also Okeke, Anyichie) (c.1962). *Adventures of the Four Stars* (Onitsha: Highbred Maxwell, Students Own Bookshop).
Aririguzo, Cyril Nwakuna. (1960a). *Miss Appolo's Pride Leads Her to be Unmarried* (Onitsha: Aririguzo and Sons).
—— (1960b). *Miss Comfort's Heart Cries for Tonny's Love* (Onitsha: Aririguzo and Sons).
Aroye, Momoh and Aliche, D. Wac. (1964). *The Lady Who Robbed her Mother to Defend her Husband* (Onitsha: n.pub.).
Asuzu, Ambrose. (1960). 'Foreword', in Cletus Gibson Nwosu, *Miss Cordelia in the Romance of Destiny: The Most Sensational Love Intricacy that has Ever Happened in West Africa* (Port Harcourt: Eastern Bookshop and Unity Bookshop), n.pag.
Austen, Jane. ([1813] 1959). *Pride and Prejudice.* (London: Thames Publishing).
Azikiwe, Nnamdi. (1977). *Civil War Soliloquies: More Collection of Poems* (Nsukka: African Book Company).
Bagot, Richard. (1905). *The Passport* (London: Methuen).
Brumder, George. (1888). *The American Letter-Writer: A Complete Guide to Correspondence on All Subjects of Every-day Life* (Milwaukee: George Brumder).
Bullock, Rev. Charles. (1870). *The Sunday School Gift: A Help to Early Prayer and Praise* (London: The Church of England Sunday School Institute).
Chiazor, Benjamin O. (n.dat.) *Back to Happiness* (Onitsha: Highbred Maxwell).
—— (c.1965). *How to be the Friends of Girls* (Onitsha: Highbred Maxwell, Students Own Bookshop).
Chinaka, B. A. (n.dat.). *The Life Story of Dr. Nkrumah, Dr. Chike Obi and Other Leaders in Nigeria* (Fegge, Onitsha: Njoku and Sons Bookshop).
Clay, Bertha M. (1890). *Beyond Pardon* (London: W. Nicholson and Sons).
Cooke, Rev. Thomas (1788). *The Universal Letter-Writer; or New Art of Polite Correspondence* (London: Osborne and Griffin).
Efiom, E. I. (1968). *The Triumphal Entry into Calabar* (Calabar: Calabar Trading Co).
Egbusunwa, R. Onwuameagbu. (1964). 'Preface', in Ralph O. Ability, *A New Guide to Good English and Correct Letter Writing* (Onitsha: R. Egbusumh and Bros), n.pag.
Ekesiobi, Eddy N. (1964). *True Love: Fineboy Joe and Beautiful Cathe* (Port Harcourt: V. C. Okeanu).
Eleonu, Emman. (c.1972). *Money is Good But Hard to Get: Old Money and New Money, Which is the Best?* (Onitsha: Sage Printers).
—— (c.1976). *Teach Yourself Everyday Good English and How to Read and Write Well* (Onitsha: Gebo and Brothers).
Emecheta, Buchi. (1982). *Destination Biafra* (Portsmouth, NH: Heinemann).
Eze, S. (1970). *How to Know When a Girl Loves You or Hates You* (Onitsha: J. C. Brothers Bookshop).

Frank, Elizabeth. (1814). *Classical English Letter-Writer; or, Epistolary Selections* (London and York: Thomas Wilson and Sons).
—— (1816). *Classical English Letter-Writer; or, Epistolary Selections* (American edn) (Philadelphia: Caleb Richardson).
—— (1821). *Classical English Letter-Writer; or, Epistolary Selections* (2nd American edn, enlarged) (Philadelphia: Caleb Richardson).
'Highbred Maxwell' (pseud.). (1960). *Our Modern Ladies Characters Towards Boys. The Most Exciting Novel with Love Letters, Drama, Telegram and Campaigns of Miss Beauty to the Teacher Asking Him to Marry Her* (Onitsha: Highbred Maxwell, Students Own Bookshop).
—— (c.1962). *Guides for Engagement* (Onitsha: Highbred Maxwell, Students Own Bookshop).
Hogan, David. ([1818] 1839). *The New Universal Letter-Writer; or Complete Art of Polite Correspondence,* (Philadelphia: D. Hogan).
Iguh, Thomas Orlando. (n.dat.). *The Disappointed Lover* (Onitsha: A. Onwudiwe and Sons).
—— (1961). *The Last Days of Lumumba (the Late Lion of the Congo): A Drama* (Onitsha: A. Onwudiwe and Sons).
—— (c.1961). *Tshombe of Katanga (A Drama)* (Onitsha: A. Onwudiwe and Sons).
—— (1970). *Dr. Nkrumah in the Struggle for Freedom* (Onitsha: Highbred Maxwell).
—— (1971). *The Struggles and Trial of Jomo Kenyatta* (Onitsha: Academy Bookshops).
—— (1972). *The Complete Life Story and Death of Dr. Nkrumah (History and Drama)* (Onitsha: J. C. Brothers).
—— (1977). *The Last Days of Biafra: A Drama.* (3rd edn)(Onitsha: Good-Way Press).
Joe, F. B. (c.1965). *The General Guide in English: Complete Compositions, Business Letters and 95 Modern Questions and Answers Made Easy* (Onitsha-Fegge: United Brothers Bookshop).
Johnson, Dr Samuel. (1751). 'No.152. Criticism on Epistolary Writings', in Dr Samuel Johnson, *The Rambler: Vol. III* (London: C. Cooke), 60–3.
Joyce, James. ([1918–20] 1997). *Ulysses.* (Dublin: Lilliput Press).
Kamalu, Sigis. (1960). *The Surprise Packet* (Port Harcourt: Goodwill Press).
Madu, Nathaniel O. (n.dat.). *Miss Rosy in the Romance of True Love* (Onitsha: A. Onwudiwe and Sons).
Millin, Sarah Gertrude. (1924). *God's Stepchildren* (New York: Boni and Liveright).
'Moneyhard' (pseud. C. N. Onuoha; also listed as C. N. Obioha). (c.1955). *Why Harlots Hate Married Men and Love Bachelors* (Port Harcourt: C. N. Onuoha Moneyhard).
Nanni, F. C. (c.1961). *Never Lose Hope* (Onitsha: Varsity Bookshop).
Njoku, Nathan O. (n.dat.). *How to Read and Write Correct English, Better Compositions, Sentences, Proverbs, Office Routine, How to Pass Examinations and General Knowledge (For Schools and Colleges)* (Onitsha: Njoku and Sons Bookshop).
—— (1960). *How to Succeed in Life: Health, Cleanliness, Truth, Honesty, Education, Manner, Ambition and Happiness are the Key to Success* (Onitsha: Njoku and Sons Bookshop).
—— (c.1960). *How to Marry a Good Girl and Live in Peace with Her* (Onitsha: Njoku and Sons).

—— (1962a). *A Guide to Marriage* (Onitsha: Njoku and Sons Bookshop).
—— (1962b). *How to Write Better Letters, Applications, Business Letters and English Grammar* (Onitsha: Njoku and Sons).
—— (1963). *The Complete Letter Writing Made Easy for Ladies and Gentlemen: Contains Love and Engagement Letters, Business and Private Letters, Invitations, Correspondences, Applications, Telegrams, Agreements, Advertisements, Good English etc.: Try to Know How to Read and Write* (Onitsha: Njoku and Sons).
—— (1964). *How to Read and Write Correct English, Better Compositions, Sentences, Proverbs, Office Routine, How to Pass Examinations and General Knowledge* (Onitsha: Njoku and Sons).
—— (1965). *How to Write Love Letters and Romance with Your Girl Friends* (Onitsha: Njoku and Sons Bookshop).
Njoku, Nathan O. and Co. (c.1964). *The Complete Letter-Writing Made Easy for Ladies and Gentlemen: Contains Love and Engagement Letters, Business and Private letters, Invitations, Correspondences, Applications, Telegrams, Agreement, Advertisements, Good English, etc.* (Onitsha: Njoku and Sons Bookshop).
Njoku, Nathan O. and Olisah, Okenwa. (c.1961). *Beware of Women* (Onitsha: Njoku and Sons Bookshop).
Nkwoh, Marius U. E. (1961). *Cocktail Ladies* (Nsukka: University of Nsukka).
—— (1963). *The Sorrows of Man* (Enugu: Okolue's Bookshop).
Nnadozie, Joseph O. (c.1962). *Beware of Harlots and Many Friends: The World is Hard* (Onitsha: J. O. Nnadozie and Bros).
—— (c.1963). *What Women are Thinking about Men: No. 1 Bomb to Women* (Onitsha: All Star Printing Press).
Nsofor, Tony Emeka. (c.1967). *Adventure on the Niger* (ed. by D.E.K. Adjepon-Yamoah) (Onitsha: University Publishing Company).
Nwachukwu, Shakespeare C. N. (1972). *The Tragedy of Civilian Major* (Onitsha: Nwachukwu Africana Books).
Nwanekezi, M. N. (c.1972). 'Preface', in *Love in a Bunker* (Onitsha: Pacific Correspondence College Bookshop), i–ii.
Nwankwo, Mazi Raphael D. A. (1964). *The Bitterness of Politics and Awolowo's Last Appeal* (Onitsha: A. Onwudiwe and Sons).
Nwapa, Flora. (1975). *Never Again* (Enugu: Nwamife).
—— (1980). *Wives at War and Other Stories* (Enugu: Nwamife).
Nwosu, Cletus Gibson. (1960). *Miss Cordelia in the Romance of Destiny: The Most Sensational Love Intricacy that has Ever Happened in West Africa* (Port Harcourt: Eastern Bookshop and Unity Bookshop).
Obiaga, C. C. (1961). *Boys and Girls of Nowadays (Jerry and Obageli in Love)* (Onitsha: A. Onwudiwe and Sons).
Obioha, R. I. M. (n.dat.) *How to Write Best Letters, Applications and Good English* (Onitsha: Highbred Maxwell).
—— (c.1962). *How to Write Better Business Letters, Good English Applications, Telegrams and Important Invitations* (Onitsha: Highbred Maxwell).
—— (1971). *A Book for Nigerian Bachelors Guide* (Onitsha: Gebo and Brothers).
Ogali, Ogali A. (1956). *Veronica My Daughter* (Onitsha: Appolos Brothers Press).

—— ([1957] 1980a). 'Long Long Ago: A Novel', in Reinhard W. Sander and Peter K. Ayers (eds), *Veronica My Daughter and Other Onitsha Plays and Stories by Ogali Ogali* (Washington DC: Three Continents Press), 14–49.

—— ([1958] 1980b). 'Okeke the Magician', in Sander and Ayers (eds), *Veronica My Daughter and Other Onitsha Plays and Stories by Ogali Ogali* (Washington DC: Three Continents Press), 50–77.

—— ([1958] 1980c). 'Eddy the Coal-City Boy', in Sander and Ayers (eds), *Veronica My Daughter and Other Onitsha Plays and Stories by Ogali Ogali* (Washington DC: Three Continents Press), 78–102.

—— ([1961] 1980d). 'Patrice Lumumba: A Drama', in Sander and Ayers (eds), *Veronica My Daughter and Other Onitsha Plays and Stories by Ogali Ogali* (Washington DC: Three Continents Press), 219–44.

—— ([1961] 1980e). 'The Ghost of Patrice Lumumba', in Sander and Ayers (eds), *Veronica My Daughter and Other Onitsha Plays and Stories by Ogali Ogali* (Washington DC: Three Continents Press), 246–72.

Ogu, H. O. (1950). *Rose Only Loved My Money* (Aba: Treasure Press).

—— (1958). *The Love That Asks No Questions* (Aba: Ofomatas Press).

—— (1960). *Okeke and His Master's Girlfriend* (Aba: Treasure Press).

—— (c.1960.) *Jonny, The Most Worried Husband* (Aba: Treasure Press).

Oguanobi, Raph. (c.1960). *Two Friends in the Romance of Runaway Lover* (Onitsha: Obi Brothers Bookshop).

Ohaejesi, Chidi Michael N. (c.1962). *The Sweetness and Kingdom of Love: A Most Exciting Exposition of Life and General Love: Without Love what is Life?* (Onitsha: Michael Ohaejesi and Bros).

—— (1971). *Learn How to Write Good English, Better Letters, Better Compositions, Business Letters, Applications, Agreements, Telegrams, and Love Letters* (Onitsha: Imperial Trading Stores).

Ojiyi, Okwudili. (1965). *The British Political Shooting of the Nigerian Coalminers in November 18, 1949: Butchered in Cold Blood to Uphold the British Prestige in the Nigerian Colliery* (n.place: n.pub.).

Okeanu, Vincent C. (1960). 'Publisher's Announcement', in Sigis Kamalu, *The Surprise Packet* (Port Harcourt: Goodwill Press), ii–vi.

—— (1971). 'Publisher's Note', in Eddy N. Ekesiobi, *True Love: Fineboy Joe and Beautiful Cathe* (Port Harcourt: V. C. Okeanu), n.pag.

Okeke, Alexander Obiorah. (1964). *I'll Rather Break My Sword and Die: A Drama* (Onitsha: Highbred Maxwell).

Okeke, Godfrey C. (1968). *The Biafra-Nigeria War – A Human Tragedy* (London: [The Author]).

Okonkwo, Rufus. (c.1961). *No Money, Much Expenses, Enemies and Bad Friends Kill a Man (The Way to Avoid Poverty)* (Onitsha: J. C. Brothers Bookshop).

—— (c.1963). *How to Make Friends With Girls* (Onitsha: J. C. Brothers Bookshop).

Oleyede, S. P. (c.1959). *The Trial of Hitler: A Play* (Aba: International Press).

Olisah, S. Okenwa. (n.dat.). *The World is Hard* (Onitsha: Chinyelu Printing Press).

—— (1960). *Drunkards Believe Bar is Heaven* (Onitsha: Chinyelu Printing Press).

—— (1961a). *Elizabeth My Lover: A Drama* (Onitsha: A. Onwudiwe and Sons).

—— (1961b). *The Life Story and Death of Mr. Lumumba* (Fegge, Onitsha: B. C. Okara and Sons Book-Shop).
—— (1962). *How to Write Good Letters and Applications* (Onitsha: Highbred Maxwell, Students Own Bookshop).
—— (1963a). *'My Wife': About Husband and Wife Who Hate Themselves* (Onitsha: Highbred Maxwell, Students Own Bookshop).
—— (1963b). *The Statements of Hitler Before the World War: His Last Words and Disappearance* (Onitsha: Okenwah Publications).
—— (1963c). *The Life in the Prison Yard: It is a Hard Life: The Prisoner Mr. Okorinta who Escaped from the White College Tells the Story* (Onitsha: Okenwa Olisah).
—— (c.1963). *Trust No-Body in Time Because Human Being is Trickish and Difficult* (Onitsha: Prince Madumelu).
—— (c.1964). *Life Turns Man Up and Down* (Onitsha: Njoku and Sons).
—— (c.1965). *Money Hard to Get But Easy to Spend* (Onitsha: J. O. Nnadozie).
Oluwide, Baba. (1968). *On the Current Divergencies* (Yaba, Lagos: The Spark Publications).
Onwudiegwu, J. Kenddys. (1965a). *English: The Language of the Modern World: How to Write Good Letters, Better Compositions, Agreements, Good Business Letters, Applications and Teach Your Self How to Speak and Write Good English* (Onitsha: Gebo Bros Publications).
—— (1965b). *The Miracles of Love* (Onitsha: Gebo Brothers Bookshop).
—— (1965c). *The Bitterness of Love (A Play of Love Tragedy)* (Onitsha: Gebo and Brothers).
Onwuka, Wilfred. (1965). *How to Study and Write Good Letters, Applications, Compositions, Telegrams, Agreements, Better Sentences, Important Letters, Speaking in Public, and Teach Yourself Good English* (Onitsha: Gebo Brothers Bookshop).
Osakwe, G. C. and Odogwu A. (c.1972). *Love in a Bunker* (Onitsha: Pacific Correspondence College Bookshop).
Oti, Penn C. I. (n.dat.). *£75,000 and 7 Years Imprisonment* (Onitsha: Chinyelu Printing Press).
Palgrave, Francis Turner. ([1861] 1944). *The Golden Treasury* (New York: The Modern Library).
Pearce, F. G. (1918). *The Indian Boy Scouts, and How They Can Help Motherland and Empire* (Madras: Commonweal Office).
Pitman, Sir Isaac and Sons. (1906). *Pitman's Office Desk-Book* (London: Sir Isaac Pitman and Sons).
'Ralph O. Ability' (pseud. prob. R. O. Egbusunwa). (1964). *A New Guide to Good English and Correct Letter Writing* (Onitsha: R. Egbusumh and Bros).
Raphael, Raja. (1965). *The Way to Grow Rich* (Onitsha: Gebo Brothers).
Sanusi, Tesilimy Adekunle. (c.1962). *Adventures of Wonderful Buja* (Onitsha: Union Press).
Sekyi, W. E. G. (Kobina). ([1915] 1997). *The Blinkards: A Play* (Portsmouth NH: Heinemann).
Shelley, Percy Bysshe. ([1820] 1847a). *The Poetical Works of Percy Bysshe Shelley* (London: E. Moxon).
—— ([1820] 1847b). *Prometheus Unbound* (London: C. and J. Ollier).

Shinn, Florence Scovel. (1925). *The Game of Life and How to Play It* (New York: Florence S. Shinn).
Simonton, Ida Vera. (1912). *Hell's Playground* (New York: Moffat, Yard).
'Speedy Eric' (pseud. A. N. Onwudiwe). (1963). *How to Write Love Letters, Toasts and Business Letters* (Onitsha: Membership Bookshop).
—— 1964. *How to Write Successful Letters and Applications* (Onitsha: A. Onwudiwe and Sons).
—— (c.1964). *Mabel the Sweet Honey that Poured Away* (Onitsha: Onwudiwe).
Spenser, Edmund. ([1590] 1981). *The Faerie Queene* (New Haven: Yale University Press).
Stephen, Felix N. (n.dat.[a]). *Be Careful! Salutation is Not Love* (Onitsha: Njoku and Sons Bookshop).
—— (n.dat.[b]). *How Tshombe and Mobutu Regretted After the Death of Mr. Lumumba* (Onitsha: Njoku and Sons Bookshop).
—— (n.dat.[c]). *The Sea of Life and How to Swim It (Experience in Life)* (Onitsha: n.pub.).
—— (1961). *How to Write Letters about Marriage* (Fegge, Onitsha: J. O. Nnadozie).
—— (c.1962a). *Experience In Life, Is Key To Success* (Onitsha: J. O. Nnadozie and Bros).
—— (c.1962b). *How to Play Love* (Onitsha: Njoku and Sons Bookshop).
—— (1964). *The Temple of Love* (Onitsha: B. C. Okara and Sons).
'Strong Man of the Pen' (pseud. Olisah, S. Okenwa). (c.1963). *Trust No-Body in Time Because Human Being is Trickish* (Onitsha: Prince Madumelu).
—— (c.1964). *Life Turns Man up and Down: Money and Girls Turn Man Up and Down* (Onitsha: Njoku and Sons Bookshop).
—— (1965). *Man Has No Rest in His Life: Since the World Has Broken into Pieces, Truth is Not Said Again* (Onitsha: B. C. Okara and Sons).
Stuart-Young, John Moray. (1904). *Merely a Negress* (London: John Long).
Thomas, I. B. ([1929–30] 2012). 'Life Story of Me, Ṣẹgilọla', in Karin Barber (ed.), *Print Culture and the First Yoruba Novel: I. B. Thomas's 'Life Story of Me, Ṣẹgilọla', and Other Texts* (Leiden: Brill), 77–259.
Townsend, G. F. (ed.). (1896). *The Arabian Nights' Entertainment* (London: Frederick Warne and Co).
Tutuola, Amos. (1952). *The Palm-Wine Drinkard* (London: Faber and Faber).
Umoh, James. (c.1971). *Before Darkness Falls* (n.place: n.pub.).
Uwanaka, Charles U. (1964). *Good Citizens, Good Country: A National Programme to End Bribery and Corruption* (Lagos: C. Uwanaka).
von Schmid, Johann Christoph. ([1859] 1870). *The Basket of Flowers; or, Piety and Truth Triumphant. A Tale for the Young.* G. T. Bedell (trans.) (London: Milner and Sowerby).
Walcott, Derek. (1990). *Omeros* (New York: Farrar, Straus, Giroux).
'Young Dynamic Author' (pseud. A. N. Onwudiwe). (1966). *A Dictionary of Current Affairs and Many Things Worth Knowing* (Onitsha: A. Onwudiwe and Sons).

Manuscript and archival collections

UK Public Record Office (PRO)
CO 879/62/13 – No.1. 'Governor Sir W. MacGregor to Mr Chamberlain received July 20 1900', *Lagos: Reports of Two Journeys in the Lagos Protectorate by Governor Sir William MacGregor, African (West) No.627*, Colonial Office. August 1900 (Confidential).
CO 879/112 – No.132. 'Gold Coast: The Governor to the Secretary of State.' *African No.999 Confidential: Africa, Further Correspondence January to June, 1913 Relating to Medical and Sanitary Matters in Tropical Africa.* April 14, 1913.
CO 879/112 – No.144. 'Southern Nigeria: The Governor to the Secretary of State for the Colonies, 12 August 1913 (Confidential)', *African No. 999 Confidential: Africa, Further Correspondence January to June, 1913 Relating to Medical and Sanitary Matters in Tropical Africa.* n.d. [1913].

Newspapers and periodicals

'A Banker'. (1904). 'A Shrouded World', *Gold Coast Leader,* 15 October 1904, 3.
'A Well-Wisher'. (1939). 'Vox Pop', *Comet,* 15 April 1939, 3.
'Adonis'. (1937). 'Vox Pop: Odeziaku and Prophesy', *Comet,* 27 March 1937, 2.
Advertisement. (1934). 'The Lagos Dramatic and Musical Society', *Comet,* 18 August 1934, 4.
Ajiṣafẹ, A. K. (1934). 'My Journey Account on Researches on Native Institutions and Arts', *Comet,* 20 January 1934, 9, 11.
Akpata, Akitola. (1933). 'Letter to the Editor', *Comet,* 28 October 1933, 17.
Alder, George. (1938). 'Letters: How to House Paper Cuttings?', *Comet,* 12 February 1938, 2.
Amon, E. B. (1933). 'Letter to the Editor', *Comet,* 11 November 1933, 17.
Anyiam, Fred Uzoma. (1938). 'Vox Pop: That Stuff was Mine', *Comet,* 10 December 1938, 2.
Arigbabuwo, Akobi. (1936). 'Vox Pop: Un-Edited Correspondence', *Comet,* 2 May 1936, 2.
Armah, Ayi Kwei. (1985). 'One Writer's Education', *West Africa,* 26 August 1985, 1752–3.
Asade, Omoteso. (1934). 'Letters: A Bound Volume', *Comet,* 1 September 1934, 1.
'B.B.' (1904). 'A Poor Man's Diary', *Gold Coast Leader,* 12 November 1904, Supp. I.
—— (1904). 'A Poor Man's Diary', *Gold Coast Leader,* 26 November 1904, 5.
'Benefited'. (1934). 'Letter to the Editor', *Comet,* 8 September 1934, 1.
'Candid'. (1935). 'Letters (Un-Edited Correspondence): Your Serial', *Comet* 13 July 1935, 1.
'Cuckoo V'. (1934). 'Letters to the Editor', *Comet,* 4 August 1934, 1.
da Rocha, Moses. (1933). 'Scotland and the Scots', *Comet,* Christmas Number 1933, 17–20.
Daniels, A. Y. (1936). 'Why Rave Against Great Britain', *Comet,* 30 May 1936, 13
'Dick Carnis'. (1904). 'Between Ourselves', *Gold Coast Leader,* 15 October 1904, 3.
Dosunmu-Ainnah, Adebesin. (1938). 'Too Many Cooks', *Comet,* 2 April 1938, 17.
Editor. (1902). 'Editorial', *Gold Coast Leader,* 5 July 1902, 4.

—— (1910). Editorial, *Gold Coast Leader*, 25 June 1910, 3.
—— (1930). 'Editorial', *Daily Times* (Nigeria), October 21 1930, 4.
—— (1933). 'Men and Matters: The Comet', *Comet*, 29 July 1933, 3.
—— (1933). 'Men and Matters', *Comet*, 7 October 1933, 3.
—— (1934). 'Men and Matters: The Boiling Cauldron', *Comet*, 17 March 1934, 3.
—— (1934). 'Men and Matters', *Comet*, 7 July 1934, 5, 9.
—— (1934). 'About It And About: The Blood Lust', *Comet*, 4 August 1934, 8.
—— (1934). 'Men and Matters: Lagos Dramatics', *Comet*, 18 August 1934, 5.
—— (1935). 'About It and About: India, Rule and Loyalty', *Comet*, 17 August 1935, 8.
—— (1935). 'About It And About: The Visit of the Stranger', *Comet*, 7 September 1935, 8.
—— (1936). 'About It and About: Below the Surface in Africa', *Comet*, 4 January 1936, 6.
—— (1936). 'About It and About: Retrogressive South Africa', *Comet*, 22 February 1936, 7.
—— (1936). 'About It and About: Carlyle and Shakespeare', *Comet*, 11 April 1936, 7.
—— (1936). 'Men and Matters', *Comet*, 18 July 1936, 5.
—— (1936). 'Men and Matters: "Civilization"', *Comet*, 19 September 1936, 5.
—— (1937). 'About It And About: The Untutored Savage', *Comet*, 13 February 1937, 7.
—— (1937). 'Men and Matters', *Comet*, 1 May 1937, 5.
—— (1938). 'His Excellency's Empire Day Speech at the Racecourse', *Comet*, 28 May 1938, 9.
—— (1939). 'Men and Matters: Dr. Harold Moody', *Comet*, 2 September 1939, 5.
Editor's Note. (1938). (M. W. Adimachi) 'Vox Pop: African Leaders', *Comet*, 7 May 1938, 2.
—— (1938). 'Ten Verandas by S.E.N.', *Comet*, 14 May 1938, 10.
'Growler'. (1933). 'The Era of the New Bolshevism', *Comet*, 16 December 1933, 2.
Hanfstaengl, Ernst. (1935). 'The German View: Why Can't You Understand Us?', *Comet*, 11 May 1935, 8–9, 17.
Ita, E. (1935). 'After India What Next?', *Comet*, 7 September 1935, 18.
—— (1936). 'Native Plays and Social Reconstruction Service in Africa', *Comet*, 21 November 1936, 6, 18–19.
'J.O.A.' (1937). 'Free-Lance Journalism in West Africa', *Comet*, 19 June 1937, 19.
—— (1938). 'Vox Pop: "S.E.N." vs Missions', *Comet*, 11 June 1938, 2.
'Kriticus'. (1936). 'Vox Pop: De-Bunking Mr. J. M. Stuart-Young', *Comet*, 8 February 1936, 12.
La Page, Gertrude. (1935). 'Africa's Greater Evil', *Comet*, 19 July 1935, 7.
'Lans, the African'. (1933). 'Letter to the Editor: After Many Years', 23 December 1933, 17.
'Literature'. (1938). 'Vox Pop: Thus Success Comes', 'Literature'. *Comet*, 3 December 1938, 2.
Litsey, Edwin Carlile. (1903). 'Success', *The Era* 11(1) January 1903, 24.
—— (1903). Edwin Carlile Litsey, 'Success', *Our Paper* 19 1903, 142.
—— (1903). 'Success', *The Summary* 31(995) 1903, 8.
—— (1903). 'Success', *The Saint Paul Globe*, 22 March 1903, 11.
—— (1905). 'Success', *The Fairfield Evening Journal*, 27 April 1905, 7.
—— (1905). 'Success', *Arkansas City Daily Traveler*, 6 July 1905, 7.
—— (1905). 'Success', *The Tiller and Toiler* (Kansas), 7 July 1905, 3.

'Mose of Owerri'. (1939). 'The Azure Blue', *Comet*, 11 November 1939, 15
—— (1939). 'The Mantle of the Night', *Comet*, 18 November 1939, 15.
Nwangoro, S. O. (1935). 'About It and About: Did She Survive?', *Comet*, Christmas Number 1935, 67–9.
—— (1938). 'The March of Civilization in Nigeria', *Comet*, 12 February 1938, 23.
—— (1938). 'The Gist of It: Sonian Reading Circle (1)', *Comet*, July 16 1938, 14.
—— (1939). 'The Gist of It: Mission Teacher (2)', *Comet*, 22 April 1939, 6.
Nwaubani, Adaobe Tricia. (2014). 'African Books for Western Eyes', *New York Times*, 28 November 2014. www.nytimes.com/2014/11/30/opinion/sunday/african-books-for-western-eyes.html [accessed 28 August 2022].
'Odeziaku' (pseud. J. M. Stuart-Young). (1934). 'An Epistle to Bekwai Bill's Sweetheart', *Comet*, 3 March 1934, 12.
—— (1934). 'West African Nights: The Bits I Remember', *Comet*, 20 October 1934, 11–15.
—— (1934). 'West African Nights: The Bits I Remember', *Comet*, 3 November 1934, 11–14.
—— (1935). 'West African Nights: The Bits I Remember', *Comet*, 9 February 1935, 11–12.
—— (1935). 'Black Man's Cradle', 16 March 1935, 11–14.
—— (1935). 'Black Man's Cradle', *Comet*, 11 May 1935, 11–15, 18.
—— (1935). 'Black Man's Cradle: A Romance of Nigeria', *Comet*, 17 August 1935, 12.
—— (1938). 'The Simple Life', *Comet*, 5 February 1938, 10–11, 17–18.
—— (1938). 'Sentimental Rhyming', *Comet*, 5 March 1938, 10–11, 14, 18.
—— (1938). 'Vox Pop: A Shameless Theft', *Comet*, 24 December 1938, 2.
Ogun, Gbadanosi. (1937). 'Under the Wrong Skin? J. M. Stuart-Young Interviewed', *Comet*, 9 January 1937, 10–11.
Ojo, G. O. (1938). 'The Book of the Week: *Ogboju Ọdẹ Ninu Igbo Irunmalẹ*', *Comet*, 1 October 1938, 15.
Opuiyo, S. D. (1938). 'African Authors Wanted', *Comet*, 5 February 1938, 18.
Oshilaja, I. W. (1933). 'The Printing Craft', *Comet*, Christmas Number 1933, 55.
'Rambler'. (1938). 'Vox Pop: Odeziaku and the African Manhood', 12 March 1938, 2.
Renwick, Vivian. (1936). 'Black and White—Or Brown? A Reply to Mr J. M. Stuart-Young', *Comet*, 11 January 1936, 12.
—— (1936). 'Black and White—Or Brown? A Reply to Mr J. M. Stuart-Young (Continued from Our Last)', *Comet*, 18 January 1936, 10.
Salami, B. B. (1935). 'Review: Dr. Edward Wilmot Blyden', *Comet*, 22 June 1935, 18.
Siggins, A. J. (1939). 'About It and About: Imperialism Versus Common Wealth', *Comet*, 5 August 1939, 7.
Stuart-Young, J. M. (1933). 'West African Journalism', *Comet*, 30 December 1933, 9.
—— (1934). 'Lonely Road to Home', *Comet*, 18 August 1934, 14.
—— (1934). 'Two Songs', *Comet*, 1 September 1934, 14.
—— (1935), 'Mist on the Moon', 17 August 1935, 9.
—— (1936). 'Black and White—or Brown?', *Comet*, 4 January 1936, 7.
—— (1936). 'Fools Tread In!', *Comet*, 25 January 1936, 14.
—— (1936). 'There is the Man Who Knows Not', *Comet*, 8 February 1936, 15.
—— (1936). 'Gee-Up, My Little Horse', *Comet*, 15 February 1936, 14.
—— (1936). 'Sunshine in the Garden of My Heart', *Comet*, 11 April 1936, 13.
—— (1936). 'Vox Pop', *Comet*, 16 May 1936, 24.

—— (1937). 'Dainty Maids of Dorset', *Comet*, 13 February 1937, 15.
—— (1938). 'I Call It God! An Essay on "Getting Your Own Back!"', *Comet*, 16 April 1938, 10–11, 20.
—— (1938). 'Somebody's Tired', *Comet*, 17 September 1938, 15.
Williams, Adisa. (1938). 'The Poems of Odeziaku', *Comet*, 13 August 1938, 10–11.
'Zambuzza'. (1936). 'Vox Pop: Black and White – Or Brown', *Comet*, 25 January 1936, 24.

Secondary sources

Abdelwahid, Mustafa. (2011). *Dusé Mohamed Ali: The Autobiography of a Pioneer Pan African and Afro-Asian Activist* (Trenton NJ: Africa World Press).
Achebe, Chinua. (1975). 'The Novelist as Teacher', in Chinua Achebe, *Morning Yet on Creation Day* (New York: Doubleday Anchor Books), 40–6.
Achebe, Nwando. (2011). *The Female King of Colonial Nigeria: Ahebe Ugbabe* (Bloomington: Indiana University Press).
Adjepon-Yamoah, D. E. K. (1967). 'Preface', in Tony E. Nsofor, *Adventure on the Niger* (Onitsha: University Publishing Company), n.pag.
Adebanwi, Wale. (2016). *Nation as Grand Narrative: The Nigerian Press and the Politics of Meaning* (Woodbridge: Boydell and Brewer).
Adeloye, A. (1974). 'Some Early Nigerian Doctors and Their Contribution to Modern Medicine in West Africa', *Medical History* 18(3), 275–93.
Adenekan, Shola. (2021). *African Literature in the Digital Age: Class and Sexual Politics in New Writing from Nigeria and Kenya* (Woodbridge: Boydell and Brewer).
Ali, Dusé Mohamed. (1911). *In the Land of the Pharaohs: A Short History of Egypt* (London and New York: St Paul).
Anafulu, Joseph C. (1973). 'Onitsha Market Literature: Dead or Alive?', *Research in African Literatures* 4(2), 165–71.
Anderson, Benedict. ([1983] 2006). *Imagined Communities: Reflections on the Origin and Spread of Nationalism* (New York and London: Verso).
Appadurai, Arjun. (1996). *Modernity at Large: Cultural Dimensions of Globalization* (Minneapolis: University of Minnesota Press).
Appiah, Kwame Anthony. (2007). *Cosmopolitanism: Ethics in a World of Strangers* (New York: W. W. Norton).
Apter, Andrew. (1998). 'Discourse and its Disclosures: Yoruba Women and the Sanctity of Abuse', *Africa* 68(1), 68–97.
Askew, Kelly. (2016). 'Everyday Poetry from Tanzania: Microcosm of the Newspaper Genre', in Derek Peterson, Emma Hunter and Stephanie Newell (eds), *African Print Cultures* (Ann Arbor: Michigan University Press), 179–223.
Azikiwe, Nnamdi. (1970). *My Odyssey* (London: C. Hurst).
Baptiste, Jean-Rachel. (2014). *Conjugal Rights: Marriage, Sexuality, and Urban Life in Colonial Libreville, Gabon* (Athens OH: Ohio University Press).
Barber, Karin. (1999). 'Quotation in the Constitution of Yorùbá Oral Texts', *Research in African Literatures* 30(2), 17–41.
—— (2007). *The Anthropology of Texts, Persons and Publics: Oral and Written Culture in Africa and Beyond* (Cambridge: Cambridge University Press).

—— (2012). 'Introduction: I. B. Thomas and the First Yoruba Novel', in Karin Barber (ed.), *Print Culture and the First Yoruba Novel: I. B. Thomas's 'Life Story of Me, Segilǫla', and Other Texts* (Leiden: Brill), 3–41.

—— (2015). 'Editorial Note', *Africa* 85(4), 569–71.

—— (2016). 'Authorship, Copyright and Quotation in Oral and Print Spheres in Early Colonial Yorubaland', in Ute Röschenthaler and Mamadou Diawara (eds), *Copyright Africa: How Intellectual Property, Media and Markets Transform Immaterial Cultural Goods* (Oxford: Sean Kingston Publishing), 105–27.

—— (2023, forthcoming). 'Print Networks and Linguistic Interaction in the Early Yoruba Press', in Caroline Davis, David Finkelstein, and David Johnson (eds), *Edinburgh Companion to the British Colonial Press* (Edinburgh: Edinburgh University Press).

—— *(forthcoming)*. *Early Yoruba Print Culture* (Oxford: Oxford University Press).

Bloom, Harold. ([1973] 1997). *The Anxiety of Influence: A Theory of Poetry* (Oxford: Oxford University Press).

Blyden, Edward Wilmot. (1908). *African Life and Customs* (London: C. M. Phillips).

Bode, Katherine. (2019). *A World of Fiction: Digital Collections and the Future of Literary History* (Ann Arbor: University of Michigan Press).

Bosah, S. I. (1973). *Groundwork of the History and Culture of Onitsha* (Onitsha: S. I. Bosah).

Bosch-Santana, Stephanie. (2018). 'From Nation to Network: Blog and Facebook Fiction from Southern Africa', *Research in African Literatures* 49(1), 187–208.

Broodryk, Chris (ed.). (2021). *Public Intellectuals in South Africa: Critical Voices from the Past* (Johannesburg: Wits University Press).

Burns, James McDonald. (2002). *Flickering Shadows: Cinema and Identity in Colonial Zimbabwe* (Athens, OH: Ohio University Press).

Burrowes, Carl Patrick. (2004). *Power and Press Freedom in Liberia, 1830–1970* (Trenton NJ: Africa World Press).

Callaci, Emily. (2017). *Street Archives and City Life: Popular Intellectuals in Postcolonial Tanzania* (Durham, NC: Duke University Press).

Coleman, James S. (1971). *Nigeria: Background to Nationalism* (California: University of California Press).

Coundouriotis, Eleni. (2014). *The People's Right to the Novel: War in the Postcolony* (New York: Fordham University Press).

Daly, Samuel Fury Childs. (2020). *A History of the Republic of Biafra: Law, Crime, and the Nigerian Civil War* (Cambridge: Cambridge University Press).

Davis, Caroline. (2021). *African Literature and the CIA: Networks of Authorship and Publishing* (Cambridge: Cambridge University Press).

de Bruijn, Esther. (2017). 'Sensationally Reading Ghana's *Joy-Ride* Magazine', *The Cambridge Journal of Postcolonial Literary Inquiry* 4(1), 27–48.

Denzer, LaRay. (1994). 'Yoruba Women: A Historiographical Study', *The International Journal of African Historical Studies* 27(1), 1–39.

Derrick, Jonathan. (2018). *Africa, Empire and Fleet Street: Albert Cartwright and West Africa Magazine* (Oxford: Oxford University Press).

Dick, Archie L. (2020). *Reading Spaces in South Africa, 1850–1920s* (Cambridge: Cambridge University Press).
Dirlik, Arif. ([1st pub. 1997] 2018). *The Postcolonial Aura: Third World Criticism in the Age of Global Capitalism* (Boulder, CO: Westview Press).
Djagalov, Rossen. (2023). 'Premature Postcolonialists: The Afro-Asian Writers Association (1958–1991)', in Toral Jatin Gajarawala et al. (eds), *The Bloomsbury Handbook of Postcolonial Print Cultures* (London: Bloomsbury), 403–19.
Dodson, Don. (1973). 'The Role of the Publisher in Onitsha Market Literature', *Research in African Literatures* 4(2), 172–88.
Dollimore, Jonathan. (1989). *Radical Tragedy: Religion, Ideology, and Power in the Drama of Shakespeare and his Contemporaries* (New York: Harvester Wheatsheaf).
Duffield, Ian. (1976). 'Dusé Mohamed Ali: His Purpose and His Public', in Alastair Niven (ed.), *The Commonwealth Writer Overseas: Themes of Exile and Expatriation* (Brussels: M. Didier), 151–69.
—— (1992). 'Dusé Mohamed Ali, Afro-Asian Solidarity and Pan-Africanism in Early Twentieth-Century London', in Jagdish S. Gundara and Ian Duffield (eds), *Essays on the History of Blacks in Britain* (Aldershot: Avebury), 124–49.
Echeruo, Michael J. C. (1977). *Victorian Lagos: Aspects of Nineteenth-Century Lagos Life* (London and Basingstoke: Macmillan).
Edoro-Glines, Ainehi. (2022). 'Unruly Archives: Literary Form and the Social Media Imaginary', *ELH* 89(2), 523–46.
Emenyonu, Ernest Nneji. (1973). 'Post-War Writing in Nigeria', *Issue: A Journal of Opinion* 3(2), 49–54.
Ezeigbo, T. Akachi. (1991). *Fact and Fiction in the Literature of the Nigerian Civil War* (Ojo: Unity Publishing and Research).
Falola, Toyin and Heaton, Matthew M. (2008). *A History of Nigeria* (Cambridge: Cambridge University Press).
Feierman, Steven. (1990). *Peasant Intellectuals: Anthropology and History in Tanzania* (Madison, WI: University of Wisconsin Press).
Fejzula, Merve. (2022). 'Gendered Labour, Negritude and the Black Public Sphere', *Historical Research: The Bulletin of the Institute of Historical Research*, 95(269), 423–46.
Frederiksen, Bodil Folke. (1991). '*Joe*, the Sweetest Reading in Africa: Documentation and Discussion of a Popular Magazine in Kenya', *African Languages and Cultures* 4(2), 135–55.
—— (2020). 'Censorship as Negotiation: The State and Non-European Newspapers in Kenya, 1930–54', *Itinerario* 44(2), 391–411.
Garcia, José Luís et al. (2017). *Media and the Portuguese Empire* (Basingstoke: Palgrave Macmillan).
Gazda, Elaine K. (ed.). (2002). *The Ancient Art of Emulation: Studies in Artistic Originality and Tradition from the Present to Classical Antiquity* (Ann Arbor: University of Michigan Press).
Gbadegesin, Olubukola A. (2016). '"True to Life:" Illuminating the Processes and Modes of Yoruba Photoplays', in Peterson, Hunter and Newell (eds), *African Print Cultures* (Ann Arbor: Michigan University Press), 251–82.

Gikandi, Simon. (2001). 'Globalization and the Claims of Postcoloniality', *The South Atlantic Quarterly* 100(3), 627–58.
—— (2012). 'Realism, Romance, and the Problem of African Literary History', *Modern Language Quarterly* 73(3), 309–28.
Gocking, Roger S. (1999). *Facing Two Ways: Ghana's Coastal Communities Under Colonial Rule* (Maryland: University Press of America).
Gondola, Ch. Didier. (2016). *Tropical Cowboys: Westerns, Violence, and Masculinity in Kinshasa* (Indianapolis: Indiana University Press).
Gramsci, Antonio. (1971). *Selections from the Prison Notebooks* (New York: International Publishers).
Grieveson, Lee and MacCabe, Colin (eds). (2011). *Film and the End of Empire* (Basingstoke: Palgrave Macmillan).
Hartman, Saidiya V. (2008). *Lose Your Mother: A Journey Along the Atlantic Slave Route* (New York: Farrar, Straus and Giroux).
Hasty, Jennifer. (2005). *The Press and Political Culture in Ghana* (Bloomington and Indianapolis: Indiana University Press).
Herissone, Rebecca. (2013). *Musical Creativity in Restoration England* (Cambridge: Cambridge University Press).
Hofmeyr, Isabel. (2004). *The Portable Bunyan: A Transnational History of* The Pilgrim's Progress (Princeton: Princeton University Press).
—— (2021). *Dockside Reading: Hydrocolonialism and the Custom House* (Durham NC: Duke University Press).
Hyde, Emily. (2023). 'Denis Williams at Midcentury: Global Modernism and the Book Form', in Toral Jatin Gajarawala et al. (eds), *The Bloomsbury Handbook of Postcolonial Print Cultures* (London: Bloomsbury), 237–49.
Igwebuike, Ebuka Elias. (2020). 'The Use of Symbols in the Praise-Naming of Chiefs in Selected Igbo Folk Music', *Journal of the Musical Arts in Africa* 1(17), 41–60.
Innes, C. L. (2002). *A History of Black and Asian Writing in Britain* (Cambridge: Cambridge University Press).
James, Leslie and Leake, Elisabeth (eds). (2015). *Decolonization and the Cold War* (London: Bloomsbury).
James, Leslie. (2018). 'The Flying Newspapermen and the Time-Space of Late Colonial Nigeria', *Comparative Studies in Society and History* 60(3), 569–98.
Jones, Rebecca. (2019). *At the Crossroads: Nigerian Travel Writing and Literary Culture in Yoruba and English* (Woodbridge: Boydell and Brewer).
Jones-Quartey, K. A. B. (1975). *History, Politics and Early Press in Ghana: The Fictions and the Facts* (Accra: School of Journalism and Communication Studies, University of Ghana).
Kalliney, P. (2022). 'Afterword: A World of Print', in F. Orsini, N. Srivastava and L. Zecchini (eds), *The Form of Ideology and the Ideology of Form: Cold War, Decolonization and Third World Print Cultures* (Cambridge: Open Book Publishers), 301–12, https://doi.org/10.11647/OBP.0254.
Kamra, Sukeshi. (2009). 'The "Vox Populi", or the Infernal Propaganda Machine, and Juridical Force in Colonial India', *Cultural Critique* 72(1), 164–202.
Kimble, David. (1963). *A Political History of Ghana: The Rise of Gold Coast Nationalism, 1850–1928* (Oxford: Clarendon Press).

King, Rachael Scarborough. (2018). *Writing to the World: Letters and the Origins of Modern Print Genres* (Baltimore: Johns Hopkins University Press).
Kingsley, Charles. (1906). *Kingsley's Andromeda; With the Story of Perseus Prefixed* (George Yeld, ed.) (New York: Macmillan and Co.).
Langmia, Kehbuma. (2016). *Globalization and Cyberculture: An Afrocentric Perspective* (Cham, Switzerland: Palgrave Macmillan).
Lindfors, Bernth. (1967). 'Heroes and Hero-Worship in Onitsha Chapbooks', *Journal of Popular Culture* 1(1), 1–22.
—— (1970). 'Amos Tutuola: Debts and Assets', *Cahiers d'Études Africaines* 10(38), 306–34.
—— (1975). *Bibliography of Literary Contributions to Nigerian Periodicals, 1946-1972* (Ibadan: Ibadan University Press).
—— (1991). *Popular Literatures in Africa* (Trenton, NJ: Africa World Press).
Macaulay, Thomas Babington. ([1835] 2003). 'Minute on Indian Education, 1835', in Barbara Harlow and Mia Carter (eds), *Archives of Empire: From the East India Company to the Suez Canal, Vol. 1* (Durham NC: Duke University Press), 227–38.
Majumdar, Rochona. (2023). 'Film Society Journals: Ephemeral Archives of Unrealized Futures', in Toral Jatin Gajarawala et al. (eds), *The Bloomsbury Handbook of Postcolonial Print Cultures* (London: Bloomsbury), 301–18.
Majumdar, Nivedita. (2021). *The World in a Grain of Sand: Postcolonial Literature and Radical Universalism* (London: Verso).
Mann, Kristin. (1985). *Marrying Well: Marriage, Status and Social Change Among the Educated Elite in Colonial Lagos* (Cambridge: Cambridge University Press).
Matera, Marc, Misty L. Bastian and Susan Kingsley Kent. (2013). *The Women's War of 1929: Gender and Violence in Colonial Nigeria* (New York: Palgrave Macmillan).
Mba, Nina. (1982). *Nigerian Women Mobilized: Women's Political Activity in Southern Nigeria, 1900-1965* (Berkeley CA: Institute of International Studies).
McCorkle, James. (2020). 'Readings into the Plantationocene: From the Slave Narrative of Charles Ball to the Speculative Histories of Octavia Butler and Nnedi Okorafor', *African Literature Today* 38, 122–33.
McGee, Micki. (2005). *Self-Help Inc.: Makeover Culture in American Life* (New York and Oxford: Oxford University Press).
Meyer, Birgit. (2003). 'Visions of Blood, Sex and Money: Fantasy Spaces in Popular Ghanaian Cinema', *Visual Anthropology* 16(1), 15–41.
Miller, Christopher L. (2020). 'Patrice Lumumba and the Past Conditional: The Virtual Reality of a Martyr', in Matthias De Groof (ed.), *Lumumba in the Arts* (Leuven: Leuven University Press), 78–93.
Morgenstern, Chana. (2023). 'A People's Literature of Palestine/Israel: Socialist Realism and the Internationalist Cultural Journal in the 1950s', in Toral Jatin Gajarawala et al. (eds), *The Bloomsbury Handbook of Postcolonial Print Cultures* (London: Bloomsbury), 57–70.
Newell, Stephanie. (2000). *Literary Culture in Colonial Ghana: 'Thrilling Discoveries in Conjugal Life' and Other Tales* (Oxford and Ohio: James Currey and Ohio University Press).
—— (2006). *The Forger's Tale: The Search for 'Odeziaku'* (Athens OH: Ohio University Press).

—— (2008). 'An Extract from "My Experience in *Cameroons* During the War"', J. G. Mullen', *Africa* 78(3), 401–9.

—— (2013). *The Power to Name: A History of Anonymity in Colonial West Africa* (Athens OH: Ohio University Press).

—— (2020). *Histories of Dirt: Media and Urban life in Colonial and Postcolonial Lagos* (Durham NC: Duke University Press).

Newell, S. and Gadzekpo, A. (2004). *Selected Writings of a Pioneer West African Feminist: Mabel Dove* (Nottingham: Trent Editions).

Ng, Michael. (2017). 'When Silence Speaks: Press Censorship and Rule of Law in British Hong Kong, 1850s–1940s', *Law and Literature* 29(3), 425–56.

Ngũgĩ wa Thiong'o. (1986). *Decolonising the Mind* (Oxford: James Currey).

—— (1993). *Moving the Centre: The Struggle for Cultural Freedoms* (London and Nairobi: James Currey).

Nolte, Insa. (2019). Unpublished paper.

Nzongola-Ntalaja, Georges. (2002). *The Congo from Leopold to Kabila: A People's History* (London: Zed Books).

Obiechina, Emmanuel. (1971). 'Foreword', in Chinua Achebe et al. (eds), *The Insider: Stories of War and Peace from Nigeria* (Enugu: Nwankwo-Ifejika), iii–ix.

—— (1973). *An African Popular Literature: A Study of Onitsha Market Pamphlets* (Cambridge: Cambridge University Press).

—— (1975). *Culture, Tradition and Society in the West African Novel* (Cambridge: Cambridge University Press).

Ochiagha, Terri. (2015). *Achebe and Friends at Umuahia: The Making of a Literary Elite* (Woodbridge: Boydell and Brewer).

Ofori-Attah, Kwabena Dei. (2006). 'The British and Curriculum Development in West Africa: A Historical Discourse', *Review of Education* 52, 409–23.

Omu, Fred. (1978). *Press and Politics in Nigeria, 1880–1937* (Atlantic Highlands, NJ: Humanities Press).

Orsini, Francesca. (2015). 'Whose Amnesia? Literary Modernity in Multilingual South Asia', *Cambridge Journal of Postcolonial Literary Inquiry* 2(2), 266–72.

—— (2023). 'A Magazine for Everyone: The Ecology of Postcolonial Indian Magazines', in Toral Jatin Gajarawala et al. (eds), *The Bloomsbury Handbook of Postcolonial Print Cultures* (London: Bloomsbury), 71–87.

Osondu-Oti, Adaora. (2015). 'An Appraisal of India-Nigeria Historical and Contemporary Relations', *Alternation* 15, 102–26.

Pick, Daniel. (2012). *The Pursuit of the Nazi Mind: Hitler, Hess, and the Analysts* (Oxford: Oxford University Press).

Plageman, Nate. (2013). *Highlife Saturday Night: Popular Music and Social Change in Urban Ghana* (Bloomington, IN: Indiana University Press).

Popescu, Monica. (2020). *At Penpoint: African Literatures, Postcolonial Studies, and the Cold War* (Durham NC: Duke University Press).

Post, K. W. J. (1964). 'Nigerian Pamphleteers and the Congo', *Journal of Modern African Studies* 12(3), 405–18.

Potter, Simon J. (2003). *News and the British World: The Emergence of an Imperial Press System, 1876–1922* (Oxford: Oxford University Press).

Primorac, Ranka. (2014). 'At Home in the World? Re-framing Zambia's Literature in English', *Journal of Southern African Studies* 40(3), 575–91.
—— (2021). 'Vivek and Mabel: Some Thoughts on African Print Cultures and World Literature', Conference: *Colonial and Postcolonial Print Mobilities: Black Periodicals and Local Publications, 1880–Present*. Newcastle Postcolonial Research Group in collaboration with the Council of African Studies, Yale University, 3–4 December.
Radway, Janice. ([1984] 1991). *Reading the Romance: Women, Patriarchy, and Popular Literature* (Chapel Hill NC: University of North Carolina Press).
Ray, Carina. (2015). *Crossing the Color Line: Race, Sex, and the Contested Politics of Colonialism in Ghana* (Athens OH: Ohio University Press).
Reddy, Vasu et al. (eds). (2020). *The Fabric of Dissent: Public Intellectuals in South Africa* (Cape Town: BestRed/HSRC Press).
Reuster-Jahn, Uta. (2016). 'Private Entertainment Magazines and Popular Literature Production in Socialist Tanzania', in Peterson, Hunter and Newell (eds), *African Print Cultures* (Ann Arbor: Michigan University Press), 224–50.
Rice, Tom. (2016). '"Are You Proud to be British?": Mobile Film Shows, Local Voices and the Demise of the British Empire in Africa', *Historical Journal of Film, Radio and Television* 36(3), 331–51.
Rosenthal, Laura J. (2015). *Infamous Commerce: Prostitution in Eighteenth-Century British Literature and Culture* (Ithaca: Cornell University Press).
Said, Edward W. (2001). *Reflections on Exile and Other Literary and Cultural Essays* (Cambridge MA: Harvard University Press).
Sandwith, Corinne. (2014). *World of Letters: Reading Communities and Cultural Debates in Early Apartheid South Africa* (Pietermarizburg: University of KwaZulu-Natal Press).
Schwartz, R. M. (2012). 'Truth, Free Speech, and the Legacy of John Milton's *Areopagitica*', *Teoria* 32(1), 47–58.
Shringarpure, Bhakti. (2019). *Cold War Assemblages: Decolonization to Digital* (London and New York: Routledge).
Sklar, Richard L. (1963). *Nigerian Political Parties: Power in an Emergent African Nation* (Princeton: Princeton University Press).
Solanke, Stephen O. (2014). 'Exploring and Bibliographing the Nigerian Onitsha Market Literature as Popular Fiction', *International Journal of English Literature and Culture* 2(11), 277–90.
Spivak, Gayatri Chakravorty. (1993). *Outside In the Teaching Machine*. (New York: Routledge).
Suriano, Maria. (2011). 'Letters to the Editor and Poems: *Mambo Leo* and Readers' Debates on *Dansi, Ustaarabu*, Respectability, and Modernity in Tanganyika, 1940s–1950s', *Africa Today* 57(3), 39–55.
Tully, Andrew. (1962). *C.I.A. – The Inside Story* (New York: Morrow).
Vail, Leroy and White, Landeg. (1991). *Power and the Praise Poem: Southern African Voices in History* (Charlottesville, Virginia and London: University of Virginia Press and James Currey).
Walcott, Derek. ([1974] 1993). 'The Caribbean: Culture or Mimicry', in Robert Hamner (ed.), *Critical Perspectives on Derek Walcott* (Pueblo: Passeggiata Press), 51–7.

Warner, Michael. (2002). *Publics and Counterpublics* (New York: Zone Books).
Wendelin, Greta. (2010). 'The Prostitute's Voice in the Public Eye: Police Tactics of Security and Discipline within Victorian Journalism', *Communication and Critical/Cultural Studies* 7(1), 53–69.
Wenzel, Jennifer. 2002. 'Intertextual Africa: Chinua Achebe on the Congo, Patrice Lumumba on the Niger', in Toyin Falola and Barbara Harlow (eds), *African Writers and Their Readers: Essays in Honor of Bernth Lindfors Vol II* (Trenton, NJ: Africa World Press), 219–53.
Westad, Odd Arne. (2005). *The Global Cold War: Third World Interventions and the Making of our Times* (Cambridge: Cambridge University Press).
Willems, Wendy. (2019). '"The Politics of Things": Digital Media, Urban Space, and the Materiality of Publics', *Media, Culture & Society* 41(8), 1192–1209.
Williams, Susan A. (2011). *Who Killed Hammarskjöld? The UN, the Cold War, and White Supremacy in Africa* (New York: Columbia University Press).
—— (2021). *White Malice: The CIA and the Covert Recolonization of Africa* (New York: Public Affairs).
Winter, Sarah E. (2011). *The Pleasures of Memory: Learning to Read with Charles Dickens* (New York: Fordham University Press).
WReC (Warwick Research Collective). (2015). *Combined and Uneven Development: Towards a New Theory of World Literature* (Liverpool: Liverpool University Press).
Yankah, Kwesi. ([1989] 2012). *The Proverb in the Context of Akan Rhetoric* (New York: Diasporic African Press).
Yékú, James. (2021). 'Chinua Achebe's *There Was a Country* and the Digital Publics of African Literature', *Digital Scholarship in the Humanities* 36(1), 209–23. https://doi.org/10.1093/llc/fqz084 [accessed 28 August 2022].
Zachernuk, Philip S. (2000). *Colonial Subjects: An African Intelligentsia and Atlantic Ideas* (Charlottesville VA: University of Virginia Press).

Unpublished PhD theses

Bosch-Santana, Stephanie. (2015). 'Forms of Affiliation: Nationalism, Pan-Africanism, and Globalism in Southern African Literary Media'. Harvard University.
Dodson, Don Charles. (1974). 'Onitsha Pamphlets: Culture in the Marketplace'. University of Wisconsin.
Gadzekpo, Audrey Sitsofe. (2001). 'Women's Engagement with Gold Coast Print Culture from 1857 to 1957'. University of Birmingham.
Redgrave, Amy. (2023 forthcoming). 'Colonial Anxieties, Local Debates, and Struggles over "Prostitution" in Southern Nigeria, 1890–1960'. University of Birmingham.
Sawada, Nozomi. (2011). 'The Educated Elite and Associational Life in Early Lagos Newspapers: In Search of Unity for the Progress of Society'. University of Birmingham.
Stroup, William James. (2000). 'Shelley and the Nature of Non-Violence'. University of New Hampshire.

Web-based sources

UN General Assembly, 'Speech by Mr. Khrushchev, Chairman of the Council of Ministers of the Union of Soviet Socialist Republics, at the 869th Plenary Meeting of the 15th Session of the United Nations General Assembly', 23 September 1960, History and Public Policy Program Digital Archive, United Nations Document A/PV.869: 65–84. http://digitalarchive.wilsoncenter.org/document/155185 [accessed 28 August 2022].

Index

'A Banker' (pseud. Charles James Lacy)   20, 22–3, 25, 27, 28
Abiakam, J. C.   8, 72, 74, 81 n.14, 111–13, 116, 124, 125, 156, 168
Achebe, Chinua   81, 82, 107, 108, 164, 183
  Things Fall Apart   82, 107, 183
Adenekan, Shola   184
Adichie, Chimamanda Ngozi   163
Adimora-Ezeigbo, Akachi   163
advertisements   1, 18, 68–9, 72, 74, 118
aesthetics   5, 7, 10, 162, 173, 175–8, 181, 185
African Times and Orient Review   33, 44
African Writers Conference (Makerere)   158
Afro-Asian People's Solidarity Organisation   157
Afro-Asian Writers Association   158
Aidoo, Ama Ata   81
Ajiṣafẹ, A. K.   62
Akede Eko   14, 36, 37, 40
Akosa, Cecilia D.   127
Ali, Dusé Mohamed   40, 44–5, 54–6, 58, 60–1, 83
  Comet (Lagos)   19, 33, 34, 43, 46, 52, 58, 62–3, 131, 176, 180
Anderson, Benedict   18, 28, 97
anglophone literature   2, 3–6, 29, 58, 62–3, 69, 83, 91, 95, 97, 99, 101, 118–19, 173–5, 182
Anorue, J. C.   81, 113, 153, 168–9
anticolonialism   3, 13, 14–17, 25, 51, 58, 176
antiracism   14, 16
anti-semitism   53–4

Anyiam, F. U.   10 n.5, 43, 47–9, 87, 97
Anyiche, Okeke   132 *see also* Okeke, Anyiche
archives   127, 129, 130, 180–1, 183, 184
Aririguzo, Cyril N.   120, 134
Armah, Ayi Kwei   81, 145 n.4
Awolowo, Obafemi   67
Azikiwe, Nnamdi   38, 44, 45, 51, 163, 164, 166

'B. B.' (pseud.)   20, 23, 25–7, 28, 29–30, 62
Balé of Ayésan   15
Balewa, Abubakar Tafawa   164
Bandung Conference   146
Barber, Karin   7, 10, 35 n.2, 36, 37–8, 38 n.5, 40, 49, 173
Baudouin, King of Belgium   152, 155
Belgium   144, 145, 152–3, 157
Bello, Ahmadu   164
Bloom, Harold   28, 96
bookshops   65, 68, 69, 72, 81, 87, 88, 123, 166, 184
Boy Scout Movement   90–1
Bullock, Rev. Charles   48
Burns, Robert   133
Byron, George Gordon   22

Callaci, Emily   7
Carmichael, Hoagy   132
censorship   74 n.12, 152, 157
Chiazor, Benjamin O.   123–4
Christianity   22, 37, 54
CIA   157
cinema   74

class   4, 6, 9, 15, 28, 52, 67, 83–4, 90–1, 95, 99, 161, 176
Clay, Bertha M. (pseud. Charlotte Mary Brame)   120, 121, 121 n.6, 123
Cold War   2, 145–6, 149–51, 152, 176
  and aesthetics   144, 157–60
  African literature and   143, 157–60, 180
colonialism   21, 58, 150
  British   4, 156, 179
  government administrators   15, 23, 183
  and literature   81–2, 95, 97, 144, 154, 175, 179
Comet (Lagos) *see under* Ali, Dusé Mohamed
communism   144, 146, 150, 154–7
'complete gentleman'   171
Congo Crisis   143, 144–57
Congress for Cultural Freedom (CCF)   157, 158
Cooke, Rev. Thomas   85, 97
copyright   100, 113, 168–9
Corelli, Marie   74, 120
cosmopolitanism   4, 25, 30, 53, 56, 58, 83, 176, 179
Coundouriotis, Eleni   163, 166 n.4, 168 n.5
cowboys   74, 132
customary rulers   15, 23, 24, 107

'D.A.L.' (pseud.)   41
da Rocha, Moses   45
Daily Times (Lagos)   17, 39
Daly, Samuel Fury Childs   163, 164, 166
decolonisation   73, 84, 180
'Dick Carnis' (pseud.)   20, 22, 23–5, 27, 28–30, 62, 176
Dodson, Don   65, 69, 74 n.11, 90, 127, 128, 129 n.2, 130, 155, 164, 168
Dosunmu-Ainnah, Adebesin   48–9
Dove, Mabel   19 n.8, 37, 38, 38 n.4

Eastern Nigerian Broadcasting Service   130
Edoro-Glines, Ainehi   184, 185
education *see* schools
Ekesiobi, Eddy N.   155
elites, educated   6–7, 16, 32–3, 57, 69, 73–4, 82, 99, 110, 118–19, 131, 175, 183
  migrants   13
  sub-elites   14, 67, 95
Emecheta, Buchi   163
Emenyonu, Ernest   164 n.1, 169
English literature   4, 21, 27–8, 30, 58, 96, 101, 108, 119–20, 122–5, 143, 160–1, 177
ephemera   2, 3, 11, 129 n.2, 178, 180–2, 184, 185
epistolarity   9–10, 31–2, 38, 85, 101, 109–18, 178, 179, 181
  epistolary fiction   3, 4, 9, 31–2, 37–9, 109–11
  epistolary manuals   9, 32, 84, 85, 87–91, 95–6, 97, 105, 108 , 111–14, 117
  letters to the press *see* newspapers *under* letters to editors
  love letters   110–12, 114–19, 124, 181
  public letter writers   10–11, 130–1
  and temporality   31, 38, 88, 101, 110–14, 179
Era, The   47
Ethiopia, Italian invasion of   2, 54
Eurocentrism   5, 84, 107, 158, 175–6, 185
Eze, S.   168
Eze, V. E.   83

Fante chiefs   23, 24
fascism   54–5
Feierman, Steven   7
Fejzula, Merve   127, 129, 130, 140 n.9
First World War   2
Frank, Elizabeth   85, 90, 96, 108
Frederiksen, Bodil   14

Gandhi, Mohandas Karamchand (Mahatma)   24
gender   5, 13, 21, 28, 38–41, 114, 128–30, 134–6, 170–6
Glen, Catherine Young   50
Gold Coast Leader   20–7, 30, 36
Gramsci, Antonio   6 n.4

Hammarskjöld, Dag   144, 149, 152
Hanfstaengl, Ernst   53
Harcourt, Lewis, 1st Viscount Harcourt   16
Hartman, Saidiya   180
'Highbred Maxwell' (pseud.)   67, 73, 133–4
highlife music   132
Hofmeyr, Isabel   49, 131
Hogan, David   81, 85, 86, 95, 96–7
humanism   14, 24, 29, 53, 58
Hyde, Emily   179

Iguh, Thomas O.   143 n.1, 144, 145 n.3, 146, 154, 155, 155 n.11, 156, 157, 160–1, 165, 168
Ikoli, Ernest S.   44
illiteracy, negative representations of   7, 10–11, 15, 26, 61–2, 84, 99, 107, 123, 131–2, 170
imperialism   3, 14, 16, 22, 27, 82, 157, 176
Independence, *see also* decolonisation
  Congo   144, 147–8, 155
  Nigeria   3, 73, 84, 128
India   90, 95, 183
Indirect rule   15
Intellectuals   2, 6–9, 128–9, 146, 158, 176
  local   2, 7–8, 10, 15, 21, 45, 128, 143, 146, 155, 169, 175, 178, 180
  organic   6 n.4
  printing presses and   2, 7, 29, 58–9, 83, 95, 99, 141, 179
internet creativity, *see* social media
Ita, E.   49

Itan Igbesi-Aiye Emi Ṣẹgilọla, see *Life Story of Me, Ṣẹgilọla* under Thomas, I. B.

'J.O.A.' (pseud.)   33
Johnson, Samuel   50, 97
journalism   33, 38, 68, 68 n.6, 127, 155

Kalliney, Peter   159
Kalonji, Albert   144
Kamalu, Sigis   82, 120–3
Kasavubu, Joseph   145, 152
Katanga   144, 145
Khrushchev, Nikita   156
King, Rachel Scarborough   34–5, 111
Kingsley, Charles   160

La Page, Gertrude   53 n.8, 60, 60 n.17
Lagos Daily News   17
Lagos Dramatic and Musical Society   61
Lagos Players, The   60
Lagos Shakespearean Society   60–1
'Lans the African' (pseud.)   33
lesbian   136, 138–40
letters *see* epistolarity
libraries   107, 121, 165 n.2, 176
Life Story of Me, Ṣẹgilọla, see under Thomas, I. B.
Lindfors, Bernth   161
literacy   83, 91, 123, 148–9
  anticolonialism and   15–16
  class and   4, 6, 9, 15, 99, 107 see *also* elites, educated *and* class formation
  English   7, 9, 15, 19, 20, 59–60, 83, 91, 107, 110, 123 see *also* anglophone literature
  gender and   130–1, 134–5
literary criticism   33, 58, 177 see *also* newspapers, aesthetic debates in literature
  and decolonisation   72

global circulation of   4, 7, 14, 25, 29,
    99–100, 119, 122, 175–7, 179
popular   3, 28, 41, 46, 69, 96, 99, 108,
    117–18, 170, 173
self-help   69, 72–3, 83, 85, 88, 95,
    100, 144
temporality and   35, 37–8, 110, 146,
    149–51, 154, 160, 178–85
'Literature' (pseud.)   43
Litsey, Edwin Carlile   43, 46, 47, 48
Lodge, Thomas   119
Lugard, Sir Frederick, 1st Baron
    Lugard   16, 17
Lumumba, Patrice   144–6, 154, 160
    assassination of   3, 67, 144–5, 146,
        151, 156
        Onitsha market literature and   3,
            144, 146–56, 157, 160–1, 166,
            168, 181 see also Onitsha
            market literature, political
            dramas
        Eisenhower administration and   144

Macaulay, Herbert   44
Macaulay, Thomas Babington   30
MacGregor, Sir William   15, 16, 17
Madu, Nathaniel O.   81
Majumdar, Rochona   183
'Marjorie Mensah' (pseud.) see Dove,
    Mabel
masculinity   5, 74, 91, 128–30, 135–6, 138,
    141, 176
'Master of English' (pseud.) see Njoku,
    Nathan O.
'Master of Life' (pseud.) see Olisah, S.
    Okenwa
McGee, Micki   72
Milton, John   23, 50
mimicry   4, 21–2, 27–8, 72, 88, 96, 177
miscegenation   52–4, 55, 57
misogyny   6, 132, 140
Mobutu Sese Seko   145, 152
Modernism   46, 179, 181, 183, 186

modernity   7, 58, 62, 74, 91, 169
'Moneyhard' (pseud. C. N. Onuoha, also
    listed as C. N. Obioha)   72, 73
Morgenstern, Chana   159
Mpolo, Maurice   145
Mullen, J. G.   36–7
Mussolini, Benito   54

Nanni, F. C.   141
narrators
    first-person   9, 38, 140
    voyeuristic   138
nationalism   150, 152
    African literature and   82, 84, 144,
        146, 151, 154, 158, 160, 176
    anticolonial   14–17, 25, 51, 145, 150, 152,
        163, 176
    Nigerian   82, 145, 146, 148
    white   54, 82
Nazism   53–4
neocolonialism   154–5, 156
neoliberalism   182
newspapers
    aesthetic debates in   2, 19, 45–6, 49, 57
    African-language   10, 13, 36, 49
    anticolonial   14–17
    bilingual   3, 13, 14, 36, 41
    censorship   16–17, 18
    creative writing in   1, 2, 7, 11, 18, 29,
        36–41, 55–7, 97
    editors   13–14, 16, 17–18, 33, 34, 55, 99
        editorials   1, 7, 9, 145
    letters   9, 10 18, 19, 32–6, 40, 56–7, 97,
        180
    poetry   3, 13, 27, 28, 44–6, 145
newsprint   2–4, 7, 11–14, 28–9, 67, 68, 82,
    99, 140, 177–8, 181
Ngũgĩ wa Thiong'o   3, 21, 25, 82, 83, 84, 158
Nigerian Civil War   164
    literature   3, 67, 81, 113, 134, 162–6,
        169–73
    women and   163–72
Nigerian-Soviet Friendship Society   157

Njoku, Nathan O. (*aka* 'Master of English')   7, 67, 72, 73, 81, 88, 90, 100, 166
Nkrumah, Kwame   74 n.12, 145 n.3, 156
Nkwoh, Marius U. E.   74, 83, 130
Nnadozie, J. O.   109, 113, 169
'noble savage'   52–3
Nolte, Insa   5
non-alignment   146, 157, 158, 160, 176
novels   28, 41, 69
Novosty Press Agency   155
Ntu, Ada Ocha (aka Esther Johnson)   67
Nwachukwu, Shakespeare C. N.   134–5, 165–6
Nwanekezi, M. N.   166, 170
Nwangoro, S. O.   8, 54 n.9, 60, 60 n.16, 61, 62, 182–3
Nwapa, Flora   127–8, 163, 166
Nwaubani, Adaobi Tricia   175, 178
Nweze, Uchenna   165–6
Nwoga, Donatus   84
Nwosu, Cletus Gibson   81, 123, 133, 134, 135, 140

Obiechina, Emmanuel   84, 164, 169, 170
'Odeziaku' (pseud.) *see* Stuart-Young, J. M.
Odogwu, A.   165, 166, 169–74
Ogali, Ogali A.   21 n.9, 56 n.11, 73, 107–8, 117, 128, 143 n.1, 146
  Ghost of Patrice Lumumba, The   149–57, 160, 161
  Veronica My Daughter   65, 122 n.7, 123, 127–9, 131, 144, 165, 168–70
Ogu, H. O.   7, 119–20
Ojukwu, Odumegwu   164
Okeanu, Vincent C.   69, 82, 110 n.1, 180
Okeke, Alexander Obiorah   61, 68, 82, 99, 110, 132
Okeke, Godfrey C.   164–5
Okigbo, Christopher   164
Okito, Joseph   145

Okonkwo, Rufus   72, 168
Olisah, S. Okenwa (*aka* 'Strong Man of the Pen' and 'Master of Life')   5, 7, 73, 81, 87, 88, 90, 100, 108, 112, 146, 148, 168
Oluwide, Baba   157
Onitsha   55, 65, 72
Onitsha market literature   2, 7, 10, 11, 26, 42, 65, 82, 87, 109
  Civil War novels   165–6, 169–73
  critical reception of   84
  newspapers and   67–8, 152
  political dramas   3, 49, 60, 143–4, 146–55, 157, 160, 178
  popular romances   3, 9, 39, 67, 99, 100, 110–11, 114–25, 165
Onwubuta, Daniel   67
Onwudiegwu, J. Kenddys   6, 72–3, 83, 87, 110–11, 117–18, 124, 133
Onwuka, Wilfred (*aka* 'Master of Pen' and 'The Strong Man of the Pen')   73
orality   11, 25, 58, 107, 129, 130–6, 141, 177
Orsini, Francesca   144, 159
Osadebay, Dennis   145
Osakwe, G. C.   165, 166, 169–74
Oshilaja, I. W.   58–60, 62
Oti, Penn C. I.   134, 136
Owerri   89, 90

Pacific Printers (Yaba)   156
Palm-Wine Drinkard see under Tutuola, Amos
pamphlets *see* Onitsha market literature
parables   40, 112, 146, 151, 162, 174
photographs   5, 74, 100
Pinheiro, Olabode   48, 49
plagiarism   27, 43, 47–50, 84, 87–96, 99, 100, 120
Popescu, Monica   158–9
Post, K. W. J.   156
printing presses   58–9, 65, 68
pseudonyms   18 n.7, 27, 29, 33, 38, 177

Queen Victoria   23
quotation   3–4, 20, 24–5, 27, 34, 47–8, 132, 161–2, 178–9, 181, 185
  and copying   96–7, 99–100, 105, 108

racism   3, 16, 53–7, 72, 82, 84, 148, 177
Radio Biafra   166
Radway, Janice   114
'Ralph O. Ability' (pseud.)   73, 83, 85–7, 95, 99, 100
'Rambler' (pseud.)   52
realism   9, 10, 22, 38, 111, 154, 160, 161–2, 173–4, 181, 186
Republic of Biafra   164
Richardson, Samuel   38–9
Robinson, Charles Seymour   23
Romantic poets   3, 22–4, 48, 97, 173

Said, Edward W.   29, 179
Sapara, Dr. O.   58 n.14
Saro-Wiwa, Ken   163
schools
  colonial   3, 4, 17, 27, 48, 65
  missionary   3, 4, 27, 65, 131, 178
  secondary   4, 7, 19, 107
Second World War   2, 14, 69, 90
'Ṣẹgilọla of the Fascinating Eyes' (pseud.)
  see under Thomas, I. B.
Sekyi, W. E. G. (Kobina)   20, 21
Senusi, Tesilimy Adekunle   128
Shakespeare, William   3, 19, 50, 120, 123, 160–1
Shaw, George Bernard   37, 51, 57
Shelley, Percy Bysshe   22, 23
  Prometheus Unbound   24
Shringarpure, Bhakti   149, 152, 160
social media   4, 5, 184–5
socialism   155, 156
songs   62, 132–6, 141, 166
South Africa   54, 55
Soviet Union   144, 150, 155
Soyinka, Wole   81

'Speedy Eric' (pseud. Onwudiwe, A. N.)   5, 73, 82, 88, 91, 100, 105, 111
  Mabel the Sweet Honey that Poured Away   132, 136–40
Spivak, Gayatri Chakravorty   179
Stephen, Felix N.   74, 83, 101, 113, 114–16, 122, 143, 144, 148, 152, 154
'The Strong Man of the Pen' (pseud.)
  see Olisah, S. Okenwa and Onwuka, Wilfred
Stuart-Young, J. M.   18, 44, 45, 50–2, 55–7, 63, 97, 109
  Black Man's Cradle   52–3

'The Teenager With Knowledge' (pseud.)
  see Onwudiegwu, J. Kenddys
Tennyson, Alfred   22
textbooks   65, 160
Things Fall Apart see under Achebe, Chinua
Thomas, I. B.   4, 9, 14, 36–41, 138, 173
  'Ṣẹgilọla of the Fascinating Eyes' (pseud.)   36, 37–41, 109, 110, 112, 113, 129, 131, 133, 134, 136, 139, 141
Times of West Africa   37, 38
Toilers Brigade   157
Tshombe, Moïse   144, 145, 152, 153
Tutuola, Amos   9, 31
  Palm-Wine Drinkard, The   31–2, 113

Ume-Ezeoke, O. G.   127
United Nations   144, 150, 156
United States   54, 95, 114, 144, 150, 153, 157
universalism   14, 23, 24, 28, 30, 62, 101
University of Lagos   130

verisimilitude   9, 35, 111, 173
vernacular literature   3, 4, 36, 39, 40–1, 49, 58, 62
Veronica My Daughter, see under Ogali, Ogali A.

Walcott, Derek   178
Ward, Rev. Fr. J.   53
Wenzel, Jennifer   161
West African Review   62
Williams, Denis   179
women   127–30, 134–6
  Congolese   148
  independence of   6, 115, 129
  in Onitsha market literature   4, 5, 115–17, 120, 128–36, 141, 170–4
  sexual morality of   36, 40–2, 52, 69, 129, 130, 132, 136, 138–9, 141
  violence against   130, 138, 139, 171–2
Wordsworth, William   22
world literature   2, 5, 11, 108, 158, 182

Yékú, James   185
'The Young Dynamic Author' (pseud. Onwudiwe, A. N.)   5, 68 n.7, 69, 73
Young Toilers Brigade of West Africa   157

AFRICAN ARTICULATIONS

ISSN 2054–5673

Previously published

Achebe and Friends at Umuahia: The Making of a Literary Elite
Terri Ochiagha, 2015. Winner of the ASAUK Fage & Oliver Prize 2016

A Death Retold in Truth and Rumour: Kenya, Britain and the Julie Ward Murder   Grace A. Musila, 2015

Scoring Race: Jazz, Fiction, and Francophone Africa   Pim Higginson, 2017

Writing Spatiality in West Africa: Colonial Legacies in the Anglophone/Francophone Novel   Madhu Krishnan, 2018. Winner of the ALA Book of the Year Award – Scholarship 2020

Written under the Skin: Blood and Intergenerational Memory in South Africa   Carli Coetzee, 2019. Winner of the ALA Book of the Year Award – Scholarship 2021

Experiments with Truth: Narrative Non-fiction and the Coming of Democracy in South Africa   Hedley Twidle, 2019

At the Crossroads: Nigerian Travel Writing and Literary Culture in Yoruba and English   Rebecca Jones, 2019. Shortlisted for the ASAUK Fage & Oliver Prize 2020, 'Honorable Mention' for the ALA First Book Award – Scholarship 2021

Cinemas of the Mozambican Revolution: Anti-Colonialism, Independence and Internationalism in Filmmaking, 1968–1991   Ros Gray, 2020

African Literature in the Digital Age: Class and Sexual Politics in New Writing from Nigeria and Kenya   Shola Adenekan, 2021

www.ingramcontent.com/pod-product-compliance
Lightning Source LLC
Jackson TN
JSHW061115250625
86703JS00004B/54